WOMEN WRITING ART THE NINETEENTH

This book sets out to correct received acc ...ergence of art history as a masculine field. It investigates the importance of female writers from Anna Jameson, Elizabeth Eastlake and George Eliot to Alice Meynell, Vernon Lee and Michael Field in developing a discourse of art notable for its complexity and cultural power, its increasing professionalism and reach, and its integration with other discourses of modernity. Proposing a more flexible and inclusive model of what constitutes art historical writing, including fiction, poetry and travel literature, this book offers a radically revisionist account of the genealogy of a discipline and a profession. It shows how women experienced forms of professional exclusion that, while detrimental to their careers, could be aesthetically formative; how working from the margins of established institutional structures gave women the freedom to be audaciously experimental in their writing about art in ways that resonate with modern readers.

HILARY FRASER is Executive Dean of Arts and Geoffrey Tillotson Professor of Nineteenth-Century Studies at Birkbeck, University of London. Her publications include *Beauty and Belief: Aesthetics and Religion in Victorian Literature* (Cambridge, 1986), *The Victorians and Renaissance Italy* (1992), *Gender and the Victorian Periodical* (with Judith Johnston and Stephanie Green, Cambridge, 2003) and *Minds, Bodies, Machines, 1770–1930* (co-edited with Deirdre Coleman, 2011).

CAMBRIDGE STUDIES IN NINETEENTH-CENTURY LITERATURE AND CULTURE

Nineteenth-century British literature and culture have been rich fields for interdisciplinary studies. Since the turn of the twentieth century, scholars and critics have tracked the intersections and tensions between Victorian literature and the visual arts, politics, social organisation, economic life, technical innovations, scientific thought – in short, culture in its broadest sense. In recent years, theoretical challenges and historiographical shifts have unsettled the assumptions of previous scholarly synthesis and called into question the terms of older debates. Whereas the tendency in much past literary critical interpretation was to use the metaphor of culture as 'background', feminist, Foucauldian, and other analyses have employed more dynamic models that raise questions of power and of circulation. Such developments have reanimated the field. This series aims to accommodate and promote the most interesting work being undertaken on the frontiers of the field of nineteenth-century literary studies: work which intersects fruitfully with other fields of study such as history, or literary theory, or the history of science. Comparative as well as interdisciplinary approaches are welcomed.

A complete list of titles published will be found at the end of the book.

WOMEN WRITING ART HISTORY IN THE NINETEENTH CENTURY

Looking Like a Woman

HILARY FRASER

CAMBRIDGE
UNIVERSITY PRESS

CAMBRIDGE
UNIVERSITY PRESS

University Printing House, Cambridge CB2 8BS, United Kingdom

Cambridge University Press is part of the University of Cambridge.

It furthers the University's mission by disseminating knowledge in the pursuit of education, learning and research at the highest international levels of excellence.

www.cambridge.org
Information on this title: www.cambridge.org/9781107428744

First published 2014
First paperback edition 2016

A catalogue record for this publication is available from the British Library

Library of Congress Cataloguing in Publication data
Fraser, Hilary, 1953–
Women writing art history in the nineteenth century : looking like a woman / Hilary Fraser.
pages cm – (Cambridge studies in nineteenth-century literature and culture ; 95)
Includes bibliographical references and index.
ISBN 978-1-107-07575-7 (hardback)
1. Art – Historiography – History – 19th century. 2. Art criticism – History – 19th century.
3. Women art historians. 4. Women art critics. I. Title.
N7482.5.F73 2014
704′.04209034–dc23
2014012704

ISBN 978-1-107-07575-7 Hardback
ISBN 978-1-107-42874-4 Paperback

For Nick

Contents

Illustrations

Acknowledgements

This is a book that, more than most, owes its existence to the family and friends, colleagues and students who have enabled me to bring it to completion. Nick Burton animated the entire project, and when he died it nearly died with him. It is thanks to the countless kindnesses and unstinting support of all those who have helped me find my way back that *Looking Like a Woman*, which for so long was looking like a defeat, recovered its focus.

My personal debts are many, but there are a few people whose support has been crucial. I wish my children – Matthew, Clair and Adam – hadn't had to experience illness and loss at such a tender age, but it taught them empathy and compassion and, in this as in many happier ways, Nick helped form the wonderful young people they are. For a while it was really only they who made life worth living; they remain constantly sustaining. My parents, Pauline and Douglas Brumwell, and my sister, Sally Clark, were rocks. Nick's family, especially Andrew Wyllie and Pat Wyllie, gave much support. Bridget Thornley, the 'Angel of the North', flew down to look after us all. Friends in Canterbury, in particular Rod Edmond, Mary Evans, Sally Minogue and Karen Shepherdson, must know how grateful I am to them for all their loving care. Old friends did what old friends do, and mine did and do it marvellously. Special thanks to Carlene Adamson, Mary Black, Jesmond Blumenfeld, Daniel Brown, Vic Burrows, Deirdre Coleman, Rob Fraser, Susan Hitch, Steven Holtzman, Clair and George Hughes, Gail Jones, Peter Kenyon, Prue Kerr, Lizzie Maisels, Keith and Jenny Page, Orna Raz, Rob Rockman, Simon Schama, Patrick Vittet-Philippe, Leon Wieseltier, Jan Wright. Their steady faith in me has made it possible to finish this book.

It has helped to have worked for the past twelve years at Birkbeck, which is, at an institutional level as well as at the more personal level of individual colleagues, a generous and generative and humane place to be. My research and my well-being have been equally supported both by the College and by the Arts and Humanities Research Council, which awarded the project a research grant back in 2002 and has patiently awaited the outcome. I am most grateful for their confidence in me and their forbearance. Likewise Linda Bree, at Cambridge University Press, and Gillian Beer, as series editor, have been wise, sympathetic and always encouraging publishers and mentors, and I thank them for accompanying me throughout the voyage and for finally steering this vessel into port. Thanks, too, to the British Library, Senate House Library, librarians at Harvard's Villa I Tatti, and especially Alyson Price at the British Institute Library in Florence.

I could not be more fortunate than to work among such brilliant and collaborative colleagues as I have in Birkbeck's School of Arts, and in particular the Centre for Nineteenth-Century Studies, which offers the most intellectually exciting and sustaining environment imaginable. I thank, especially, Isobel Armstrong, Nicola Bown, Laurel Brake, Carolyn Burdett, Luisa Calè, Patrizia Di Bello, David Feldman, Roger Luckhurst, Helen Maslen, Vicky Mills, Laura Mulvey, Lynda Nead, Heather Tilley, Ana Parejo Vadillo and Carol Watts. Sonny Kandola and Vicky Mills were exceptionally resourceful and meticulous research assistants at an early stage of the project and remained involved long after their formal association ended; and David Gillott gave invaluable assistance in the final stages, particularly with the preparation of the index. Alison Finlay kindly stepped up to be Head of Department when I had to step down; Sue Wiseman particularly encouraged me later to make space for scholarship amidst my labours as Dean; and Anthony Bale, by deferring his own sabbatical, enabled me to act on her advice and take a month's study leave. Others at Birkbeck – especially Verity Hutton, Tricia King and Miriam Zukas – and former colleagues – Ella Dzelzainis, Holly Furneaux, Tom Healy – and to dear Sally Ledger, who also died too young, have played their part as well. Beyond Birkbeck, friends have engaged generously with the project and helped me frame my ideas: Kate Flint and Gail Jones were helpfully stringent critics in the early stages of the project; Anna Gray and Judy Johnston allowed me to draw on their deep expertise; and Meaghan Clarke, Stefano Evangelista, Catherine Maxwell and Lene Østermark-Johansen shared their extensive knowledge of nineteenth-century visual culture. Kate and Meaghan gave wise and precise guidance as readers of the complete script. I owe a great debt to Steven Holtzman, who reached out a helping hand and got me started again. Martin Sixsmith encouraged me when I lost heart, and was an attentive critical reader in the final stages of writing. Thanks to you all.

This book is deeply informed, of course, by a lifetime of looking at pictures. Looking at art, looking like a woman, is something I have done for as long as I can remember, often with people I love. Particularly moving and formative gallery experiences include Titian in Venice with my Mother in 1990; Edward Hopper with Matthew; Frida Kahlo with Clair; *Whistler's Mother* at the Musée d'Orsay (via Mr Bean) with Adam; the Isabella Stuart Gardner Museum with Steven Holtzman, *Las Meninas*, San Gimignano and, later, Diego Rivera in New York; Anthony Gormley with Russell Celyn Jones and our respective children, Kenwood House (and walks on Hampstead Heath); Eugène Atget and Artemisia Gentileschi in Paris with Martin Sixsmith, Pre-Raphaelites from Port Sunlight to *Pegwell Bay*. Often looking at art involves tears, and I have wept over art with many a dear friend: over Rodin with Gail Jones, when I had to leave the exhibition because, like George Eliot before the *Sistine Madonna,* it 'made my heart swell too much for me to remain comfortably'; over Kathe Kollwitz in Berlin with Orna Raz; over Rothko with Chris Leich; over Matisse and Picasso, especially their love of women's breasts, with Trish Crawford, who had lost her own, and has since lost her life, to cancer; over Brancusi with Prue Kerr and Nick.

Memories of looking at art with people now dead are especially precious and enable vividly specific reconnection. I recall my father's good-humoured indulgence whenever I now experience a surfeit of Madonnas; and recollections of a 'Victorian Ladies' expedition to the Millais Exhibition in 2007 with Nicola Bown, Ella Dzelzainis and Sally Ledger encapsulate all that I treasure about working with a group of women who are close friends as well as professional colleagues – something that Sally especially fostered, and I miss her. Looking at art with Nick taught me how to see afresh, and left me with a fund of the dearest memories, especially of our intensely happy summer in Florence researching the female art historians who worked there in the nineteenth century. Nick is gone, but is everywhere present in this book, and I dedicate it to his memory.

Note

My thinking for this book has taken place over a number of years, and I have explored aspects of my project in a number of earlier articles that I wish to acknowledge here: 'Women and the Ends of Art History: Vision and Corporeality in Nineteenth-Century Critical Discourse'.

Victorian Studies 42, 1 (1999): 77–100; 'Regarding the Eighteenth Century: Vernon Lee and Emilia Dilke Construct a Period'. *The Victorians and the Eighteenth Century: Reassessing the Tradition*, ed. Francis O'Gorman and Katherine Turner. Aldershot: Ashgate (2004), pp. 223–49; 'Interstitial Identities: Vernon Lee and the Spaces In-between'. *Marketing the Author: Authorial Personae, Narrative Selves and Self-Fashioning, 1880–1930*, ed. Marysa Demoor. Houndmills Basingstoke and New York: Palgrave Macmillan (2004), pp. 114–33; 'Writing a Female Renaissance: Victorian Women and the Past'. *Victorian and Edwardian Perspectives on Renaissance Italy*, ed. John E. Law and Lene Østermark-Johansen. Aldershot: Ashgate (2005), pp. 165–84; 'Art History'. *Companion to Women's Historical Writing*, ed. Mary Spongberg, Barbara Caine and Ann Curthoys. Houndmills Basingstoke and New York: Palgrave Macmillan (2005), pp. 29–38. 'A Visual Field: Michael Field and the Gaze'. *Victorian Literature and Culture* 34 (2006): 553–71; 'Through the Looking Glass: Looking like a Woman in the Nineteenth Century'. *Strange Sisters: Literature and Aesthetics in the Nineteenth Century*, ed. Francesca Orestano and Francesca Frigerio. Oxford, Bern etc.: Peter Lang (2009), pp. 189–209; 'Women Writing Art History: The Art of Fiction'. *Yearbook of English Studies* 40, 1 and 40, 2 (2010): 61–82.

Introduction

In 1893, Bernard Berenson wrote from Venice to his friend, the poet Edith Cooper. Berenson was then at the very beginning of his career as a connoisseur and art historian, and he expresses his admiration for the established writer's perceptive appreciation of art: 'There is perhaps no person living whose company before a work of art I covet so much as I do yours', he writes. He finds 'something so profound, & earnest in the effort you make to suck out the soul of a picture that it really makes me feel as if my own powers of appreciation had received a new set of feelers'. In Venice more than anywhere, he declares, he would find her 'sympathy stimulating' to his own ability to respond to the city's art: 'Before the best Bellinis & Carpaccios, the best Tintorettos, & Veroneses you would make me feel as I have felt these days having had the luck to see mirrors throwing a light upon them which revealed in them whole tracts I had not seen before.' The effect of the warm Italian light reflected on the Venetian paintings puts him in mind of Cooper's own power to illuminate and transform his experience of art: 'The mere addition of warmth given by the light was in itself something never to be forgotten when looking again at these pictures. Well, you have in a subtle way, & emotionally, nearly the same effect on a picture, for me, that these mirrors had.'[1] In the previous year Edith Cooper and Katharine Bradley, writing under their authorial signature Michael Field, had published a volume of ekphrastic poetry entitled *Sight and Song*, based on their collaborative response to a series of paintings in British and Continental public galleries. Cooper was an experienced art critic, yet in Berenson's account she is assigned a wholly reflexive role. She figures as a 'mirror' that enables the connoisseur to see more, and more profoundly, what is present in the picture. She is valued for her sympathy and her warmth, qualities that enhance his own emotional encounter with these art works in the same way that the mirrors do. The letter nicely exemplifies how a woman's talent as an art critic could be at once acknowledged and complimented, and at the same time regarded as inevitably subsidiary to a man's expertise. It is an attitude expressed more succinctly in a private comment Berenson made to his partner (later wife) Mary Costelloe about another female writer more established than himself, the art historian and critic Vernon Lee: 'Vernon said something *worthy of me* yesterday ... she somehow makes you feel that she is intelligent.'[2] Anna Jameson did not merit even such equivocal praise from John Ruskin, who confided contemptuously to his father that the popular critic 'has some tact & cleverness, & knows as much of art as the cat'.[3]

My aim in what follows is to correct the partial and distorted view of the emergent discipline of art history, formulated in the nineteenth century and recapitulated in most modern accounts, that art criticism was a masculine intellectual field in which a handful of women played a merely secondary role. In fact, according to the nineteenth-century French art historian Alexis-François Rio, Jameson had a greater influence on the artistic education of the British public than any of her contemporaries, including Ruskin.[4]

The high value placed on art writing by the Victorians makes the neglect of women's contributions especially egregious. Art criticism had an unprecedentedly important public function in nineteenth-century Britain. Writers such as Ruskin and Walter Pater formulated and disseminated an entirely new concept of the cultural and moral value of looking at art. The capacity to respond critically to paintings, sculpture and architectural forms was enshrined as a crucial dimension of human experience.[5] So my book will investigate the part female writers played in developing a discourse of art notable for its complexity and cultural power, its increasing professionalism and reach, and its integration with other discourses of modernity. It will ask how women looked at art in the nineteenth century and how they participated in the mainstream writing of art criticism and art's histories. The past few decades have witnessed a growing intellectual preoccupation with vision and visuality, and with the related issue of the gendered gaze. There has been a steady scholarly interest in the art-historical work of writers such as Charles Eastlake, Walter Pater, and Ruskin and Berenson themselves. But relatively little attention has been paid to women's art criticism and history and to what it can tell us about female visual experience, in all its diversity, and about the patterns and strategies of women's cultural engagement in the nineteenth century.[6] The submerged history of women's relationship to art offers a compelling instance of Deborah Cherry's observation that 'feminine spectators have remained beneath the surface of historical discourse'.[7]

History has frequently been identified as the 'master' discourse of the nineteenth century, while vision has been described by Martin Jay as 'the master sense of the modern era'.[8] The emergence of the new discipline of art history in Victorian Britain combined both. It became uniquely eloquent of the cultural moment and it cast new light on the gender politics of both visuality and history. Because my book is concerned with the intersection of vision, art and history in writing by women, it focuses some of the most momentous questions about how gender shapes ideology in Victorian cultural history. How could women claim visual agency and make space for themselves as observers under the Victorian gender order? In what ways were the female observer's relations to institutions, professions and discourses regulated and circumscribed? And how did female art historians, in particular, participate in the epistemic shift identified by Jonathan Crary, who argues that a new kind of observer took shape in the nineteenth century? Crary's influential study of vision and modernity, *Techniques of the Observer*, speaks of a new understanding of the physiology of human perception, and new interests in the ways in which optical phenomena are mediated by the body. Female art historians and critics provide, as a category, a good example against which to test his theory.[9] To what extent are their experiences as observers marked by gender in ways that distinguish them from the homogeneous 'dominant model' of the modern observer that he proposes? My aim is to re-evaluate the large body of generically diverse art-historical writing by Victorian women that has been written out of literary and art history. My hope is that this will allow the recovery of what Elspeth Probyn calls '"submerged" knowledges', and that in reading these women writers alongside the more mainstream male authors 'we can begin to trace out what is sayable at any one moment', to develop a sense of their differences, and hence of our own.[10]

My focus, then, is on nineteenth-century women observers and specifically on women who looked at and wrote about art. These women, I suggest, have become invisible to the modern gaze. They have barely crossed the sightline even of second-wave feminist art historians who were so concerned with reconceptualising how we write the past that they had little patience for what they saw as the deficiencies of first-wave critical interventions and the putative collusion of their grandmothers in the establishment of a male canon.[11] Yet it is undoubtedly the case that Victorian women wrote about art in ways that anticipate the more systematic approach of twentieth-century feminist scholarship, and which lend themselves to analysis using the tools and concepts of modern gender theory. In the course of my work on the relationship between modern feminist scholarship on the gendered gaze and nineteenth-century art-critical practice, I encountered a suggestive genealogy grounded in a particular family history. Laura Mulvey, Professor of Film and Media at Birkbeck, whose work has done so much to expand our thinking about gender and visuality, is the great-granddaughter of the prominent Victorian poet, journalist and art critic Alice Meynell. Although it must be said that Meynell herself had little time for 'Professors [who] have written of the mental habits of women as though they accumulated generation by generation upon women, and passed over their sons. Professors [who seem to] take it for granted … that women derive from their mothers and grandmothers, and men from their fathers and grandfathers',[12] I do find this particular line of descent irresistible. It seems wonderfully apt that Alice Meynell's pioneering excursions into the realms of visual pleasure should have been renewed three generations on. Laura Mulvey's groundbreaking article in *Screen*, 'Visual Pleasure and Narrative Cinema', is an essay that has generated much debate around the question of the gender of the gaze. Mulvey's work helps frame the questions we might ask about how people looked in the nineteenth century. Her own focus is on Hollywood film, but her argument about its enshrinement of 'woman as image, man as bearer of the look', and about the '"masculinisation" of the spectator position', has been extended into other visual and textual fields.[13] We might similarly ask to what extent patriarchal ideologies, conventional interpretations of sexual difference and heterosexual desire structured the form and discourse of art history and criticism in the nineteenth century. How can such work help the modern reader approach the work of her own great-grandmother, for example?

Alice Meynell, one of numerous women who looked at and wrote professionally about art and aesthetic matters in the nineteenth century, was married to the writer and journalist Wilfred Meynell and mother of their eight children. She was loved by (among others) the poet Coventry Patmore, who gave her the manuscript of his poem *The Angel in the House.* She came to be regarded as a real-life model for this domestic paragon, despite her actual professional identity as an energetic and high-profile figure in the busy world of Victorian journalism and letters. How did such a woman write about art? Why, having commanded a considerable reputation in her own day, is she now so neglected?

In her introduction to the Centenary Volume of essays and poems by Alice Meynell, published in 1947, Vita Sackville-West describes the difficulty of writing about someone whom one never knew, when 'a multitude of the personally well-informed exists to ululate in protest'. 'Like an army of friends and relations invited to view a posthumous painting', she writes, 'they fill the artist's studio with their cries of objection.'[14] Although

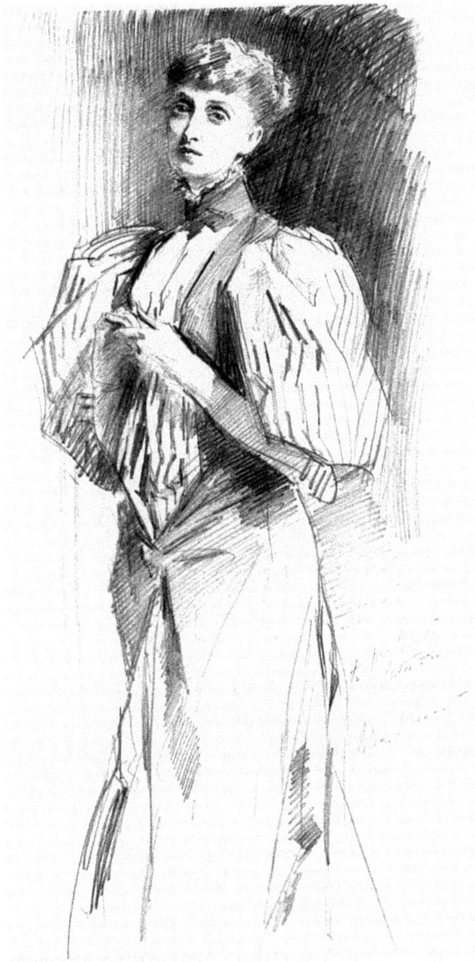

Fig. 1. John Singer Sargent, *Alice Meynell* (1894)

Sackville-West never met her subject, and claims only to be able to put together a 'composite image' of her, she nonetheless makes of her a visual object. She invokes an imaginary portrait, one of the visual forms that most engaged Meynell herself (she wrote, for example, with great insight about the work of John Singer Sargent, whose drawing of Meynell was used as a frontispiece for her books (Fig. 1)).[15] Yet this woman who was the subject of several portraits was also an artist in words. 'She wrote, one might believe, with an etching pen', says Sackville-West, who quotes from a contemporary review that labels her an 'observer of genius', like a jeweller with 'a cylindrical magnifying-glass fixed in one eye'.[16]

Meynell's lyrical essays are full of evocative descriptions of visual phenomena and the process of perception. This woman with, by all accounts, spectacular eyes devoted a whole essay to the subject, called simply 'Eyes'.[17] They are everywhere in her work. Sometimes they are the passive recipients of nature's dazzling special effects, as in the essay 'Rain', where 'nature flashes on our meditative eyes'; where '[t]here is no need for the impressionist to make haste, nor would haste avail him, for mobile nature doubles upon him, and plays with his delays the exquisite game of visibility'.[18] More often, though, eyes are active players in this visual game. They *make* the world, as in her essay on 'The Horizon', which explains: 'All things follow and wait upon your eyes', even, it seems the horizon, for '[t]o mount a hill is to lift with you something lighter and brighter than yourself or than any meaner burden. You lift the world, you raise the horizon; you give a signal for the distance to stand up.'[19] For Meynell the early landscapes of Jean-Baptiste Corot, conceived 'at the time when sleep and dreams claimed his eyes', contain 'the very light of dreams'.[20] Elsewhere, thinking about shadows and clouds, she is intrigued by the way light and darkness are entangled and reversible, and by how painters, such as those of the Newlyn School, represent light in their work.[21]

Meynell's literary essays are scattered with illustrative references to the visual arts – 'Solitude', Millet has painted it; 'Walls', the Norwich painters knew the value of them.[22] But she also wrote dedicated art-historical pieces and notices of art exhibitions, and was well known as an art critic. She contributed regularly to a range of periodicals, including specialist art journals such as the *Magazine of Art* and the *Art Journal*. An article 'Art Critics of To-Day', published in the *Art Journal* in 1892, informs us that 'a good many ladies are to be found' at 'Press Views', and Mrs Meynell heads the list of 'regular critics of well-known weekly and daily journals … who are invariably visible on these and the like occasions'.[23]

In this crowded and notably masculine space, the normally invisible female viewer is made into a visual object. Meaghan Clarke identifies Meynell as one of the women who appear in the accompanying illustration showing 'Press Day at the Royal Academy, 1892' (Fig. 2): 'Meynell is in the top centre with her back to the viewer, wearing a hat and veil.'[24] A friend recalled her appearance at a Royal Academy private view in the 1890s 'wearing a flounced skirt of smoke-grey crepe and a simple black hat. She moved among the women there, many of whom wore eccentric and startling costumes, as if she were a being belonging to another, and

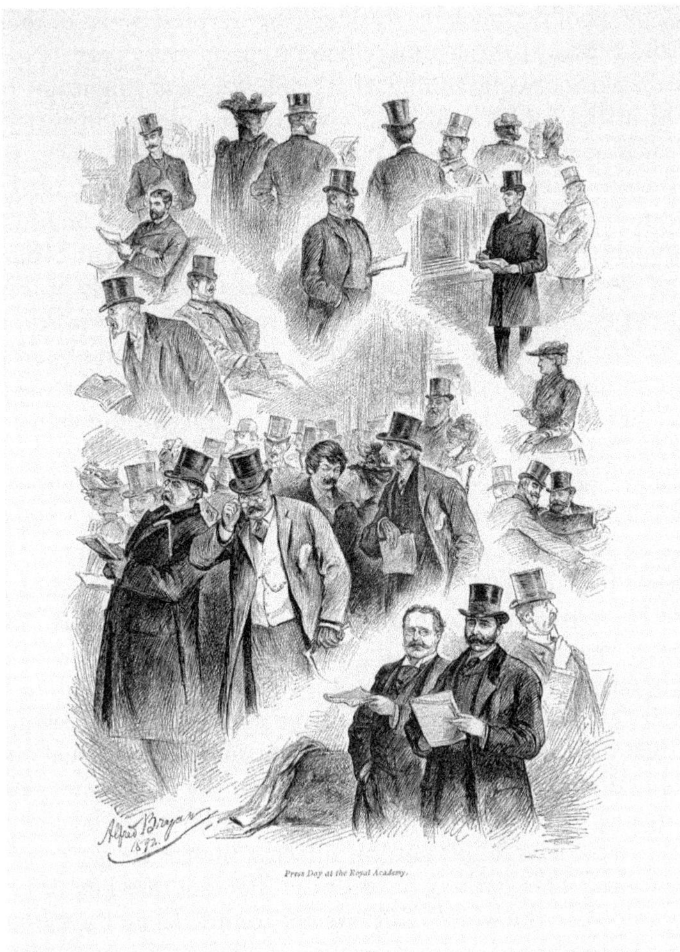

Fig. 2. 'Press Day at the Royal Academy', *Art Journal* (1892)

more rarified, sphere.'[25] This rather distant and ethereal woman was not above making wittily acerbic comments in the margins of the exhibition catalogues. Against *The Judgement* by Burne-Jones, whose work she disliked, she notes: 'So difficult to tell the damned from the blessed'; and at a later exhibition she wrote beside his *The Star of Bethlehem*: 'Angel Trained to carry his feet perpendicularly'.[26] Alice Meynell knew all about being a (domestic) Angel, but it didn't prevent her being a dispassionate critic, even in the case of her friend and mentor John Ruskin. A contemporary review observes of her book on Ruskin: 'The warmest praise of the Master is there and yet courteous alarm-bells are rung on every page.'[27]

She believed, notwithstanding, that while England might not have led the world in the genius of its art, it was, as she wrote, 'in the literature of art that modern England [is] pre-eminent'.[28] Meynell's own contribution to the literature of art is certainly most distinctive, particularly in the attention it gives to the role of the viewer and the analysis of visual pleasure. In this she resembles her contemporary Vernon Lee, who believed that 'the life of all art goes on in the mind and heart, not merely of those who make the work, but of those who see and read it', that '*the* work, the real one', is 'a certain particular state of feeling, a pattern woven of new perceptions and impressions and of old memories and feelings, which the picture, the statue or poem, awakens, different in each different individual'.[29] Like Lee, Meynell creates a space for herself, for herself not least as a woman, to look at art. Writing on Velázquez, whom she accords the title 'the first Impressionist', she declares: 'So little … are we shut out from the mysteries of a great Impressionist's impression that Velásquez requires us to be in some degree his colleagues … he leaves my educated eyes to do a little of the work. He respects my responsibility no less … than I do his.'[30] Meynell identifies in Velázquez's art qualities that Foucault, writing half a century later, elaborates in his discussion of *Las Meninas* in *The Order of Things*: the painter's emphasis on the reciprocity of the gaze, and his disruption of the idea that painting is the representation of an objective visual order.[31] In her introduction to *The Works of John S. Sargent*, Meynell writes eloquently about Sargent's 'manner of seeing and of perceiving what he sees', and of the idiosyncratic 'look' of his portrait subjects, such as the great Italian tragedian Eleanora Duse, whose 'eyes under their sombre lids have … the most direct look in the world'. But it is her comments on the viewer of his work, on 'we spectators', that are most memorable: 'A certain education', she writes, 'makes us able to see well, and that is our art and needs our attention. It is our contribution, and we owe it. Life, light, form and colour in a picture, and indeed in nature, must have our intelligent eyes.'[32]

Alice Meynell was evidently a 'looker', in all senses of the word. But to what extent might her gaze be seen to be gendered; to what extent did sexuality enter her field of vision? She was undoubtedly aware of gender issues, and was, from a young age, a feminist. She believed that women had equal rights with men to work and vote (she was a leading suffragist). Her essays, both those written under her own name and those published anonymously as part of the radical column 'The Wares of Autolycus' in the *Pall Mall Gazette*, are replete with examples of her intolerance of the ill-treatment and the patronising of women. She was alert to the injustices, great and small, routinely suffered by women, and she was active in exposing and opposing them. She recognised that literary and artistic canons are shaped by unexamined critical assumptions and gender biases. So she was far from gender blind, particularly in relation to the gaze. In 1885 she turned a journalistic controversy over the propriety of looking at and painting the nude into a feminist polemic. She deplored the exclusion of women from life classes at public art schools, pointing out the irony of an edict which ensured that, '[o]n the grounds … of conventional propriety, women are deprived of an advantage which could not possibly do them any harm, while men receive with altogether unnecessary abundance, facilities which might conceivably be dangerous'.[33] In the context of women's rights to the life class, she was more than willing to enter into public debate on the question of the 'visual pleasure' that men and women derive from looking at the nude – potentially 'dangerous' for men; 'harmless' for women.

But she was also an Angel, trained – if not to carry her feet perpendicularly – then to maintain a certain upstanding position, schooled to uphold feminine values, such as modesty and discretion. In her own critical writing, she deployed oblique devices and strategies to write about topics such as nudity, focusing on abstract painterly qualities like colour, line or form rather than on the naked body or on her own response as a woman. In her essay 'The Colour of Life', as Talia Schaffer has so deftly argued, she displaces her vision of naked boys swimming in the Serpentine into a disquisition on colour and shape, in which the London gamin 'makes, in his hundreds, a bright and delicate flush between the gray-blue water and the gray-blue sky'.[34] It is only through such abstractions that the watching woman and the naked object of her gaze become subtly connected. In a fascinating counter-narrative, what began as a meditation on colour modulates into a powerful statement about female political agency. Now the colour red, with which the essay opens, 'the colour of violence, or of life broken open, edited, and published', is made figurative in the broken body of a woman. Red is made to signify both the 'flush' of a properly modest woman and the violent death by guillotine of Olympe de Gouges, who wrote 'The Declaration of the Rights of Woman': 'The blood wherewith she should, according to Robespierre, have blushed to be seen or heard in the tribune, was exposed to the public sight unsheltered by her veins.'[35]

To what extent did a woman such as Alice Meynell connect the sexual economy and the visual economy? How far did she acknowledge the politics of the gaze? In an essay such as 'The Colour of Life', whose theme is the viewing of bodies – a woman looking at naked boys, another woman's body viscerally displayed – the sexed body of the female observer is not explicitly invoked. Questions of gender and sexual difference are seemingly disavowed until the bitter violence of the end, which has the effect of retrospectively colouring the entire piece. It is only ostensibly about 'The Colour of Life'. Such displacements are characteristic of women's writing about the body at this time, whether in art-historical discourse or writing about visual experience more generally. They are at once symptomatic of their ideological positioning and discursive circumscription, and, I suggest, an indirect critique of masculine conventions of visual knowing.

Writing such as this raises questions that will inform my thesis about women's writing about art in the nineteenth century. Was there a specific mode, or spectrum of modes, of looking at art that was specific to women? And, if so, how might we understand the conditions that gave rise to gendered spectatorship? How far, in other words, are aesthetics the product of historically and culturally specific social conditions? One of this book's most significant findings, for example, is that while women experienced a variety of forms of professional exclusion that were detrimental to their careers, writing from the margins of established institutional structures often had the effect of freeing up their prose styles, liberating their assumptions and encouraging more adventurous tastes. What might be taken as lightweight, conversational or anecdotal may also be read as – in the broadest sense – experimental.

This range of styles in art writing reflects another distinguishing feature of my study: my emphasis on the diversity of genres in which women discussed art. These included reviews for newspapers and magazines; periodical articles; histories; guide books and travel writings; letters and diaries; novels, short stories and poetry. I do not restrict the category of 'art criticism' to formal treatises on art history, exhibition catalogues and reviews, artist biographies and more abstract aesthetics. Acknowledging the generic flexibility of women's writing about art has the effect of recalibrating our definition of what constitutes art history.[36] And this means the inclusion of many more women – not only those who are recognised as art critics, such as Anna Jameson, Emilia Francis Dilke and Vernon Lee, but many far less familiar names. In adopting this approach I am following the example of feminist work on nineteenth-century life writing. This elected to include not only formal biography and autobiography but also diaries, letters, novels and so on, and has radically altered the gender profile of the canon. Similarly, the contours of Romanticism changed significantly when critical categories defined by what Jerome McGann identified as the Romantic ideology were loosened. Romanticism was found to embrace many more than the great five poets, including dozens of previously neglected female authors. Giving proper weight to the range of women's writing as well as to the celebrated male art historians changes our understanding of the whole landscape of Victorian art writing. Berenson's circle included not only Edith Cooper but also his wife Mary, and their neighbours Vernon Lee and Maud Cruttwell, all art historians. Ruskin's included not only Alice Meynell but also Katharine Bradley and the formidable art historian Emilia Dilke. Reading the work produced by these women helps us to understand nineteenth-century art scholarship and appreciation in more nuanced ways.

This book asks about whether women *saw* differently from men. My answer is tied in part to my contention that, for some women, writing from a position of exclusion meant seeing outside the categories and value judgements that structured the writings of their male counterparts. These men were, themselves, involved in consolidating and professionalising the field of art writing, and this involved setting up certain enduring distinctions. Women challenged these both implicitly and openly, especially the distinction between 'art' on the one hand, and 'crafts' and 'interior design' on the other. Indeed, some women expanded their definition of art to include not only the domestic arts, but also activities such as fashion and cookery. I do not, however, intend to stereotype art criticism in terms of gender. I emphasise throughout the book that women moved comfortably between the fine arts, new forms of art such as photography, and the arts of the home – as, increasingly, did male critics. When women encountered painting and sculpture in different social and cultural circumstances from men, this could have a considerable impact on the nature of their viewing. Different protocols could come into play in writing about the naked form, for example, as we have seen in the case of Alice Meynell. Expectations about modesty and propriety undoubtedly led women to emphasise abstract qualities rather than subject matter. I am also interested in the lesbian gaze that Michael Field turned upon art, as it is displayed in the conversations between Katharine Bradley and Edith Cooper – in poetry and in prose – about painting.

The chapters that follow explore the many ways in which women negotiated masculine conventions of visual knowing and critical discourse in order to write about art. They investigate how women inhabiting different subject positions and employing different modes of visual consumption developed strategies for articulating their experiences of and experiments with art, visuality and aesthetics; how they wrote and performed across a wide range of genres, cultural contexts and media. My book reassesses the contribution and critical impact of these women, who have too often been accorded a secondary or derivative role in modern art historiographies. In many cases their writing was in ephemeral forms, such as the periodical press, and their impact may also have been ephemeral. I suggest, though, that they played a critical role, for example, in the 'uneven development' of ideology. In other cases their interventions were important and original, and their legacies enduring. From Anna Jameson and Lady Eastlake to Julia Cartwright and Vernon Lee, women have contributed in imaginative and scholarly ways to the historiography of art and the formation of an academic discipline.

Because the social and institutional position of women had such an important influence on their writing, I begin my book with a consideration of the place of female writers in the emerging profession and intellectual discipline of art history. Chapter 1 examines the professional lives and reputations of pioneering women from Anna Jameson, Mary Merrifield and Elizabeth Rigby (later Lady Eastlake) to the art specialists Francis Pattison (later Emilia Dilke), Julia Cartwright and Maud Cruttwell, who were active towards the end of the century. While the specialist professional field was still in the process of definition, British art history in the second half of the nineteenth century was still in many respects at a pre-disciplinary stage. This made it easier for women to claim a professional identity. At the same time, the audience for art and the appetite for learning about it were expanding across all classes. By the middle of the century, Britain had become a nation of spectators and critics, as exhibition attendance figures and the number of visual and textual depictions of the new museum culture attest. Fine art images made their way into shop windows and into the home, not only in the fashionable streets of London or via educated networks such as the Arundel Society, but in provincial towns and in the pages of the penny press. The art historian Anna Jameson observed in 1843 that 'the *Penny Magazine* [could] place a little print after Mantegna at once before the eyes of fifty thousand readers'; the fine arts were made democratically available to an entirely new viewing public.[37] Looking at art, writing about it and reading about it were no longer the reserve of an aesthetic elite but at the very centre of Victorian cultural life. This was widely reflected in its literature, not least literature by women.

Although numbers of women engaged in formal art criticism and historical research, and some published in scholarly forms, it remained more acceptable for them to publish in certain genres than in others. Some writers, for example, wrote about art and artists in fiction, and this is the subject of my second chapter. Many novels took art and artists as a central theme, both fictional (for example, Anne Brontë's *The Tenant of Wildfell Hall* (1848), Dinah Craik's *Olive* (1850) and Mary Elizabeth Braddon's *Lady Audley's Secret* (1862)) and historical (as in George Eliot's *Romola* (1862–3) and Anne Thackeray Ritchie's *Miss Angel and Fulham Lawn* (1876)). The ways in which individuals respond to art can be a crucial marker of character.[38] Jane Eyre is a seeing subject, an artist and a lover of art. She is introduced to the reader as a girl who consoles herself for the fact that '[t]here was no possibility of taking a walk that day' by immersing herself in a book, 'taking care that it should be one stored with pictures', and displaying less interest in the letterpress than in the images.[39] Jane's drawings have considerable symbolic power, and Rochester's engagement with them is a crucial feature of their courtship.

My third chapter, on 'Girl Guides', focuses on other genres of art writing with which women are particularly associated – guidebooks, travel books, letters, exhibition guides, translations, popular histories, ekphrastic poetry. Some of the women who would go on to write as professional art critics, such as Anna Jameson and Elizabeth Rigby, began their writing careers as translators and travel writers; a number wrote introductory historical surveys of art for popular audiences, including female readers. So this chapter provides an occasion for thinking about art criticism as a mediating agent between different genres, enabling the metaphorical translation of one form into another, of images into texts, and the turning of spectators into readers.

Chapter 4, 'Women's Periods', turns to more formal examples of art criticism and historical writing to consider ways in which historical periodisation is gendered. Focusing on women's writing about the Middle Ages, the Renaissance and the eighteenth century, and looking particularly at the art-historical work of Emilia Dilke, Vernon Lee, Anna Jameson and Julia Cartwright, it addresses the question of how women reconceived these historical periods. They all, for example, discuss the cultural roles assumed by women. Sometimes, as in the case of Cartwright, they draw on women's historical archives to demonstrate how this altered perspective changes our modern sense of a period in art history. What happens, for instance, when the history of the Renaissance is viewed through the eyes of Beatrice or Isabella d'Este? And they all experimented with voice, style and methodology. Anna Jameson wrote about art in a fictional diary, in travel narratives, and in a study of Marian iconography, while Vernon Lee summoned the ghosts of the past through her reading of portraits and the evocation of the *genius loci*. Emilia Dilke offered new perspectives on eighteenth-century French culture by broadening her definition of art to include furniture and the decorative arts of the home.

The final chapter turns to the so-called 'Feminine Arts'. It looks not only at women's articles and books on the art of the home and the art of dress, but also at their writing about photography, an art form that was feminised in nineteenth-century critical discourse, and at their responses to contemporary movements in the fine arts. Much of the work by women such as Florence Fenwick Miller, Rosamund Marriott Watson and Elizabeth Robins Pennell was published in the periodical press which, by the final decades of the century, had become an important medium for female art criticism. In a review of an exhibition on 'Les Arts de la Femme' in Paris in 1892, Pennell reports: 'seldom have I been disappointed more woefully … The arts of woman, in this case, did not mean the work of her hands, but any and everything with the least claim to beauty, made for her benefit.'[40] The chapter concludes with a discussion of how, in addition to writing about the arts designed for women's pleasure and benefit, female critics also wrote about 'feminine arts' in the sense of contemporary art produced and exhibited by women.

CHAPTER I

The profession of art history

> Given that we can define art history as a hegemonic discourse, we are forced then to ask: can feminists be 'art historians' – that is, professionals within its extended remit of curation, history and criticism? Or does that not of itself imply self-identification with the hegemonic tradition embodied in institutionalised art history, with the canonical as a systematic pattern of inclusions and exclusions which are generated from and sustain deep structures of social and economic power?[1]

In the middle of the nineteenth century, opportunities for the public to view the fine arts in Britain, as well as in Continental Europe, expanded on an unprecedented scale. The National Gallery more than doubled the size of its collection between 1843 and 1855, and initiatives such as the contest for the decoration of the new Palace of Westminster in 1843 provided a catalyst for major exhibitions of public art. The Manchester Art Treasures Exhibition of 1857 meant that even works in private collections were made available to the public gaze, and reached mass audiences. This new exposure to the fine arts enabled an explosion of visual pleasure, but the novel experience of viewing painting and sculpture in such rich abundance induced anxiety among some spectators. One visitor to the Manchester Exhibition, New England novelist Nathaniel Hawthorne, records:

> I was unquiet, from a hopelessness of being able fully to enjoy it. Nothing is more depressing than the sight of a great many pictures together ... We went first into the gallery of British Painting, where there were hundreds of pictures ... but I could not fix my mind on one more than another; so I left my wife there, and wandered away by myself ... it was dreary to think of not fully enjoying this collection, the very Flower of Time, which never bloomed before, and never by any possibility can bloom again.[2]

To be sure, Hawthorne is registering here in part the problem of excess: how to appreciate the single, discrete work of art amidst such plenitude. But here, and elsewhere, he also conveys a deeper aesthetic anxiety about his ability to respond appropriately to art that seems endemic to his times, an 'unquiet' that his wife, the painter and illustrator Sophia Peabody Hawthorne, who remains in the gallery when he makes his escape, seemingly doesn't share. Indeed her own journals, published as *Notes in England and Italy* in 1869 (after her husband's death, since he disapproved of female authorship), make it clear that she was an enthusiastic and discerning critic of art.[3] This was something that Hawthorne, who had to work hard to educate his own visual sensibilities, readily acknowledged, and celebrated in the attributes he gives to the young American artist Hilda in his novel *The Marble Faun*, of whom we are told:

> She was endowed with a deep and sensitive faculty of appreciation; she had the gift of discerning and worshipping excellence, in a most unusual measure … She saw – no, not saw, but felt – through and through a picture; she bestowed upon it all the warmth and richness of a woman's sympathy, not by any intellectual effort, but by this strength of heart, and this guiding light of sympathy, she went straight to the central point, in which the Master had conceived his work. Thus she viewed it, as it were, with his own eyes, and hence her comprehension of any picture that interested her was perfect.[4]

Hawthorne's highly gendered account of Hilda's exquisite 'womanly' sensibility to the beautiful, albeit her own visual agency is entirely subsumed into the vision of the Master painter, is widely regarded as modelled on Sophia's own (both were copyists, adept at capturing and translating the essence of a work of art), and seems informed by his own experience of museum and gallery visits in England and Italy, especially Rome, with his wife:

> Happy were those … whom she ever chose to be the companions of her day; they saw the art-treasures of Rome, under her guidance, as they had never seen them before. Not that Hilda could dissertate, or talk learnedly about pictures; she would probably have been puzzled by the technical terms of her own art. Not that she had much to say about what she most profoundly admired; but even her silent sympathy was so powerful that it drew your own along with it, endowing you with a second-sight that enabled you to see excellencies with almost the depth and delicacy of her own perceptions.[5]

The professional status of art history in the nineteenth century

In this new age of tourism and ever-expanding museum, gallery and exhibition culture, there must have been many who would have appreciated such a companion to give critical guidance on how to respond to art. It was within such a milieu that art journalism and the modern academic discipline of art history originated and began to become professionalised and institutionalised. Writers produced a dazzling array of literature on the visual arts, and art criticism was accorded an extraordinarily influential public role, unprecedented in modern history. Among those who wrote articles for the periodical press, monographs on artists, historical surveys, guidebooks and other kinds of art literature designed to aid, direct, regulate and inspire modern readers and spectators were female art specialists, both historians and critics. Some, like Elizabeth Eastlake, Emilia Dilke and Julia Cartwright, made the 'intellectual effort' required to develop technical expertise and a critical language to 'dissertate' and 'talk learnedly' about pictures, as professional art historians. Many more, like Sophia Hawthorne herself, moved beyond the 'silent sympathy' admired by her husband, and published their writing about art in the form of travel journals, journalism, diaries, letters, poetry and other less academic genres than the formal art-historical treatise. Others again, like Hilda, inhabit works of fiction, and in this form mediate their authors' views on the contemporary art world. Women's engagement with art was thus articulated across a variety of genres.

Although in their day women made a significant contribution to mainstream contemporary aesthetic debate, as well as working within women's artistic and intellectual networks, and forming distinctively female cultural discourses, much of their critical and historical work on art has fallen out of view for modern readers. Yet the 'first professional English art historian' was, according to Adele Holcomb, a woman: Anna Brownell Jameson (1794–1860), widely read author of a major three-volume study of religious iconography in the arts and numerous popular art treatises and guidebooks.[6] Three decades after her death, the writer of an article already referred to in the introduction, 'Art Critics of To-Day', published in the *Art Journal* in 1892 declares, 'We have not yet forgotten Mrs. Jameson', but by this point many more names can be added to the list of women known principally for their contribution to art history. As the pseudonymous author notes, 'Several of the most admirable writers on Art during recent years have been, and are, highly cultivated women … among our contemporaries the names of Mrs. Oliphant, Miss Julia Cartwright, Miss Helen Zimmern, and others occur readily.' These writers are specifically distinguished as art historians as opposed to 'the regular critics of well-known weekly and daily journals', among whom 'a good many ladies are to be found' (eight prominent female art journalists are cited by name, including as we have seen Alice Meynell).[7] The world invoked by this writer is one in which women play an active and seemingly integral role. They are to be seen in the illustrations accompanying the article, both as single figures contemplating art works and among the crowds of journalists on press day at the Royal Academy, and other names could be added to his roll call of female art historians producing substantial scholarly studies in the latter part of the nineteenth century, such as Emilia Dilke, Vernon Lee and Maud Cruttwell.

While acknowledging the extensive participation of female art historians and critics of the intellectual stature of Dilke in late nineteenth-century artistic networks, some prominent modern feminist scholars have, however, argued that they were complicit in the formation of a professional discipline that is deeply and fatally gendered. Germaine Greer, for example, observes that female artists have been betrayed by the very women who might have bought and promoted their work, including female art historians working in the nineteenth and early twentieth centuries:

> Women are consumers of art; they are also art historians, but they have not so passionately espoused their own cause that they have become a market that will impose its own values. They did not as a result of the 1906 exhibition [Une Exposition retrospective d'Art feminine] begin to haunt the salerooms on the qui vive for any scent of an Artemisia Gentileschi; they did not force the prices of women's work up by bidding at auctions.[8]

Deborah Cherry focuses even more specifically on the failure of nineteenth-century women art historians to exercise influence at this important moment of canon formation, noting that '[t]heir writings participated in the discipline of art history at a crucial stage in its development, and their silence contributed to the structural exclusions of women artists in the history of art and the public collections of the early twentieth century'. She concludes: 'in refuting sexual difference and refusing women artists, these writers assisted in the framing of those discourses of art which became hegemonic in the later nineteenth century, in which masculinity was inscribed as the central area of study and the pivotal term of reference'.[9] Paradoxically, then, it seems, the pioneering women art historians of the nineteenth century played a significant part in creating the ideological construct of art history that it is the project of modern feminist scholars to undo. In light of this, Griselda Pollock's feminist refusal of the title art historian, and her question 'can feminists be "art historians"', constitute an ironic riposte to Jameson's first-wave claim to a professional identity.

It is the project of this book to reassess the historiographical work of these nineteenth-century women writers on art and their interventions in academic discourses, not only in the context of canon formation but also in light of *how* they write about art and its histories, and how they shape, disrupt, negotiate and critique – theoretically, methodologically, strategically and politically – the professional discipline of art history at the very moment of its emergence. But such a project must begin with the question: 'What did it mean to be a professional art historian in the nineteenth century?' The term 'professional' is itself, of course, semantically unstable, shifting and changing over time, and specifying, as N. N. Feltes argues, a 'field of ideological tension'.[10] Professionalism is a category that is neither meaningful outside history nor empty of ideological signification; indeed, it is constitutive of ideology, a critical site for the negotiation and contestation of cultural values and norms. In the nineteenth century, its positive connotations, such as guaranteed adherence to mutually agreed standards of practice, were heavily counterbalanced by its associations with commoditisation, from which the amateur, free of the pressures of commercial production and the need to make a living, was absolved.

Furthermore, art history as a distinct disciplinary category, at least as it was practised in Britain in the nineteenth century, itself had a curiously uncertain professional status. While some European universities began teaching the history of art as an academic subject early in the nineteenth century, and Chairs were established in Göttingen in 1813, Berlin in 1844 and Vienna in 1851, it was not until the twentieth century that undergraduate programmes in art history were developed in British universities, despite the foundation of the Slade Professorships in Oxford, Cambridge and University College London in 1869. Although it was clearly associated with the emergence of a new kind of historical consciousness at mid-century that galvanised the profession of history, and was becoming increasingly professionalised in Continental Europe, in Britain art history was slow to adopt the new, more culturally contextualising or more technically and scientifically based methodologies of modern historiography, curatorship and connoisseurship. Laurie Kane Lew goes so far as to describe this period as a 'preprofessional age, before art history had acquired disciplinary identity or an institutional structure, before Roger Fry created the modern specialised art critic', noting 'the unspecialised amateurism of art criticism as a discursive practice', particularly in the early to mid nineteenth century.[11]

These are the very conditions within which we might expect women to be able to prosper as art historians, since they were ostensibly as free as men to claim cultural authority and enter the field despite their lack of specialist knowledge, and there were undoubtedly some who took that opportunity. Yet such a sanguine view of the opportunities for women to make a career as art historians should be tempered by what we know of the obstacles facing women who wished to pursue a professional writing life of any kind. For being a professional writer, even if the term is used loosely to refer to anyone who earned an income from writing, meant different things for men and women in this period, not least because of the legal constraints and social taboos surrounding women's rights to earn and own an income that reforms such as the Married Women's Property Acts only began to lift later in the century.[12] And of course women's access to institutions, professions and discourses remained highly regulated and circumscribed throughout the nineteenth century, which made it hard for them to claim the kind of authority that a university education, for example, or membership of a professional association conferred upon men. When Ruskin identified himself on the title page of the first volume of his first book *Modern Painters* (1843) as a 'Graduate of Oxford', he was announcing himself not only as an amateur but as a scholar and a gentleman. It was a descriptor that endowed him with a kind of intellectual authority and independence that was simply unavailable to women at this time, as the later title Slade Professor was to do even more decisively. 'High' art, as Lew reminds us, 'remained, throughout the eighteenth and nineteenth centuries, under the discursive and institutional control of men'.[13]

But there is another reason why we should qualify the notion that the quasi-amateur status of art history in the nineteenth century made it attractive and accessible to women, and that is the intriguing fact that the most serious and informed female art historians, working both early and late in the period, tended, almost to a woman, to promote the more specialist and professional style of art criticism practised in Continental Europe in preference to the more literary and generalist mode favoured in Britain. Arguably this was precisely to escape the confines of their societal circumstances. Often self-educated, or educated at home, such women read widely in the most current European critical literature in the field, consuming and reproducing knowledge in what Lew calls 'a circulating economy of art',[14] mediating it for a British reading public used to a different mode of art criticism. Anna Jameson herself is a case in point. In her preface to a translation of Gustav Waagen's life of Rubens, she wrote in 1840: 'Neither our English artists nor our English public are as yet accustomed to that *many-sided* and elevated spirit in criticism with which the Germans have long been familiar.' She goes on:

> To know *what* a picture represents, and with what degree of propriety and success it is represented, may be sufficient critical skill for the consideration of nine-tenths of the pictures which yearly cover the walls of our Academy: but to enable us to appreciate the creations of genius, and to reap all the

> pleasure and improvement which art can bestow, we must go far higher and deeper.[15]

The tendency to concentrate principally on the subject that Jameson notes here was only reinforced by the cultural phenomenon of Ruskin, who was about to launch his brilliantly eclectic and highly subjective and literary account of modern painters to the critically one-dimensional British readership she describes, and who was to exercise such peculiar cultural authority in Britain over the middle decades of the century.

Ruskin was, unsurprisingly, disparaging about Jameson's own art-historical knowledge and practice. In 1845 he declared in a letter to his parents, as we have seen, that she 'knows as much of art as the cat'.[16] A couple of years later, they coincidentally stayed at the same hotel in Venice as she completed her notes on Venetian painting for her book *Sacred and Legendary Art* and he researched *The Stones of Venice*. Later, in his autobiography, *Praeterita*, he retrospectively dismissed her as wholly unoriginal and derivative, pronouncing: 'Mrs Jameson was absolutely without knowledge or instinct of painting (and had no sharpness of insight even for anything else); but she was candid and industrious, with a pleasant disposition to make the best of all she saw, and to say, compliantly, that a picture was good, if anybody had ever said so before.'[17] Ruskin's view of her importance as an art historian has been radically challenged by more recent scholarship,[18] but it is true that Jameson was not in the fortunate position of being independently wealthy, as Ruskin was, and she had to support not only herself but also several dependants by her writing on art, and so she was obliged both to be industrious and to write books with popular appeal. However, while it must be conceded that her early work, in particular, is heavily larded with references to distinguished (and generally male) scholars (to the extent that, as Lew notes, 'There is no single voice in her writings: rather, her critical identity is established by affiliating herself with the expertise of others – connoisseurs, artists, scholars like Waagen and Eastlake, or "our mutual friend N—"')[19], it is instructive to look at which authorities she most often invokes, and to think, therefore, about how she is announcing herself as an art critic, and how she is aligning herself professionally.

Intriguingly, as becomes evident when we look at the kinds of approach to art most admired by Jameson and other female art historians writing through the century, we find that they are typically drawn to the new, the Continental, the more 'scientific' and technical studies that carefully research and historically locate the art work. They are attracted by a seemingly more professional mode of art history and criticism, one that attends carefully to questions of attribution, date and place, and is more closely associated with curatorial practice. Jameson herself was influenced not only by Waagen and Eastlake, directors respectively of the Berlin Gallery and the National Gallery, but also by a number of contemporary French and German art historians, most notably Alexis-François Rio, Adolphe-Napoléon Didron, Félicie d'Ayzac, J. D. Passavant, and Karl Friedrich von Rumohr, whose *Italienische Forschungen* (1827–31) provided her with an up-to-date source on Italian painting and modern German art-historical methods when she wrote her own *Memoirs of the Early Italian Painters* (1845).[20] Holcomb draws attention to '[t]he originality of Jameson's historical sense', and to her appreciation of the modern, by contrast with Ruskin or with the prevailing tenor of Murray's Handbooks – why, she asks in her essay 'The House of Titian' (1846), 'should we be always looking back?'[21] These are characteristics that locate her intellectually within Continental rather than British art-historical research at this time.

Elizabeth Eastlake, who had already established a reputation for her writing on art as Elizabeth Rigby before her marriage to Charles Eastlake, moved in similar intellectual circles to Jameson, whose close friend and, later, literary executrix she was, and whose last unfinished book, *The History of Our Lord*, she completed.[22] In May 1850, she writes in her journal of the visit of the German art historian Passavant to London, and of the dinner they hosted in his honour, at which she placed him 'next to Mrs. Jameson, whom he knows'.[23] Lady Eastlake was fluent in German, having spent two years in Heidelberg and, as Elizabeth Rigby, she had translated Passavant's account of his earlier tour through the English collections, undertaken 'for the purpose of ascertaining the state of art in that country', and published it in 1836 under the title *Tour of a German Artist in England with Notices of Private Galleries, and Remarks on the State of Art*.[24] The Eastlakes also entertained Gustav Waagen, with Jameson, in London in the summer of 1850, and, like her friend, Elizabeth Eastlake transmitted his work to a British readership through her translation in three volumes of his *Treasures of Art in Great Britain* (1854).[25]

Elizabeth Eastlake admired Jameson's genuine scholarship, but drew a very clear distinction between those whom she considered to be serious art historians and critics and mere amateurs, including women, whose work was derivative and ill-informed. In an article on Leonardo da Vinci in the *Edinburgh Review* in 1875, for example, later incorporated with others into the volume *Five Great Painters* (1883), she is critical of the recent book on the artist by Mary Margaret Heaton: 'An English work was also compiled by a lady in 1874, giving much that had previously been published on the life and work of the great master; including, it must be owned, anecdotes and conclusions long disproved, and lacking also the discriminating criticism requisite in such an undertaking.'[26] In her later essay on Titian, she makes a more general comment about the quality of contemporary British critical writing on art:

> For if it be very rare to meet with one with the power to advance a really critical opinion – and such all connoisseurs will readily respect – it is far rarer to find another with the discretion to abstain from any opinion at all. In this dilemma, each borrows the best ideas he can gather from his neighbour, who, if the truth were known, has obtained them by the same secondhand process himself. In short, the chief result is a faithful illustration of Hans Andersen's fable of the 'Emperor's Clothes' – minus the child. It is only just to add that, this unanimous agreement in what Carlyle would call 'a great sham' has been fostered by a class of modern literature which has reduced, or rather expanded, a limited vocabulary into little better than a fashionable jargon.[27]

As her polite but firm corrections and criticisms of such second-rate work demonstrate throughout her long critical career, Eastlake was keen to distance herself from the kind of unscholarly recycling of Vasarian anecdote that passed as art history in some English circles. As a woman, she was particularly anxious not to be associated with what she viewed as the popularising histories of art by women such as Heaton or, worse still, the amateur compilations of women like the American feminist historian Elizabeth Ellet, whose 1859 book *Women Artists in All Ages and Countries*, though adjudged by Pamela Gerrish Nunn to be 'an important book … which had particular value for female readers', was severely reviewed in the *Athenaeum* in a way that threatened to throw all such women's work into disrepute:

> Nothing is easier, or, in general, more unsatisfactory, than this summarizing, significant of a few visits to a public library, the ransacking of one or more bibliographies, with a vague amount of raw reading and discursive transcript. Mrs Ellet … is purely and simply a collector and assorter of rough materials.[28]

Nor would she have wished to be patronised, as Ellen Clayton was in the review of her 1876 study *English Female Artists*, for her womanly treatment of a womanly topic: 'Without any attempt at Art-Criticism, Miss Clayton tells the stories, long or brief as they may happen to be, of our Art sisters very pleasantly and very creditably both to them and to herself.'[29] Lady Eastlake's own critical models were for the most part male,

European and rigorously professional. Travelling with her husband in Italy to acquire paintings for the National Gallery gave her the opportunity to meet in 1864 one of the most influential of the modern scholars defining the profession of art history at mid-century, Giovanni Morelli, 'one of those extraordinarily clever men whom even the slavery of Italy did not extinguish'. Later, in 1882, she wrote a paper on Raphael for the *Edinburgh Review* for which she drew heavily upon Morelli's *Die Werke italienischer Meister*, confessing to her friend Sir Henry Layard: 'It was difficult to say anything new about Raphael, except what Morelli supplies.'[30] Morelli's controversial ideas, and his practice of basing attributions on the exact study of an artist's rendition of apparently minor details such as fingernails or ears, were to become more widely known the following year in England with the translation of this work by Louise Schwab Richter as *Italian Masters in German Galleries* (1883). Significantly, for it was an important part of Morelli's method, Eastlake made careful use of photographs and prints, rather than drawings or engravings which were less accurate, and regrets that 'there is not a sign' of the 'recently published records' pertaining to Raphael advertised by Crowe and Cavalcaselle in the first volume of their new book, showing her eagerness to benefit from the latest research.[31] Morelli was, for Eastlake, not only a good friend, but 'the ablest connoisseur of art of his time', and following his death in 1891 she wrote an important account of his life and work, entitled 'Giovanni Morelli: The Patriot and Critic', for the *Quarterly Review*, in which she draws attention to the 'sympathy between modern Italian connoisseurship and modern Italian patriotism' in his work, and claims that he 'create[d] a revolution in the history of criticism'.[32]

The article celebrates the 'modern profession' of connoisseurship that Morelli had inaugurated, opposing his meticulous scientific method with 'the haphazard arguments, which, in what has been called the pre-Morellian period, have been dignified with the name of "authority"'.[33] Eastlake had, in 1857, written a pioneering account of photography for the same journal, and here she stresses the role of this still new form of representation and reproduction as 'an invaluable ally to the connoisseur', in that it enables the close comparison of different works by the same painter, and therefore increases the likelihood of accurate attribution.[34] She concludes her piece with the hope that 'we have convinced the reader that true Connoisseurship, or the identification of a master, may be indirectly a matter of intuition, tradition, and documentary evidence; but it is directly dependent on a mode of research infinitely more intellectual, exact, and not altogether independent of common sense and conscientiousness'.[35] Interestingly, she twice in her letters refers to Anna Jameson's 'conscientiousness',[36] recalling Ruskin's damning description of her as 'industrious', but here conscientiousness is recuperated and made into a respectable virtue that any professional art historian who subscribes to Morelli's empiricist emphasis on close looking must needs have. Certainly it is a quality that, like common sense and exactness, it is not beyond the reach of the female historian of art to acquire.

Writing from the margins/at the cutting edge

In the same year that Lady Eastlake wrote her celebratory article on Morelli's connoisseurship and his renovation of the study of art, another woman, Mary Whitall Costelloe, left her husband and children to move to Italy and, declining 'merely to dabble in it',[37] to make a professional study of art (and a new relationship) with the up-and-coming art historian Bernard Berenson. Within a few years, in an article for the *Nineteenth Century* in 1894, we find her, like Eastlake and Jameson before her, mounting the case for 'the new' art criticism vis-à-vis the old. She writes disparagingly about the literary-rhetorical kind of art criticism practised by Ruskin and Pater and their followers, and about 'our bad national habit of jumping at the obvious literary meaning of a work of art, instead of waiting until we have mastered the actual forms in which the artist has incarnated his ideas, and which alone can reveal them'. Instead, she celebrates the 'new scientific school of art criticism' (exemplified, of course, by Berenson, whose first book on Renaissance art, *The Venetian Painters of the Renaissance*, was published in that year, but inaugurated, she explains, by Morelli) which improvements in photographic technology and modern travel have only recently made possible, and which confers upon art history for the first time a kind of professional legitimacy equal to that of the natural sciences, or philology or history.[38]

Elizabeth Eastlake had written privately to her younger colleague in 1893 of the importance of Morelli's influence: 'Our friend Morelli has created what is called "a new departure" in Art, & the present generation is fortunate in being born to it.'[39] But of course women of her own generation, like Eastlake herself in her critical work on photography, had also been in the vanguard of this new more technical and professional departure. Mary Merrifield, for example, had in the 1840s developed a knowledge of ancient traditional painting techniques that was unparalleled in her day, and which led the government to employ her to conduct research associated with the work of the Royal Commission on the Fine Arts set up in

1841 in connection with the rebuilding of the Houses of Parliament. The two major books emerging from this research, *The Art of Fresco Painting* (1846) and *Original Treatises on the Arts of Painting* (1849), amount to what Merrifield's modern editor describes as 'a very thorough collection of early technical information and recipes on all the arts, which have still not been superseded'.[40] Merrifield's government-funded research involved going to Northern Italy to collect manuscripts relating to the 'processes and methods of oil-painting adopted by the Italians' and also oral testimony by living Italian artists, which she then compared to 'many of the best English and foreign works connected with the fine arts, in order to ascertain how far the statements and practices of these artists were supported in their view of the practice of the old masters', only including in her published volumes information that was strictly verifiable.[41]

By the later nineteenth century it was standard practice for female art historians to research their books and articles using original archives and on the basis of first-hand technical knowledge. Julia Cartwright, for example, worked on the correspondence of Isabella d'Este, in the Gonzaga archives at Mantua, a cache of material, she writes, that throws '[a] flood of light … on the history of Italy in the fifteenth and sixteenth centuries', with the result that in her own studies of Isabella and Beatrice d'Este, 'public events and personages have been placed in a new aspect; the judgments of posterity have been modified and, in some instances, reversed'.[42] Cartwright explains how she brings together for the first time in her study 'the vast number of letters which passed between [Isabella d'Este] and the chief artists of the day', which have 'hitherto lain buried in foreign archives or hidden in pamphlets and periodicals, many of them already out of print'.[43] Working thus with original materials proved to be not without its difficulties. Cartwright carefully acknowledged the work of the Gonzaga archivists Alessandro Luzio and Rudolpho Renier; however, envious of her success, they accused her of stealing their work and violating international laws of copyright. Although Cartwright was publicly vilified, she was eventually completely exonerated, but the originality and professionalism of her published work was achieved at some cost, ironically, to her professional reputation.[44]

Maud Cruttwell, starting out on her career as an art historian and determined to be professional in her approach, was mortified to discover that the secondary sources she had used for her book on *Luca and Andrea Della Robbia* (1902) were inaccurate, even studies by the eminent French scholar Emile Molinier. She wrote despairingly to her friend and mentor Mary Berenson from Paris: 'I'm disappointed with Molinier … Every quotation is wrong – full of the grossest mistakes – all of which I've copied into my book to my eternal shame & never shall I get Dent … to go to the expense of correcting them.' Having learned to her cost that she cannot trust even the most distinguished of secondary sources, she is more careful with her next project, telling Mary crossly: 'Every French book I open contradicts the last – the documents are all misquoted – the dates all different. It's unravelling a skein of knots & how to find out the most reliable of these unreliable people I don't know.'[45]

Emilia Dilke was a more experienced scholar by the time she published her monumental four-volume study of eighteenth-century French art around the same date, and in it she acknowledges but also quibbles with other scholars, such as the Goncourt brothers, and draws attention to the meticulousness of her research and how long it has taken her.[46] She is concerned that her work be understood for what it is: an original study rather than a 'mere compilation' of second-hand ideas, proudly asserting 'I have described nothing, I have criticised nothing that I have not seen for myself', and accusing others of cutting corners and depending on unverified secondary sources.[47] Her text is heavily freighted with footnotes and references to the primary and secondary sources she has used, and the reader who does not have a good knowledge of French would find it hard to follow. Dilke pursued modern research methods in her numerous publications on French art from the Renaissance on, and as a consequence she had to endure the criticism that she excessively paraded her learning in her work.[48] She was anxious, like Elizabeth Eastlake, to differentiate herself as a serious art historian from the mere popularisers of art, and she does indeed take an uncompromisingly academic approach to her subject in all her art-historical studies. As one critic observes, hers is '[a] positivist orientation, keyed towards an objective perspective, devoid of … maundering and prettification'.[49] The extraordinarily comprehensive ambit of her work was based on her belief in the importance of original primary research, of a knowledge of the social and economic conditions under which art was produced, and of examining all the arts of an epoch, both the fine arts and the so-called minor arts, in order to gain a more accurate understanding of the period style. It also perhaps suggests her anxiety about being accepted as a serious art historian.

Dilke insisted on her professionalism as a researcher and critic, and she was undoubtedly a scholar working in the vanguard of modern art history. Like Elizabeth Eastlake before her and Mary Costelloe after, she wrote from the perspective of the European intellectual tradition about which she was so knowledgeable, and was critical of the prevailing mode of art-historical writing in England. She famously criticised Pater's *Studies in the History of the Renaissance* (1873) in the pages of the *Westminster Review* for failing to be properly historical and scientific in its methods: 'For instead of approaching his subject, whether Art or Literature, by the true scientific method, through the life of the time of which it was an outcome, Mr Pater prefers in each instance to detach it wholly from its surroundings, to suspend it isolated before him, as if indeed it were a kind of air-plant independent of ordinary sources of nourishment.' For all that she admires Pater's *Studies*, 'they are not history', she pronounces, 'nor are they even to be relied upon for accurate statement of simple matters of fact'.[50]

At the time that she wrote this piece, she was the wife of the Oxford don Mark Pattison, Rector of Lincoln College. The Pattisons' marriage was famously unhappy, allegedly the model for the *mésalliance* of Dorothea Brooke and Edward Casaubon in George Eliot's *Middlemarch* (1871–2) and of Belinda and Professor Forth in Rhoda Broughton's *Belinda* (1883). George Eliot was of course herself well-versed in Continental intellectual culture, and her heroine Dorothea is made to confront the fact that the man she had married because of his scholarly eminence is hopelessly old-fashioned in his approach, and doomed to obscurity because of his refusal to acknowledge 'the necessity of knowing German' in order to engage with modern scholarship. As Will Ladislaw explains to her, despite his great knowledge and the antiquity of his material, 'The subject Mr Casaubon has chosen is as changing as chemistry: new discoveries are constantly making new points of view.'[51] Though loyal to her husband, it is no surprise that, faced with a choice between his dull and barren scholarly labours, so perfectly symbolised by the unfinishable and unpublishable *Key to All Mythologies*, and Will Ladislaw's modern German thought and preference for Nazarene painting, Dorothea is instinctively drawn towards the latter. It was to be another seven years after the publication of *Middlemarch* before Emilia Pattison published her own first book, *The Renaissance of Art in France* (1879), but it was a work that ineluctably demonstrates that the putative model for Dorothea had, like her fictional counterpart, come to understand the importance of engaging with the most current European research, for it is a work that is both based on meticulous archival research into primary and unpublished sources and deeply versed in modern French thought. Indeed, life was uncannily to imitate art, for by this time she had renewed an old friendship with the liberal politician and periodical proprietor Sir Charles Wentworth Dilke, whom she had first met in 1858 as a fellow art student at South Kensington, and who shared her interests in radical politics and in French culture, and, like Dorothea and her dashing Will, they were to marry, much more suitably, after her elderly husband's death.

One of the themes of *Middlemarch* and of Eliot's other greatest novels, is, of course, the tragic exclusion of women from the world of culture and learning that confers legitimacy on their sometimes less able menfolk, and the consequent denial of intellectual fulfilment. Emilia Pattison/Dilke is one woman who throughout the twenty-three years of her first marriage must have been very conscious of her intellectual marginalisation as a woman at Oxford, although this did not prevent her engaging critically with both her early mentor Ruskin, the 'Graduate of Oxford' and eventually namesake of a college, and Pater, the Fellow of Brasenose, or pursuing her own independent intellectual career. Even those women writing at the end of the century and into the next did not do so under the auspices of an academic institution, as Virginia Woolf was to note in 1929 in *A Room of One's Own*. While Bernard Berenson was, and remains, closely associated with Harvard, his wife's own college education was interrupted by her first marriage and never resumed. Maud Cruttwell seems to have got her education at the feet of Vernon Lee, among the many 'cultes' who surrounded her at her villa outside Florence. It was not until the next generation that such women began to enter the university strongholds – although Mary Berenson would have preferred her daughter Ray Strachey, who read Mathematics at Newnham and was to become a leading feminist activist, to have pursued the more cultured route followed by Julia Cartwright's daughter, Cecilia Ady, who became a Classics don at Somerville.[52]

Claire Richter Sherman suggests in her 1981 study *Women as Interpreters of the Visual Arts, 1820–1979* that the lack of institutional employment for women in prestigious universities and their 'marginal position' in the new centres of academic art history may have 'discouraged women from taking new or controversial positions'.[53] But equally one might argue (with the benefit of post-colonial hindsight) that writing from the margins confers a kind of freedom that those who inhabit centres do not have. Women did not have to take the institutions that would not have them as seriously as those who were held in their ideological embrace. Not formally recognised as belonging to a discipline, they could be more undisciplined. Writing from the sidelines, from the verge, their work is, we should not be astonished to discover, more often at the cutting edge, more likely to refuse conventional categories. And so while many of them observed the canon, their approach to mainstream art was sometimes inflected very differently from the more conventional approaches of those who were more centrally positioned. They did indeed, as Cherry argues, assist 'in the framing of those discourses of art which became hegemonic in the later nineteenth century', but their location within the frame, rather than in the picture, their own exclusion from the hegemonic masculinity of 'the central area of study', meant that, like their modern counterparts, they worried at the edges of an institutionalised art history with which they engaged critically but did not identify.

Art history was not, it is clear, a discourse that women felt prohibited from engaging in, or indeed defining, and their writing troubles, I suggest, the notion implied by Pollock's account of the impermeability of art history's borders, of a kind of professional and disciplinary hegemony that has the power to resist such incursions. Even in the mainstream forms of critical prose (and in the next chapters I will look at other genres and discourses for women's writing about art), we find important contributions by women to the critical literature and history of art from the 1820s through the century. For example, Maria Graham (later Lady Callcott) published *Memoirs of the Life of Nicholas Poussin*, the first monograph in English on the French Baroque painter, in 1820, and was also responsible for the first publication of Giotto's Paduan fresco cycle, the *Description of the Chapel of the Annunziata dell'Arena*, illustrated by her husband, the painter Augustus Callcott, in 1835. She followed up these very focused works in 1836 with a collection entitled *Essays Towards the History of Painting*, which was directed specifically at 'those of my sex and country who love the good and the beautiful'. This text explicitly distinguishes itself from specialist histories of art by 'professors' of art and art criticism, and identifies itself as something new, a popular guide to art for women, aiming to take 'an unpretending path, yet untrodden, by which those who love art may be led sufficiently near her temple to enjoy her beauties, understand her virtues, and be blessed by her happy influence, without encroaching on the province of her professed servants, or engaging in combat with her false or mistaken friends, or avowed enemies'.[54] Yet it is a survey that is clearly very deeply informed by the author's own knowledge of art, as were the art monographs of many other women writing in the nineteenth century: Lady Morgan's 1824 biography of the Italian Baroque artist, *The Life and Times of Salvator Rosa*; Anna Jameson's *Memoirs of the Early Italian Painters, and the Progress of Painting in Italy* (1845) and her widely read studies of visual iconography in the arts; Maria Farquhar's 1855 biographical catalogue of the principal Italian painters; Mary Margaret Heaton's *History of the Life of Albrecht Dürer*, the first biography of the artist published in English; Emilia Dilke's study *Claude Lorrain: Sa Vie et Ses Oeuvres*

(1884); Julia Cartwright's on Mantegna and Francia (1881), Raphael (1895 and 1905), Sandro Botticelli (1903) and the nineteenth-century painters Jean-Francois Millet (1896), G. F. Watts (1896) and Edward Burne-Jones (1894); Maud Cruttwell's books on Signorelli (1899), Verrocchio (1904) and Pollaiuolo (1907); Helen Zimmern's on Sir Lawrence Alma-Tadema (1902); and Mrs Russell Barrington's *Reminiscences of G. F. Watts* (1905) and *The Life, Letters and Work of Frederic Leighton* (1906). In both mainstream periodicals and the specialist art magazines these women, and others such as Margaret Oliphant in *Blackwood's* and Hannah Lawrance in the *British Quarterly Review* at mid-century and, at the end, Louise Lander in the *Art Journal* and Elizabeth Pennell in the *Nation* and elsewhere, wrote major critical articles and reviewed significant exhibitions and books on art and aesthetics. Women also engaged in the central public debates about art that characterised the period, weighing into the great controversies, and in the case of writers such as Lucy Crane, in *Art and the Formation of Taste* (1889), and Mrs Russell Barrington, in *Essays on the Purpose of Art* (1911), exploring the definition and philosophy of art.

But were such women considered to be professional art historians? To take the case of Anna Jameson as an example, Judith Johnston points out that reviewers of her earliest art publications differed in how they placed this new writer on art and her work, and how they viewed her expertise. Her *Handbook to the Public Galleries of Art in and near London*, published by John Murray in 1842, was, as Johnston notes, 'reviewed in all the noted journals of the day', often in the distinguished company of Franz Kugler's *A Handbook of the History of Painting* and Alexis-François Rio's *De la Poésie Chrétienne*. On the one hand, there was the *Gentleman's Review*, which began what was notwithstanding a substantial seventeen-page review with the wish that 'we hope before long to see [a handbook] executed by some person *professionally* acquainted with the subject, under the sanction of the trustees, and at the national expense'.[55] On the other, the *British and Foreign Review* praised her for her professional approach, criticising her only for her excessive quotation of others 'to the exclusion at times of criticisms which we would have gladly received from her own pen'.[56] Modern critics are also divided on the matter of Jameson's professional status. Is she to be seen, as Adele Holcomb claims, as the first professional English art historian, or does her writing, as Lew argues, 'anticipate the development of what has come to be known as "middlebrow" culture', in its '*performed* anxiety over what constitutes a cultured taste and a cultivated eye' and its self-representation as 'a new form of amateurism'.[57] Lew's discussion of 'the liminality of Jameson's status as a critic'[58] can usefully be extended to the many other female art historians and critics who, in positioning themselves as observers and interpreters, were required to negotiate the boundaries between amateurism and professionalism, and high and popular culture, as well as between verbal and visual culture.

One of those who reviewed Jameson's work, and who occupied a similarly liminal position, was Mary Merrifield. In her discussion of *Legends of the Madonna* in the *Edinburgh Review* she does not call into question Jameson's professionalism, claiming rather that 'it is impossible that they could have found a better interpreter'.[59] Interestingly, she places the general English reader outside of the field of knowledge that Jameson, and she herself by implication, command, asking rhetorically: 'how is the English visitor in Italy to understand these symbolical meanings and the traditionary legends of the old painters?' Thankfully, 'Mrs. Jameson will inform us.'[60] The review is a notable example of the operation of a female professional network which ensures that, contrary to the negative notices of Ellet's and Clayton's books on women artists which seemed to condemn the feminine topic along with the female authors, women's work on female topics is promoted in decidedly gendered terms. Merrifield emphasises the fact that Jameson offers a particularly privileged, because feminine, perspective on her subject, quoting her words: 'And let me speak for myself. In the perpetual iteration of that beautiful image of THE WOMAN highly blessed, – *there*, where others only saw pictures or statues, I have seen this great hope standing like a spirit beside the visible form.'[61] She concludes her thoughtful and positive review by declaring that 'some knowledge of these legends is absolutely essential to the student of Italian art', and recommending 'this beautiful and instructive volume' unreservedly.

Writing authoritatively of this female art historian and the feminine subject matter of her book in one of the mandarin quarterlies, the formidably knowledgeable Merrifield seems firmly situated at the centre of her discipline. Yet even the most scholarly examples of her own work bear traces of her precarious professional status. Of her *Original Treatises on the Arts of Painting*, for example, she writes in the preface that 'the work has been begun and finished under the presence of great domestic anxiety and ill health, which sometimes rendered it scarcely possible to give that attention which so arduous a task required', and she fears that 'many errors have crept in, or been overlooked, and that many links in the chain of evidence as well as in the technical processes are still wanting'.[62] Furthermore, the hybrid form of her volumes on fresco painting, which include translations from ancient treatises, narrative history, recipes, and tables of weights and measures, signifies the uncertainty of their textual status. At once authoritative history and practical manual, Merrifield's work negotiates between the realms of the artist and the artisan, and between past achievements of high culture and the cultural aspirations of the nineteenth century, in an attempt to make the arcane knowledges of the 'Old Italian and Spanish Masters' assimilable for the modern reader. Other writings by Merrifield move still further out of the mainstream of art-historical writing while still drawing on her professional expertise as an art historian. In her volume *Dress as a Fine Art* (1854), for example, she uses the old 'Masters' as a measure of aesthetics in modern female dress, adapting the discourse of high culture to women's fashion.[63] Through the discursive heterogeneity of her text, which draws on art history and criticism, contemporary colour theory and women's fashion, Merrifield insists upon a reciprocity between high art and women's experience. Her distinctive critical perspective, and, in particular, the device of using the old 'Masters' in the service of modern women, unsettles established dominant critical discourses and appropriates the history of art for domestic culture.

As it is hoped the chapters to come will show, the liminal status of women at the edges of the profession arguably gave them the creative freedom to imagine other ways of writing about art and its histories than were available to those who were contained by its boundaries, whether to follow different, Continental critical and theoretical models or to extend their range in other ways. As we will see, it was characteristic for women writing about art to be drawn to forms and methodologies that, in a way that seems intriguingly to reflect their own marginal positionality, are charged by the idea of the spaces in between. For Elizabeth Eastlake, it was photography, 'that new form of communication between man and man – neither letter, message, nor picture – which now happily fills up the space between them',[64] that fascinated her. For Maria Callcott, it was that 'unpretending path, yet untrodden', between the specialist and the popular reader that she determined to take. For Mary Merrifield, it was the sartorial aesthetic that connected the woman at the exhibition and the painting on the wall that appealed. While for Vernon Lee, it was the interstitial ficto-historical spaces between the 'real' Renaissance and its simulacra, the 'daubs of paint' on the 'flat and chilly stucco', that enticed her into the period.[65] And of course many women there were, such as George Eliot and Michael Field, who wrote about art from a position altogether outside the profession, flouting the idea of professional boundaries altogether, and appropriating the critical discourses of art for their own discursive, fictional or poetic uses.

The struggle for professional recognition

But for all that we might appreciate and applaud the imaginative resourcefulness of such border negotiations, and understand, from our postmodern and post-colonial perspective, the creative possibilities of those '"in-between" spaces' which for Homi Bhabha 'provide the terrain for elaborating strategies of selfhood ... that initiate new signs of identity',[66] we must forget neither the urgency of the desire these women had for professional recognition nor their particular individual struggles to establish a critical identity that commanded respect and, crucially for some, brought in an income. Margaret Oliphant, cited in the *Art Journal* in 1892 as one of 'the most admirable writers on Art during recent years', and at the time at work on her book *The Makers of Venice*, wrote in her diary on Christmas night, 1887: 'It is dreadful in the morning when I wake and try to keep the vultures off ... I want money, I want work, work that will pay, enough to keep this house going which there is no-one to provide for but me.'[67] Women such as Oliphant and Jameson, who had sole responsibility for supporting large families, had particularly pressing reasons to seek professional success, but undoubtedly even those who did not lack means would have liked to locate themselves firmly and unequivocally within the emerging profession. From Anna Jameson and Elizabeth Rigby/Eastlake to Margaret Oliphant, Emilia Pattison/Dilke and Vernon Lee, they made the most of their connections to develop professional networks, publicise their work and enhance their reputations.

Letters in the Berenson Archive at the Villa I Tatti give a fascinating insight into the personal and professional lives of a number of women who wrote on art in the late nineteenth century, including Mary Berenson herself, her friends Katharine Bradley and Edith Cooper (who wrote poetry collaboratively under the signature 'Michael Field'), her neighbour Vernon Lee, and a younger woman Maud Cruttwell, who was also part of the Anglo-American artistic community in Florence. Maud Cruttwell was, at the time these letters were written in the 1890s, a single woman still very new to the profession and trying to make her name, and her experiences are therefore of particular interest in the context of thinking about women and the profession of art history. We first hear of her in a spiteful letter from Bernard Berenson to 'Michael' (Katharine Bradley), in which he tells her:

> [Mary] has torn a lamb out of the wolf's mouth, & is nursing it up to be a sheep. In this allegory Vernon Lee is the wolf, & the lamb a certain Miss Crutwell, a young girl of 33. Mary takes to her as one takes to anything one

> nurses, & the young lady is in ecstatic admiration, altho' she is Vernon's guest, & fed therefore on k-k-ulture the livelong day.[68]

Berenson's relations with Vernon Lee, who was a close neighbour on the outskirts of Florence, were tense and competitive, and he no doubt took pleasure in Mary's poaching the affections of her friend even though, according to Vineta Colby, he considered Cruttwell 'stupid' and 'a lineal descendant of Miss Bates [in Jane Austen's *Emma*]'.[69] Katharine Bradley and Edith Cooper were more generous in their assessment of her when, as by this time Mary's housekeeper, she took care of them during a visit to Florence in 1895, when they stayed at the Villa Rosa. As they wrote to Mary, 'we both greatly like Miss Crutwell. She could not possibly be more kind or thoughtful, & she nourishes us exquisitely – & gives us our freedom'.[70] She also took them to visit Vernon Lee, with whom she remained very close, continuing to attend the afternoon symposia held at her home Il Palmerino. Cruttwell is described by Ottoline Morrell's biographer Miranda Seymour as, at the time of her subject's visit to Lee in 1899, 'one of the *cultes*, a stout and lively young art historian'. We are told that even Ottoline 'was startled by her fondness for wearing men's clothes and smoking cigars in public'.[71]

When she was not taking Vernon Lee's visitors off to the Uffizi or entertaining Mary's guests, or doing research for Bernard Berenson, Maud was writing her own art-historical books – the first of which, on Luca Signorelli, appeared in 1899 – and scholarly articles. Letters written to Mary in 1900 from Paris, where she was doing some work for Bernard, give a strong sense of the importance to her professional survival of her personal connections with the Berensons and Vernon Lee, about whom she engages in rather bitchy gossip but is anxious lest it reaches her ears. She tells Mary that, thanks to her recommendations, she has been able to gain access to various collections in Paris, and is clearly having a marvellous time. She confides to her friend and mentor, 'it's so seldom one gets a chance of really enjoying living as I am now. For the last 3 years life & enjoyment have meant work. I know you will understand.'[72] Meanwhile, Mary has forwarded reviews of Cruttwell's work, which are obviously important to the newly published author as an indication of public esteem, though she regrets that they don't engage with her work as rigorously as she would have liked. She thanks Mary – 'How nice of you to send me the "gratifying" notice of the Standard' – adding 'these notices certainly do give me a lot of pleasure but I would like to get some discussive ones'.[73]

One of the most interesting exchanges between Cruttwell and the more established and influential Mary Berenson reveals the younger woman as a strategist with a keen sense of the need to market herself and of the usefulness of such friendships. She is 'delighted', she writes, 'about the Gazette', the editor of which 'sent for me & told me that you had kindly offered to write a critique of my book for it & that he was delighted to have it'. She now has a favour to ask of Mary:

> He has chosen 6 of the plates which he wants to reproduce, the list of which I give below & he wants me to ask Dent to send the clichés for these to him. Now you know what Dent is like & how ignorant he is. I am so afraid that my word alone as to the importance of this criticism and the massive good it will do me & also the sale of the book, will not be enough & that he will refuse to trust these plates, so I am writing to ask you to be very kind & tell him also what a fool he will be to refuse. I am so keen about it. I want you to say all you can about the value of this criticism & the importance of the paper, everything you can that will make him send them … Will you do this great kindness to me & write to him as soon as you get this, enlarging on the advantage it will be to him to send them & on the increase of the sale this criticism would bring.[74]

It is interesting to see here the operation of a female network, which enables the more established art historian to support and promote her protégée.

However, it is perhaps not quite as simple as that, for Mary Berenson has not, after all, herself been an established figure for all that long, and the authority of her name is perhaps more to do with her husband's growing reputation. A note of uneasiness creeps into the next letter, when Cruttwell has to explain that she has asked the editor to postpone publication of Mary's notice of her book in order that one of her own articles might appear in the next number first. The younger woman is clearly embarrassed as she explains that her piece on Robbia had been delayed since July, that it was important to her to get it out before another article on Robbia, by Allan Marquand, pre-empted it, and that the editor was just using Mary's review of Cruttwell's book as a way of procrastinating about the article she would prefer to see in print first. 'I have already got beyond that Robbia article of mine & it will resurrect like an old corpse', she tells her friend, who has had her own piece put aside in order that Cruttwell can publish something more useful to her. Cruttwell breezily admits to her opportunism: 'I am as free-lance as my temperament insists on my being, & that I shall remain always.' She is devoted to the Berensons, she assures Mary; 'Only at the same time I do want to get on – I began so late, & I must accept the good offers that come. You do understand, don't you?'[75]

By the end of the series of letters, the image of a mutually nurturing female network that sustains these women has become rather tarnished, for Cruttwell is revealed by her own words to be as self-preoccupied and competitive as Bernard Berenson himself. Describing the argument of a piece she has just completed, Cruttwell anticipates and tries to circumvent the possibility that she might, like Vernon Lee and her companion and co-author Kit Anstruther-Thomson, be accused by Berenson of plagiarism:

> It was the only connecting thread I could weave satisfactorily & when I had finished, I found that I had unconsciously just stolen from Mr Berenson's Florentine Painters to an extent that would merit imprisonment on the score of plagiarism. But que voulez vous! I'm fed on his ideas they are bred in the bone & I can't put at the end – 'All this I owe to the first Father of criticism – the onlie begetter ie B. B.' Really I begin to wonder whether Miss Thomson consciously plagiarized or was only like me saturated with his ideas![76]

Writing in the certain knowledge that any ridicule of Lee will meet with the approval of the Berensons, she is uncharitable equally about Lee's new collection of essays, *Hortus Vitae*, and her lovers and hangers on, and disrespectful towards the intellectual interests of the woman at whose feet she had sat, referring to the German psychologists who so absorbed her mentor at this time as 'Lipps (is that how you spell it) & her other abstruse writers'. Cruttwell declares, 'Now I'm going to shake off art subjects & write a pot-au-feu',[77] but this is the correspondence of a woman who is clearly determined to make her career as an art historian, and is as motivated and driven as any of her male contemporaries.

Maud Cruttwell's letters to Mary Berenson give a strong sense of how a woman entering the profession at the end of the century used her contemporary female networks at a particular time and place, but the archive contains another very interesting correspondence, between Elizabeth Eastlake and Mary Costelloe, which demonstrates the existence of a different kind of inter-generational women's network that operates across time. Eastlake, by now an elderly woman, writes to the younger woman in 1892–3 with, it is clear, a strong sense of their being connected as part of a nineteenth-century female tradition of art-historical writing. 'How glad I am', Eastlake writes, 'that there is a lady who can take up where I left off, & pursue the absorbingly interesting road much further and much abler!' adding ruefully, 'There are few such pleasures left me now as to read & hear such fresh experiences as yours. Indeed it will be a great boon to me if from time to time you wd. write me or, better, come & tell me what you have most enjoyed, or latest discovered.'[78] The older woman has clearly followed the younger one's career with interest, and read her work carefully, and she is gratified to discern similarities between their respective readings of various artists and their works. Remarking on their kinship, she observes: 'This love of the Old Masters & of art altogether which you and I are blessed with, is what few know in the same degree.'[79] She notes in particular of Mary's article on 'Venetian women & Venetian pictures', 'Some of your conclusions have crossed my mind before. The fact that the beautifully arranged hair was simply a wig, tells a significant tale.'[80]

The younger couple certainly seem to have seen themselves as inheriting the Eastlakes' mantle. Mary remembers how they were inspired by Lady Eastlake's account of the art discoveries she and her husband had made when they 'turned pictures to the light from the lumber room of the Uffizi and whispered incredulously to each other "Botticelli – Fra Filippo"'. According to Mary, 'Bernhard and I looked at each other with shining eyes that confirmed each of our secret resolutions to follow in our humbler way the example of Lady Eastlake.'[81] The Berensons' passion for art in turn recalls to Elizabeth Eastlake her own youthful enthusiasms – 'I remember well when we began to "discover" Lotto', she writes, referring to Berenson's book on the subject – and she writes with a consciousness of the centrality of them all to the developing discipline of art history: 'each generation (as you will know 50 years hence) have new loves & enthusiasms and discoveries, not quarrelling with the former generations, but continuing & widening them'.[82] Mary Berenson had, it seems, written to Lady Eastlake for advice and assistance in getting published, but the older woman's view is that her help is not necessary, for, as she encouragingly tells her, 'You write so well & brightly that you have no reason to apply to a friendly "Editress" to publish.'[83] However, she does offer to recommend Bernard Berenson's book on Lotto to Murray, though she warns him: 'You are only too profound & too sincere for English readers. I fear we have not the public for it. I fear Mr Murray will think the same.'[84]

At the end of her professional life, Elizabeth Eastlake is interestingly making the same kind of distinction between English readers of art history and their professional counterparts in Europe that she and others were making fifty years earlier. Throughout that period she moved confidently in the world of which she writes with such authority, praising Morelli, criticising Crowe and Cavalcaselle for their unreadable style ('for more pedantic and intolerable writing was never perpetrated'),[85] recommending younger writers to the younger Mr Murray as she herself had been recommended to his father decades earlier. And yet she clearly regarded herself as having special connections with other women art historians, whether

Anna Jameson in her own generation or Mary Berenson in the next. Her letters reveal that she saw younger women like Mary to be entering a profession that she herself helped found, and that she identified with a female tradition and critical practice, as well as locating herself squarely within the mainstream profession of art history. It is with the tensions between these connected but different professional identities for female art historians in the nineteenth century that this study is concerned.

CHAPTER 2

The art of fiction

True to her promise in 1900 to Mary Berenson to 'write a pot-au-feu', Maud Cruttwell did indeed eventually turn her hand to fiction, but in so doing, far from carrying out her threat to 'shake off art subjects',[1] she made art (and women) the subject of her potboiler. When *Fire and Frost* appeared in 1913, although it did represent a new departure generically from its author's earlier critical work, the novel told the highly wrought tale of a young female art historian living and working among the Anglo-American community in Florence, even (like Cruttwell) writing a book on Mantegna, who seems remarkably like an idealised portrayal of Maud Cruttwell herself. Clare Glynne is described as 'a young woman of about twenty-eight, built on the lines of a Greek ephèbe, tall and straight, with blue eyes that looked you full in the face, and a fair skin slightly tanned with exposure to the Italian sun'. She and her American friend Sibyl are portrayed as 'energetic, healthy young women, clad in tailor-made serge of faultless cut'.[2] Cruttwell's heroine is an independently wealthy, forward-thinking, 'new' woman of 'good birth' who, after the fashion of Mona Caird's and Kate Chopin's fictional prototypes, inhabits aesthetic interiors, smokes 'blonde Turkish cigarettes', and has 'a horror of marriage, considering it a fetter which chains the body, hampers the mind, and necessitates the complete sacrifice of the personality on one side or the other'.[3] Early in the story she tells her friend that she might perhaps marry 'if I found someone with exactly the same temperament and ideas as myself. But that is impossible, since he would have to be a man and I'm a woman, and there is nothing in the world so dissimilar as a man and a woman.'[4] Despite this unambiguous announcement of her proclivity for women, and emphatic disavowal of marriage, she is inveigled into marrying an Egyptian 'boy', declared to be 'exactly like Pollaiuolo's bust of a young warrior in the Bargello'.[5] He turns out to be a bad lot, shaped (despite Clare's best efforts to educate him through art) by the 'old Koranic teaching of his childhood' that 'Man is the only being that really counts in the world! Women were created merely to minister to his needs, like his horses and dogs.'[6] They eventually are divorced, and Clare ends the novel as a successful writer and collector, with her own gallery at her villa in Florence – like Cruttwell's friends the Berensons.

Fire and Frost is of interest for this study in that it conjures a world that, despite its extravagances and melodrama, is recognisably that of the late nineteenth-century Anglo-Florentine art circles in which Cruttwell moved. It fictionalises aspects of her own and her friends' professional and personal lives in ways that allow her to address feminist issues that are eschewed in her formal art-historical writing but which intersect with that body of work in interesting ways. Figures such as Vernon Lee and the Berensons are absorbed into the text at every level. Like Lee, whose youthful precocity is revealed in her juvenilia and early publications, Clare is said to have 'adored art' from a young age:

> and her adolescence was a kind of spiritual orgy, during which her soul rioted impartially in the music of Wagner, or Bach, and of Beethoven, in the painting of the Italian Renaissance and the modern Impressionist, in the sculpture of Ancient Greece, of Michelangelo and Rodin. Everything that was great pleased her and she darted like a dragon-fly from one to the other unable to fix her insatiable mind. She wanted to know everything, see everything, feel everything, that was famous in Nature and Art.[7]

The friends with whom Clare shares her passion for art are a husband–wife couple named Maryx (Mary X?). Interestingly, Ferdinand Maryx, who had helped Clare in her art studies and whose restored Florentine home is filled with art like a museum, is portrayed as sexually indeterminate: 'a small man, delicately built as a girl',[8] yet who looked like 'a cross between Don Quixote and an Assyrian bull, with his dark flashing eyes, above which the eyebrows nearly met, his hooked nose, black moustache, and pointed beard'.[9] Cruttwell's description of the Hungarian-born Maryx calls to mind the appearance and tastes, not to mention the lineage, of her Polish-American Jewish friend and mentor Bernard Berenson.

Clare's self-consciously aesthetic descriptions are suffused with a 'keen visualising faculty which made her life so full of incident' that also recalls Berenson and, especially, Lee. And so a passage that begins 'The high road to Settignano [where the Berensons lived] is an odd mixture of beauty and ugliness [the title of Lee's co-publication with Kit Anstruther-Thomson]' describes how the heroine sees in this scene of the *Decameron*, 'as if they were really there, "the dainty youths and maids pacing with slow step, weaving garlands and singing amorously"'.[10] Vernon Lee had written of the pleasures of having 'an historical habit of mind', of 'supplementing our present life by a life in the past; a life larger, richer than our own, multiplying our emotions by those of the dead', and of 'the sense of being companioned by the past, of being in a place warmed for our living by the lives of others',[11] and for Clare too the Italian hillside is haunted by its past, which seems palpably present, mediated by the artistic legacies that survive and immortalise it:

> the *lieta brigata* of Boccaccio gave place to the gorgeous procession which Benozzo Gozzoli has painted on the walls of the Medici Chapel winding up this very hill. Her vivid imagination conjured up the gay group of nobles and pages – the boy Lorenzo reining in his steed, the courtiers with hooded falcons and spotted leopards prancing behind. One of the charms of such day-dreams is that these historic personages, instead of holding themselves coldly aloof, as they probably would have done in real life, became one's intimate friends, and her imaginary Lorenzo with his fresh face ... threw her a familiar greeting as he rode by, old Cosimo smiled benevolently, and the gay young angels nodded to her with charming affability.[12]

Such a passage, in which literary and historical figures, suggested by the Renaissance art that surrounds her, come to life for the sensitive modern observer, might have come straight from the pages of any of Vernon Lee's historical studies of Italian culture.

Cruttwell's novel provides as much evidence as her art-critical writings of her saturation with Berenson's and Lee's aesthetics, and also shows the fictional influence of the 'new woman' writers of the turn of the century; but what is of interest to me here is the way the novel form enables her to address the question of her professional life as a female art historian in ways that are virtually completely expunged from her critical work. For Cruttwell, as for Lee herself, and indeed for a number of other women who wrote about art in the nineteenth century, fiction offered an alternative medium of expression to the more ideologically circumscribed discourse of art history, one that enabled women to rehearse with greater freedom issues relating not only to the gender politics of their profession and the writing of art's histories, but to sexuality, visuality and intersubjectivity. Like many female art historians in the nineteenth century, Cruttwell was a feminist, but she directly articulated her feminist politics and her engagement with women's issues and questions of gender in arenas other than her art-historical writing. We similarly find Helen Zimmern, for example, translating Gemma Ferrugia's New Woman novel *Woman's Folly* (of which Edmund Gosse writes: 'The Graven image called Man lies at the feet of Gemma Ferrugia, and she has ground him to dust'); Mary Merrifield publishing articles not only on women's dress but also on 'The Need of

Sanitary Knowledge to Women'; Louisa Twining writing essays on the condition of women and on the female poor; Emilia Dilke writing and lecturing on trade unionism for women, and women's suffrage; Vernon Lee publishing on pacifism; and Elizabeth Pennell publishing a *Life of Mary Wollstonecraft* and reviewing 'A Century of Women's Rights'.[13] For all these women, writing in forms and discourses other than the standard art-historical treatise appears to enable a different, more overtly gendered, in some cases feminist voice to emerge. Indeed, our reading of other genres, such as biography and autobiography, suggests that we need to look outside mainstream art-historical writing in order to appreciate the full extent of women's contribution.[14] It is to an exploration of some of these other generic forms – sometimes closely connected to formal art-historical writing, like the guidebook, the travelogue, the artist's biography or the translation, sometimes displaced into fiction – and of the whole project of 'translating' visual experience into verbal and other forms, that the next two chapters are devoted.

This chapter will consider some of the ways in which women, including those who did not write either principally or professionally about art, introduced the visual arts and artist figures in critically distinctive ways into their fiction, and can be said in this form to have contributed to nineteenth-century art discourse more broadly conceived. Importantly, they convey, in a fictional form, the experience of art. Art and artists, including female artists, feature prominently in Victorian women's novels, and if, as Deborah Cherry contends, women were indeed complicit in the exclusion of historical female artists from the canon of great Masters, it might equally be said that their novels fully articulate the multifarious modes of that exclusion within both the profession and institutions of art and the culture at large.[15] Furthermore, any student of the Victorian novel will be aware of key scenes in which an encounter with the visual arts is used by a female author to convey something profound about her fictional heroine and more generally about women's lives. Lucy Snowe's encounter with the paintings of Cleopatra and 'La Vie d'une Femme' in *Villette*; the unveiling of Lady Audley's portrait at the heart of her boudoir and her mystery in *Lady Audley's Secret*; the challenges posed by ancient statuary and modern painters to Dorothea Brooke on her wedding journey to Rome in *Middlemarch*: these are only the best-known examples. To what extent can such fictional texts be viewed as complementing and supplementing the formal literature on art by nineteenth-century women so disparaged by Cherry and others? Was it in Victorian women's fiction, indeed, that some of the questions most urgently addressed by modern feminist art historians were first, as it were, sketched out? It is by reading the art of fiction, I suggest, that we can make the most effective counter-claim against the charge of women's 'silence' or at best their docile acquiescence in the gender blindness of art history in the nineteenth century. In their writing about female art and women artists, their fictional use of encounters with works of art, and in their representation of the nineteenth-century art world, female novelists contributed to contemporary critical debates about art. We can reframe the questions we ask of these iconic aesthetic encounters, picturesque ateliers, artistic heroines, and their fictional dealers and patrons by locating them within a broader discursive context of nineteenth-century art history in which women looked at and wrote about art.

Fictional portraits of female artists

In the large body of literature addressing the pressing question of what an impecunious middle-class woman is to do to earn her living (written often by women who were themselves making a career as writers in order to support themselves and their families), one of the few genteel professions represented as open to her, alongside that of writer, governess or needlewoman, was of course to become an artist and sell her work. Fiction abounds with heroines who, finding themselves abandoned, orphaned, widowed, married to or obliged to flee from a profligate husband, resort to art as a means of support, compromising their reputations in the manner so iconically suggested by Emily Mary Osborn in her painting *Nameless and Friendless* (1857, Fig. 3).[16]

Helen 'Graham', for example, the heroine of Anne Brontë's *The Tenant of Wildfell Hall* (1848), retreats with her son to the remote moorland mansion of the title, where in order to support them both she sets up her studio, adopts an assumed name, and must even sell her pictures under false names – 'Fernley Manor, Cumberland, instead of Wildfell Hall' – doubly displaced, lest she be tracked down by her husband.[17] Nameless and friendless indeed. Olive Rothesay, the eponymous heroine of Dinah Mulock Craik's novel *Olive* (1850), obliged to support herself and her ailing and eventually blind mother on the death of her father, seizes the opportunity to develop her natural talent for and interest in art when they become lodgers in the house of a professional painter, Michael Vanbrugh, and his sister Meliora, and becomes a successful artist. While Margaret Oliphant, in her 1870 novel *The Three Brothers*, portrays in Mrs Severn the young widow of a second-rate artist who is supporting herself and her

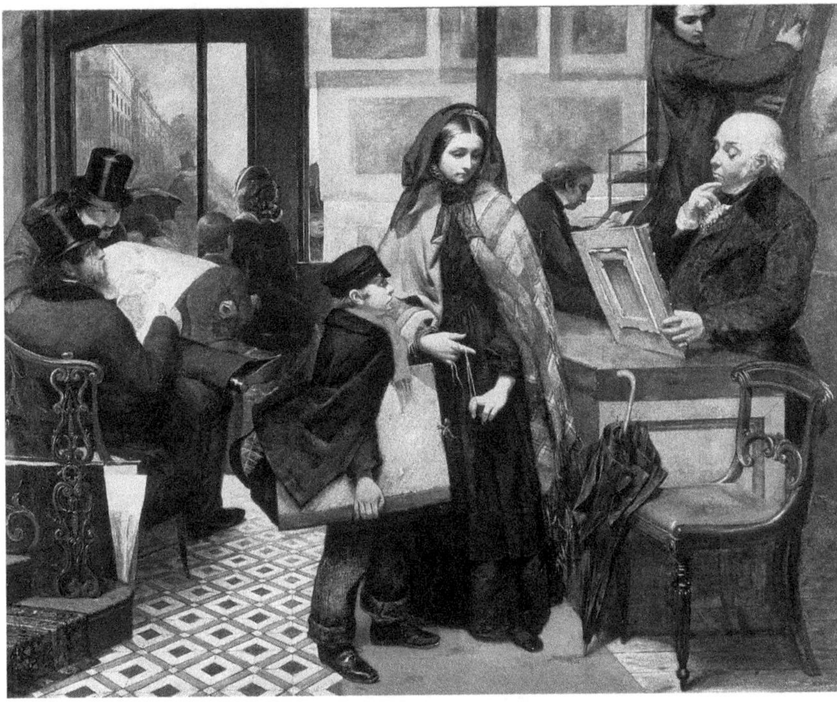

Fig. 3. Emily Mary Osborn, *Nameless and Friendless* (1857)

children through her own art work, Mrs Severn, the reader is reassured, 'was not a partisan of work for women, carrying out her theory, but a widow, with little children, working with the tools that came handiest to her for daily bread'.[18] In each case, their status as fee-earning artists is legitimated by need, rather than a consequence of ambition: Olive, explicitly, is not driven by 'yearning after fame' or 'genius-led ambition, but from the mere desire of earning money' – a motivation scorned by her mentor, whose lofty disregard for pecuniary reward is heavily ironised by Craik (his refusal to compromise his art for the market eventuates in his sister's death from starvation – 'the painter dreamed his dream, the little sister stayed at home and starved').[19] Notably, in each case, the creator of the fictional artist-heroine – Anne Brontë, Dinah Craik, Margaret Oliphant – herself wrote out of economic necessity, in order to support herself and her family.

Just as Brontë's knowledge of art benefited from her brother Branwell's artistic training, and Oliphant's from her husband Frank's (only moderately successful) career as a professional artist, so we are shown in these fictional portraits of women artists how crucially dependent they were on having indirect access, through the male artists in their immediate domestic circle, to the formal education they themselves were denied. Craik had herself studied drawing at the Government School of Design in 1843, but her heroine has no access to formal training. Simply being around Vanbrugh's studio increases Olive's passion for art and, we are told, 'while her hand secretly laboured to attain perfection, her mind was expanding, so that the deeper things of Art were opening unto her' (p. 113). Vanbrugh, culpably obtuse and contemptuous of the needs of the women who tend him, observes, with some surprise and despite himself, when Olive demonstrates her artistic sensibility and understanding, 'you seem to know all about it … You might have been an artist's daughter or sister' (p. 113). Indeed, his own sister, though she has no aspirations to become an artist herself, 'had quietly gathered up a tolerable critical knowledge of' art. She explains to Olive: 'You see, when I was a girl, I "read up" on Art, that I might be able to talk to Michael. Somehow, he never did care to talk with me, but perhaps he may yet' (p. 117). When Olive asks why she didn't become an artist herself, she agrees that 'plenty' of women have been painters: 'There was Angelica Kauffman [*sic*], and Properzia Rossi, and Elizabetta Sirani. In our day, there is Mrs A____ and Miss B____, and the two C____s. And if you read about the old Italian masters, you will find that many of them had wives, or daughters, or sisters, who helped them a great deal' (p. 118). She herself clearly falls into this latter category, but the erasure of the names of contemporary women artists eloquently conveys how they too are marginalised and liable to be written out of history.

'The young woman has a pretty talent', reports Mr Welby, RA, patronisingly of Mrs Severn, 'and her husband taught her after a fashion how to use it' (*The Three Brothers*, p. 86). The dependence of such women as Olive and Mrs Severn upon a kind of arbitrary coincidence of their 'pretty talent' and the education and experience of a man willing to teach her 'after a fashion' is a theme that emerges in other stories too. In Anna Mary Howitt's serially published novella '*The Sisters in Art*' (1852), a once successful Italian sculptor, now fallen on hard times, helps raise the sights of the female artist-heroine and her friends, and gives them access to casts they can copy, and to a kind of artistic ambition and professionalism that Alice Law cannot hope to find at the private academy of art for young ladies that she attends (although it should be noted that Alice and her friends do reciprocate by helping the impoverished sculptor to make a living, doing detailed anatomical sketches for him from which he can make wax models for medical demonstrations).[20] In this respect Victorian fiction confirms what modern feminist art historians tell us about the importance of women having an entrée into the Victorian art world via their artist-fathers, brothers, husbands or family friends, and how inadequate such arrangements often are (*The Sisters in Art* is about the setting up of a School of Art and Design that provides a proper education for women of all classes and backgrounds). But it also tells us, as do modern feminist critics, of the importance of *female* networks in enabling women to become artists. In *The Sisters in Art*, Alice is mentored, to be sure, by Giuseppe and by a male landscape painter from her native Yorkshire, but she explains how she was also well instructed as a child by her female guardian, 'a lady who had herself a very noble power in art' (p. 286). And it is the collective talent of the three young women at the centre of the story, together with the warm-hearted support of Alice's aunt, the generosity of their landlady and, above all, the financial assistance and patronage of Mrs Cohen – their 'sisterhood in art', in other words – that enables them to realise their ambition of setting up a Female School of Art which will mean that young women with talent will no longer have to depend on such ad hoc and contingent arrangements. Similarly in *Olive*, it is the artist's sister, Meliora, who acts not only as the heroine's teacher, but as her agent, negotiating the sale of her first painting for her, and it is a woman, Mrs Fludyer, who becomes her patron.

But if such novels convey something of how, in reality, as well as in utopian idealism, women played a prominent and active role in the Victorian art world as recent feminist art historians have shown us, they also represent the barriers women faced, not only in terms of acquiring a thorough education in art, to equal that of their male counterparts, but also in relation to the prejudices they had to battle. Women, it was felt by many, were not capable of being great artists. They could only manage, at best, so-called 'female' subjects. As Mr Welby, RA, opines in Oliphant's *The Three Brothers* (1870), 'a woman may content herself with the homely sort of work she can do; but a young fellow aims at high art' (p. 86). Even by the end of the century, the view expressed so paradigmatically by Charles Tansley in Woolf's *To the Lighthouse*, 'women can't paint, women can't write', widely prevailed.[21] The heroine of Ella Hepworth Dixon's novel *The Story of a Modern Woman* (1894), Mary Erle, who has ambitions to become a painter, has a suitor, Vincent Hemming, who considers painting 'especially in water-colours' to be 'an eminently lady-like occupation'. Even her feminist friend, Alison Ives, observes: 'No woman ever made a great artist yet … but if you don't mind being third-rate, of course go in and try.' Her jaundiced view that, for a female artist, South Kensington and the Royal

Academy will be followed inexorably by 'portraits of babies in pastel or cottage gardens for the rest of your life' suggests Dixon's understanding of the ways in which the ideological limitation of women's capacity to engage in cultural production to 'third-rate' domestic and floral subjects had been internalised even by many enlightened women.[22] Unsurprisingly, Mary abandons her painterly ambitions.

The fullest exploration of how such ideological barriers operated is to be found in Craik's *Olive*, in which the artist Michael Vanbrugh is the mouthpiece for all the institutionalised prejudices against women becoming anything more than, like Mrs Severn, painters of 'pretty groups of children' or vapid landscapes (p. 86). His very name vests him with the authority of the Old Masters, and he is fully cognisant of his place in a kind of Apostolic Succession of genius. 'He took his art for his mistress', we are told, and emulated the great Florentine master who was his namesake (p. 112). Olive herself 'regarded the old artist with as much reverence as if he had been Michelangelo himself' (p. 112). He decides eventually to move to Rome where, he rhapsodises, 'Once again I will lie on the floor of the Sistine, and look up worshippingly to Michael the Angel' (p. 145). He fantasises with Olive about 'how we should go together to the City of Art, dwell together, work together, master and pupil ... We should be like the brothers Caracci – like Titian with his scholar and adopted son.' Warming to his theme, and rolling out the myth of succession, he sighs: 'Would that you had not been a woman! That I could have made you my son in Art, and given you my name, and then died, bequeathing you the mantle of my glory' (p. 157). He invites her to be his wife instead, as the only role he can fit her into, since he already has a sister. She declines.

Vanbrugh, the type of the male artist genius, 'had reduced the womankind about him to the condition of perfect slaves' (p. 156). His sister's 'whole life had been pervaded by one grand desire – to see her brother president of the Royal Academy. When she was a schoolgirl and he a student, she had secretly sketched his likeness – the only one extant of his ugly, yet soul-lighted face – and had prefixed thereto his name, with the magic letters, "P.R.A."' (p. 117). The world they inhabit is one in which women's potential for talent is subsumed by the imperative to give every advantage to the son of the family – as, in real life, Branwell Brontë, for example, was given a privileged education over and above his more talented sisters. Naturally, such men would be anxious to protect their privileges, and Michael, when his sister introduces the idea that Olive might be a painter, 'stood, flourishing his mahl-stick and palette – looking very like a gigantic warrior, guarding the shrine of Art with shield and spear'

(p. 121). Michael is predictably dismissive of such a preposterous proposal, and at first refuses to look at that 'rubbish' (p. 121), her work. Far from acknowledging her creative identity as an artist, he instead wants to capture her look of 'passive misery' for a painting of his own, adding insult to injury by casting Olive as the mother of Alcestis, who is to be modelled by her own mother (p. 122). When he does look at her drawings, he reluctantly admits to finding some talent there, but he doesn't hold back on the subject of women painters:

> I am not such a fool as to say that genius is of either sex, but it is an acknowledged fact that no woman ever was a great painter, poet, or musician. Genius, the mighty one, does not exist in weak female nature, and even if it did, custom and education would certainly stunt its growth. (p. 123)

It is 'impossible' for a woman to become a *great* artist, according to Vanbrugh, because the term implies:

> Not only a painter, but a poet; a man of learning, or reading, of observation. A gentleman – we artists have been the friends of kings. A man of high virtue, or how can he reach the pure ideal? A man of iron will, unconquered daring, and passions strong – yet stainless. Last and greatest, a man who, feeling within him the divine spirit, with his whole soul worships God! ... This is what an artist must *be* by nature. I have not spoken of what he has to make himself. Years of study such as few can bear lie before him – no life of a carpet-knight, no easy play-work of scraping colours on canvas. Why, these hands of mine have wielded not only the pencil, but the scalpel; these eyes have rested on scenes of horror, misery – even crime. I glory in it; for it was all for Art. (pp. 124–5)

Although Vanbrugh himself is ironised in the novel, his views on the gender of genius are ostensibly endorsed by the narrator, who avers: 'The hierarchies of the soul's dominion belong only to man, and it is right they should. He it was whom God created first, let him take the pre-eminence.' For woman's 'sphere is, and ever must be, bounded; because, however lofty her genius may be, it always dwells in a woman's breast. Nature, which gave to man the dominion of the intellect, gave to her that of the heart and affections.' And, he adds, 'there scarce ever lived a woman who would not rather sit meekly by her own hearth, with her husband at her side, and her children at her knee, than be the crowned Corinne of the Capitol' (p. 126).

It is a familiar enough view of woman's 'nature' and capacities, but interestingly subverted in a novel which has an artist-heroine, one who, moreover, is shown to be capable of moving beyond 'the mere prettiness of most women-painters to the grandeur of sublimer Art', one who works in a range of genres, including History painting and allegory, and who through her arduous labour makes herself 'worthy of being ranked among those painters who are not of the passing hour, but for all time' (p. 127). What makes this possible, of course, is that Olive is defined less by her womanhood than by her disability. It is repeatedly stated throughout the novel that Olive is 'deformed', expected by no one (least of all herself) to marry and enjoy the 'normal' womanly satisfactions of life, which frees her to devote herself to art, like a man can, and to become a 'genius', as he can. For some women, the narrator tells us, 'chance, or circumstance, or wrong, sealing up her woman's nature, converts her into a self-dependent human soul. Instead of life's sweetnesses, she has before her life's greatnesses' (p. 126). Olive is one such, and her disability becomes enabling, placing her in a position from which she can overcome the disabilities faced by other women who wish to become professional artists:

> Olive could do many things with an independence that would have been impossible to beautiful and unguarded youth. Oftentimes Mrs Rothesay [her mother] trembled and murmured at the days of solitary study in the British Museum, and in various picture galleries; the long, lonely walks, sometimes in wintertime extending far into the dusk of evening. But Olive always answered, with a pensive smile.
>
> 'Nay, mother; I am quite safe everywhere. Remember, I am not like other girls. Who would notice *me*?' (p. 127)

Her disability unsexes her, and so does her 'genius'. Eventually Vanbrugh 'never thought of her sex at all' (p. 127). She had an 'almost masculine power of mind', an 'ardent, almost masculine genius' (p. 145). 'Though you are a woman', he tells her, 'you have a man's soul – the soul of genius' (p. 157). Olive, then, becomes a successful artist, although she remains to all intents and purposes very womanly, and shows none of the monstrous egotism that characterises the self-styled modern master Vanbrugh. She continues to position her studio in one half of the living room, to tend her mother and anyone else who needs her, and indeed proves to be enough of a woman that the hero falls in love with her. She confesses to her mother, 'Mamma, I think, on the whole, I am happier here than I was at Woodford Cottage. I feel less of an artist and more of a woman' (p. 185).

The sense of conflict between womanhood and artistic identity articulated in *Olive* – one that is familiar to us from, for example, *Aurora Leigh* (1857) and Gaskell's *Life of Charlotte Brontë* (1857) – is very particularly inflected in the case of the visual arts. In Anne Thackeray Ritchie's

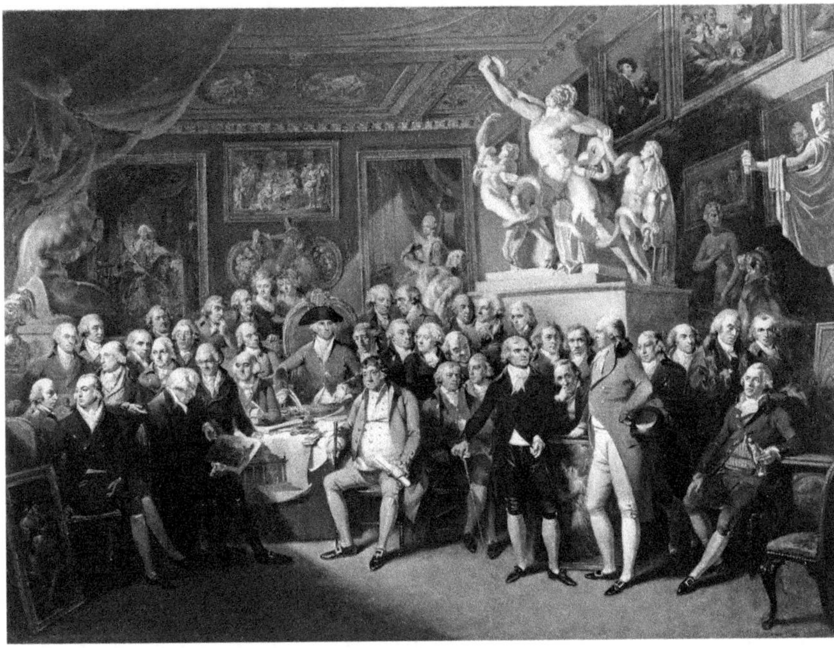

Fig. 4. Henry Singleton, *The Royal Academicians in General Assembly* (1795)

intriguing novel *Miss Angel* (1876), the heroine is fatally divided between her art and her social success as a woman and object of desire. It is of particular interest because it is explicitly based on the life of Angelica Kauffmann, who with Mary Moser was one of the signatories to the petition to King George III for the establishment of a Royal Academy of Painting and Sculpture, and a founding Fellow. (She is represented among the gathered academicians in Henry Singleton's painting of 1795 – both in person, and, significantly, in a framed portrait (Fig. 4).)

Miss Angel constantly draws attention to the tension between its heroine's professional ambitions on the one hand, and her 'womanly' social and romantic ambitions on the other; between her artist's gaze, and her to-be-looked-at-ness as a woman. The title, ironically suggesting a female counterpart to 'Michael the Angel', alludes to Joshua Reynolds's nickname for the young painter, and much is made of the relationship between the two artists, each of whom painted portraits of the other. When she is first taken to Reynolds's studio, she admires professionally the light and the painter's palette and pencils, but 'then, with some sudden impulse, she sprang up into the sitter's chair'.[23] In a key scene, Angelica leaves a glittering party at Reynolds's house, at which she has been described as both his 'living Muse' and his 'rival', to go to his studio to 'enjoy a different feast' (pp. 115–16). He, clearly smitten with her, finds her looking at one of his paintings, with a painter's eye: we are told that 'Angelica had in that instant become a painter again, as some people do who have two lives to lead. She was looking at the picture, and for a moment she had forgotten the painter, and was wondering at his work, at the breadth and grace of that lovely combination of colour, of feeling, of flowing ease' (p. 116). She gazes at the painting (Reynolds's full-length portrait of Lady Elizabeth Keppel, portrayed as a bridesmaid making sacrifice to Hymen) 'with some sort of hope that she could look, and admire, and try to realize the gracious mystery of this new master's art' (p. 117). But while hers is explicitly the look of an artist at that moment, she becomes the object of Reynolds's, and the narrator's, gaze, like another picture in his gallery (and indeed a painting by Margaret Isabel Dicksee, entitled *'Miss Angel' – Angelika Kauffmann, introduced by Lady Wentworth, visits Mr. Reynolds' studio* (1892, Fig. 5), depicting an earlier scene from the novel, does actually make a picture of her in his studio, although, notably, she is not in the sitter's chair).[24]

This is a manoeuvre that occurs throughout the novel, from the very first page, where the narrator enters the story of the artist's life via an engraving of Reynolds's portrait of Angelica Kauffmann, probably by Francesco Bartolozzi:

> It was the picture of a lady some five or six and twenty years of age. The face is peculiar, sprightly, tender, a little obstinate. The eyes are very charming and intelligent. The features are broadly marked; there is something at once homely and dignified in their expression. The little head is charmingly set upon its frame. A few pearls are mixed with the heavy loops of hair; two great curls fall upon the sloping shoulders; the slim figure is draped in light folds fastened by jeweled bands, such as those which people then wore. A loose scarf is tied round the waist. Being cold, perhaps, sitting in Sir Joshua's great studio, the lady has partly wrapped herself in a great fur cloak. (p. 1)

Thereafter, we are repeatedly shown the artist-heroine with '[t]he little head … charmingly set upon its frame' as if she is indeed the framed subject of a painting. She is a 'sweet living picture' for her friend Antonio, the Italian painter whom she will eventually marry, as she stands, brush and palette in hand, before Titian's magnificent *Assumption*, hung above the high altar of the Frari Chapel in Venice, which she had been commissioned to copy (p. 12). Yet by dint of imagining herself into the painting, as

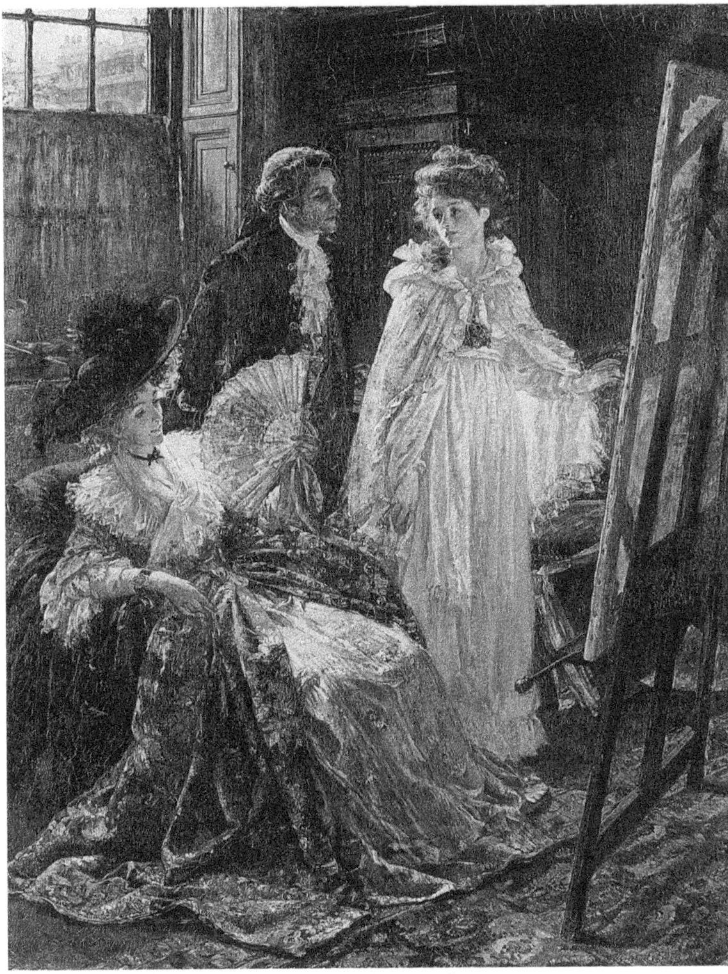

Fig. 5. Margaret Isabel Dicksee, *'Miss Angel' – Angelika Kauffmann, introduced by Lady Wentworth, visits Mr. Reynolds' studio* (1892)

'one of the women in the crowd looking on with the amazed apostles', she seems to evade his gaze, avoid being framed by him, and become absorbed into the noble art to which she aspires, a witness to its elevating power, like the women onlookers she empathetically imagines beyond the frame of the painting (p. 13). Later, in the sacristy of the same church, as Angelica gazes upon Giovanni Bellini's *Madonna and Child with Sts Nicholas, Peter, Benedict and Mark*, wondering at 'the noble Pesari heads [bent] in reverent conclave before the gracious and splendid Madonna', and observing especially '[h]ow measured and liberal it all is; what a stately self-respect and reverence for others', the woman who is to become her own first patron, Lady W, looks admiringly at Angelica herself and, interrupting the young painter's still concentration on the painting, says: 'I wish I could paint you as you are now, child' (p. 54). The fictional Angelica is, then, it is emphasised, both painter and the subject of paintings, as was the historical Angelica Kauffmann. She is known not only for her large-scale historical and allegorical subjects, but also for her self-portraits, of which there are many, but of course in these it is the female artist who has control over her own representation, and they do convey a sense of self-possession that the fictional Miss Angel, at least, lacks.

In Craik's *Olive*, it is the heroine's mother, Sybilla Rothesay, rather than her 'pale, deformed' self, who is the great beauty, and who is described throughout the novel as the subject of painting: 'Any poet, painter, or sculptor, would certainly have raved about Mrs Rothesay.' She is 'a Venus de Medici transmuted from the stone' (pp. 18, 7, 9). Olive herself is, by contrast, described as possessing 'scarce one charm that would prove its lineage from the young beautiful mother, out of whose sight it instinctively crept' (p. 18). When her father first saw her, he 'turned away, putting his hand before his eyes, as if to shut out the sight' (p. 23). The visual objectification of Sybilla Rothesay is played out in the novel as she becomes the actual model for both Vanbrugh and her daughter and, more, as she herself loses her sight, rendered unable to see her daughter's paintings of her. Visuality and subjectivity are closely aligned, and being shut out of the sight of both her parents seems to enable the development of Olive's own vision. But even as she finds visual agency, and becomes more confidently the mistress of her art, training the eye for beauty that attracts her among other things to her young neighbour Sara Derwent, and hiring professional models to sit for her, poor, unattractive Olive herself even, within this visual economy, becomes the object of the gaze: 'as she sat with her hands crossed on her knee, her bending head and pensive eyes out-gazing, [Olive] added no unmeet picture to the still beauty of the scene. Many a lovely woman might have coveted the meek yet heavenly look which cast sweetness over the pale features of the deformed girl' (p. 96).

Subjects and objects

As with other artist-heroines such as Miss Angel, there is some reciprocity of vision in the case of Olive. She is 'watched – long and earnestly; but by an innocent watcher', Sara's young brother Lyle Derwent (the formulation here implying that there may be male watchers who are not so innocent), while in turn the boy's own delicate beauty 'pleased her artist's eye' (p. 97). However, for professional models, this and other novels of the period suggest, the objectification is complete, and they often come to a bad, or at least a sad, end. Olive is taken by Vanbrugh's sister to visit a 'strange foreign-looking woman' who goes under the name Mrs Manners, and who Meliora explains was one of her brother's models and had sat for his *Cleopatra* (p. 129). Ironically, in light of her own future fate, she tells her friend that the woman is 'slowly dying, and I shouldn't wonder if it were of sheer starvation; those models earn so little' (p. 129). Olive recalls seeing her at the time of the painting, in all her magnificence: 'Oh, she was a grand, beautiful woman, like an Eastern queen … What an eye she had, and what a glorious mouth!' (p. 129). They find the wrecked beauty even now 'on a grand scale', reclining half-dressed; 'the large but perfect proportions of her form reminded Olive of the reclining figure in the group of the "Three Fates"' (pp. 129–30). It transpires that Celia Manners was the discarded mixed-race mistress of Olive's own father, acquired when he worked away in the West Indies.

Olive has frequently been read as, in Cora Kaplan's words, 'both a companion and a countertext to *Jane Eyre*' (p. x): Celia Manners is clearly a fictional relative of Bertha Mason, and blindness, as Heather Tilley argues in a fine discussion of the two texts, a key trope of both novels.[25] But it also bears comparison with Brontë's *Villette*, published three years later in 1853. During a visit to a gallery in Villette, Lucy Snowe stands before a painting of Cleopatra that could have been Vanbrugh's, in which the 'huge, dark-complexioned gipsy-queen' similarly reclines in a state of undress and is painted on a 'grand scale' – she estimates her weight at 'fourteen to sixteen stone'.[26] Much has been written about this scene, of course: M. Paul's shock at seeing her sitting 'coolly down, with the self-possession of a garçon' before such a painting, and his referral of her to the more suitable subject of 'La Vie d'une Femme', while he, she notes, 'looked at the picture himself quite at his ease, and for a very long while' (p. 277). He admits of 'des dames' looking at the Cleopatra in mixed company, but not a 'demoiselle'. The exchange resonates with Frances Trollope's account of her visit to the antique statue gallery at the Pennsylvania Academy of the Fine Arts, in *Domestic Manners of the Americans* (1832), where she is shocked to discover that men and women are not permitted to view the antique casts together, and is informed that 'the ladies like to go into that room by themselves, when there be no gentlemen watching them'. 'I never felt my delicacy shocked at the Louvre', she reports, 'but I was strangely tempted to resent as an affront the hint that I received, that I might steal a glance at what was deemed indecent.'[27] Lucy Snowe brings a similarly critical eye not only to the vulgar morality of Belgian museum culture, and to the artistic deficiencies of works such as the Cleopatra that fail to meet the requirements of her thoroughly realist aesthetic, but also to the very conventions of the nude. She observes caustically of the Cleopatra:

> She lay half-reclined on a couch; why, it would be difficult to say; broad daylight blazed around her; she appeared in hearty health, strong enough to do the work of two plain cooks; she could not plead a weak spine; she ought to have been standing, or at least sitting bolt upright. She had no business to lounge away the noon on a sofa. She ought likewise to have worn decent garments; a gown covering her properly, which was not the case: out of abundance of material – seven-and-twenty yards, I should say, of drapery – she managed to make inefficient raiment. (p. 275)

The painting which, she complains, 'seemed to consider itself the queen of the collection', is dismissed as a 'coarse and preposterous canvass', 'an enormous piece of claptrap' (p. 276). Lucy is prepared to question the received view that this is good painting, and apply her own judgement. We come away from this scene with a sense less of the objectified women on view in the gallery, the Cleopatra and La Femme, than of the keen-eyed spectator and independently minded art critic, Lucy Snowe, who preferred to be left alone rather than endure the sociability of gallery culture, for, permitted to look properly at the art works displayed, she was 'happy; happy, not always in admiring, but in examining, questioning, and forming conclusions', that is, developing a critical attitude towards art (p. 274).

Sculptural representations of Cleopatra provide the *mise en scène* for numerous novelistic disquisitions on 'womanhood' in the period. Two of the artist-protagonists in Hawthorne's *The Marble Faun*, Miriam and Kenyon, discuss the latter's (fully clothed) sculpture of Cleopatra, with her 'full Nubian lips, and other characteristics of the Egyptian physiognomy', in a key scene of the novel in which the exotically beautiful Jewish painter almost confesses her dark secret to the American sculptor (p. 98). The Cleopatra, and Miriam herself, both racialised and sexualised, are explicitly contrasted with the New England puritan Hilda, whose 'womanhood is of the ethereal type' (p. 99). Statuary is deployed to point up a similar contrast in George Eliot's *Middlemarch*, when the fictional German Nazarene painter Naumann draws his friend Ladislaw's attention to a young woman he wishes to paint, who is standing in 'the hall where the reclining Ariadne, then called the Cleopatra, lies in the marble voluptuousness of her beauty'. She is not looking at the sculpture by which she stands, but providing, with her quakerish spiritual beauty, a model for 'the most perfect young Madonna'.[28] Her dreamy inattention to the art works around her is later explained. Dorothea Brooke, or Mrs Casaubon as she now is, who had hitherto been 'fed on meagre Protestant histories and on art chiefly of the hand-screen sort', is utterly overwhelmed by 'the weight of unintelligible Rome' on her disastrous wedding journey, experiencing 'Titanic life gazing and struggling on walls and ceilings' and 'the long vistas of white forms whose marble eyes seemed to hold the monotonous light of an alien world' as a nightmarish assault.[29] These scenes magnificently convey, through the scopophilic objectification of Dorothea and her own lack of visual agency when confronted with the bewildering visual surfeit of Rome, how her lack of education renders this potentially strong, independent and ambitious young woman vulnerable and passive when she is exposed to a cultural world beyond the sheltered life of her girlhood. Without knowledge and visual agency she can only be subject to what others make of her, like the model Naumann would like her to be.

The issue of women's education is at the heart of *Middlemarch*, of course, and of other fiction by Eliot, as it is of *Villette*, and it is a theme of many other mid-nineteenth-century novels. The specific question of women's education in art is taken up by other writers too. The focus of *Sisters in Art* by Anna Mary Howitt, herself a painter and author of the autobiographical *An Art Student in Munich* (1854), is on the development of a new ethos in art education for women according to which the teaching of art and design are integrated, and embedded in a broader education in humanities and science; where women are envisaged as working collectively and collaboratively, and, importantly, as having the education to approach art critically. The very form in which Howitt's story was published, serially in the *Illustrated Exhibitor and Magazine of Art* (a journal that announces itself as being devoted to painting, sculpture, architecture history, biography, art-industry, manufactures, invention and discoveries, local and domestic scenes, and ornamental works, and has a 'Ladies Department', mainly concerned with embroidery), by the same token, signifies this ethos. Howitt, herself a painter, inserts her utopian fictional vision for women's art into a mainstream art journal, both thematically and formally proposing an alternative to the very concept of a 'Ladies Department'. The story realises an alternative role for women in art than that of the model and muse. Lizzy Wilson, for example, is educated to become a productive and self-supporting artist rather than a model, like Giuseppe's daughter, who had disappeared and was feared fallen and lost (though even she is sought out by the 'sisters', and her own daughter and granddaughter are rescued from sharing her fate).

Lizzy is frequently identified as a fictional correlative of Howitt's friend Elizabeth Siddall, here represented as an artist rather than as the mythologised wife of Dante Gabriel Rossetti she was to become after her death from a laudanum overdose in 1862. The 'legend' of Siddall was at the centre of a new wave of feminist work on the Pre-Raphaelites in the 1980s, initiated by Deborah Cherry and Griselda Pollock's article 'Woman as Sign in Pre-Raphaelite Literature: A Study of the Representation of Elizabeth Siddall' (1984). Like Howitt, these critics recuperated Siddall as an artist in her own right, but they also probed the larger question of 'woman as sign' in the Pre-Raphaelite imaginary. They argue that Rossetti's drawings of Siddall's and other female faces are not portraits, rather: 'Operating within an emergent regime of representation of Woman in the 1850s, they signify in the ideological process of a re-definition of woman *as image*, and as *visibly* different.' In short, 'They are ... symptoms of and sites for the renegotiation and redefinition of femininity and sexuality within the complex of social and gender relations of the 1850s.'[30]

This is an insight that women novelists contemporaneous with Pre-Raphaelitism intriguingly anticipate. Mary Elizabeth Braddon, for instance, in her sensation novel of 1862, *Lady Audley's Secret*, creates a protagonist who exemplifies precisely the doubleness of the 'femme fatale' that Pollock identifies in those obsessively repetitious Rossettian images of female faces: an angel/fiend, who signifies at once the spiritualised bourgeois feminine ideal and a dangerous conjunction of perverse sexuality, erotic fantasy and class infiltration. Indeed, the discovery of Lady Audley's secret begins when George Talboys penetrates her boudoir and recognises his ostensibly dead wife in a Pre-Raphaelite portrait of the angelic lady of the house:

> Yes, the painter must have been a pre-Raphaelite. No one but a pre-Raphaelite would have painted, hair by hair, those feathery masses of ringlets with every glimmer of gold, and every shadow of pale brown. No one but a pre-Raphaelite would have so exaggerated every attribute of that delicate face as to give a lurid lightness to the blonde complexion, and a strange sinister light to the deep blue eyes. No one but a pre-Raphaelite would have given to that pretty pouting mouth the hard and almost wicked look it had in the portrait.
>
> It was so like and yet so unlike; it was as if you had burned strange-coloured fires before my lady's face, and by their influence brought out new lines and new expressions never seen in it before. The perfection of feature, the brilliancy of colouring were there; but I suppose the painter had copied

> quaint mediaeval monstrosities until his brain had grown bewildered, for my lady, in his portrait of her, had something of the aspect of a beautiful fiend.[31]

Robert Audley declares that he doesn't like the portrait: 'there's something odd about it'. His cousin Alicia suggests that 'sometimes a painter is in a manner inspired, and is able to see, through the normal expression of the face, another expression that is equally a part of it, though not to be perceived by common eyes', adding: '*We* have never seen my lady look as she does in that picture; but I think that she *could* look so' (p. 73).

Pollock observes of the kind of Pre-Raphaelite painting from which this description derives: 'The myth of woman is that she is simply revealed by the genius of the artist' (p. 122). In this text, Lady Audley/Lucy Graham/Helen Talboys is of course literally revealed in the painting. Its meticulous realism enables George Talboys to identify her as his wife, and its lurid and fantastic exaggeration of her features and colouring suggests the madness that is eventually discovered to lurk within the beautiful form. But Braddon deploys the generic Pre-Raphaelite iconography of woman in her description of Lady Audley's portrait in ways that also suggest her appreciation of how, in its peculiar conjunction of bourgeois realism and hallucinatory fantasy, Pre-Raphaelitism initiated a new regime of representation that played a crucial role in shaping Victorian ideas about womanhood. Not only does George recognise his wife in the portrait, and Alicia recognise the ruthlessness and insanity that the artist reveals within her apparent perfection, but, I suggest, Braddon herself recognises something 'odd' about Pre-Raphaelite representations of women, and understands the role of such visual images in the maintenance of a gender order in which women are fetishised as angels and demonised as fiends.

Vernon Lee was to tackle the issue of the Pre-Raphaelite woman more directly two decades later, not in her art criticism, but in her controversial novel *Miss Brown* (1884). The novel's chief interest lies in its dissection, over three volumes, of the artist Hamlin's scopophilic obsession with the beautiful young nursemaid with the Pre-Raphaelite looks whom he makes his model, and who has no more identity for him than as the object of his eroticising gaze. It reveals Lee's acute awareness of the constitution of woman as spectacle in the contemporary visual economy. Anne Brown is constantly described in terms of art works: her head is likened to 'certain mournful and sullen heads of Michaelangelo'; she is 'a picture by an old master'. At one point she asks herself bitterly: 'Did he care for her only as a sort of live picture?'[32] It is men who are endowed with visual agency in this text, and Lee does not allow her trapped heroine any escape. Anne dreams of going to Girton, and has her opportunities for freedom. At one point in the story, her philanthropic cousin Richard Brown, who, significantly, is losing his eyesight, tells her he will have to engage a young man as his secretary. But she cannot act: 'Anne felt a lump in her throat. Oh that she had been a man, instead of being this useless, base creature of mere comely looks, a woman, set apart for the contemplation of aesthetes' (3, p. 63). She succumbs at the end of the novel to the pressure to become Hamlin's wife.

Miss Brown is a novel in which the visual field is definitively masculine (although it does contain an intriguing vignette of an advanced young woman 'studying eye-surgery with a famous Rhenish oculist (1, pp. 211–12)), and in which the female protagonist's abject dependence upon a man is explicitly connected to their specular relation. It firmly links the visual economy with the sexual economy. While it is the male artist protagonist, Hamlin, who has the 'delicate, handsome features', and the 'fair, almost beardless complexion' of the corrupt and 'effeminate' male family line (2, pp. 48, 51), and his model and protégée Anne Brown whose features are 'monumental' (her nose 'massive, heavy', her lips 'thick, and of curiously bold projection and curl', her neck 'round and erect like a tower', and her chest, again, 'massive' (1, pp. 24–5)), it is in the feminised artist and aesthete that patriarchal power is vested. Hamlin's ancestors were slave owners in the West Indies, and Miss Brown's name bespeaks her racial origins. When Hamlin wonders if she is Jewish, or 'some Eastern, dashed with Hindoo or Negro' (1, p. 27), she explains that she has Moorish blood, and at one point sees herself as having a 'strange, half-southern, half-Jewish, and almost half-Ethiopian beauty' (2, pp. 48–9). In Lee's story, as in the novel with which this chapter began, Maud Cruttwell's *Fire and Frost* (1913), the play with physical tropes of masculinity and femininity and the inscription of exoticism in the novel are mechanisms by which critique is established.

In their novels and stories, then, Victorian women such as Lee and Cruttwell articulated a profound awareness of difference that was often not apparent in their formal art-historical writing. Other female novelists *imagined* and gave substance to the female artists and patrons that would have a place in some future history of art, even if actual female painters are largely absent from women's accounts of art past. Through their deft use of narrative voice and a range of characters they are able to convey competing views about the place of women in the Victorian art world, and especially to dramatise the conflicted identity of the woman artist. Plot and tone, especially irony, are effectively deployed to show the barriers to women's full professional engagement in art practice. Inventive narrative forms enable the exploration of experiences that cannot be so effectively rendered in the factual historical prose expected of either art criticism and history or popular guides to art. Fictional encounters with invented works of art can convey the experience of art more than accurate catalogues of artefacts in galleries, and the ways in which that experience may be gendered. A proper account of art-historical writing by women in the nineteenth century, then, must include the much wider range of genres in which they wrote about art than simply their formal treatises which, while in themselves much more interesting I think than some critics suggest, represent only one dimension of their contribution to the historiography of art.

CHAPTER 3

Girl guides: travel, translation, ekphrasis

Fiction was a popular literary form that enabled women to explore issues relating to the professional lives of female artists and critics and the gendering of aesthetic experience, but it was only one of the many genres in which women wrote about art in the nineteenth century. Being a writer in the nineteenth century, equally for major authors and minor players and hacks, generally involved engaging in a number of different kinds of writing practice, so it should not surprise us that women who established reputations as professional art historians and critics published in other forms and fields. Nevertheless, the breadth and diversity of their literary and cultural interests, and the sheer range of genres in which they wrote, are very striking. Claire Richter Sherman points out that

> Lady Callcott wrote a popular children's history of England; Lady Morgan, plays, songs, and best-selling novels; Mary Margaret Heaton, children's poetry. Elizabeth Rigby, Lady Eastlake, was the first woman to write on a variety of artistic, literary and social topics for the prestigious *Quarterly Review*. With her edition and translation of *The Mabinogian*, Lady Charlotte Guest (later Schreiber) inspired interest in Celtic folklore and Arthurian romances.[1]

We might add many more examples of women's generic fecundity, and note the fact that Mary Merrifield, in addition to being an expert in fresco, had research interests in natural history, frequently contributed papers to *Nature* and became an authority on seaweeds, having learned Danish and Swedish in order to read Scandinavian scientific papers on the subject; that Ellen Clayton wrote on women warriors and women vocalists as well as on women artists; that Elizabeth Pennell was a well-known cookery and travel writer as well as a regular contributor on art subjects, writing under the signature 'N. N.', to the *Nation*; and that, in addition to her art-critical work, her biographies and translation of New Woman novels, Helen Zimmern translated Nietzsche and Schopenhauer, as well as volumes of Persian poetry and the comedies of Goldoni.

Their range, productivity and the extent of their popular impact on a wide spectrum of audiences was indeed impressive, and reflects the fact that this was a generation of writers not constrained to be narrow and specialist by the etiquette of modern professionalism: however, one explanation for the diversity of their published output and for the particular publishing trajectories of many of these energetic, imaginative and resourceful women is that female writers were subject to particular discursive constraints. If it was not uncommon later in the century for women to experiment creatively with different forms in writing of art and its histories, early in the period it was pragmatic, if not essential, for them to find informal paths into art history. Women were more readily acknowledged as professional writers in some fields and genres than in others, and so if they wished to write about art they practised circumspection. Writing in less prestigious genres where they had already established a legitimate claim, such as the 'low-status' arenas of translation and travel writing,[2] or that were perceived, like the novel, journals and letters, to be feminised forms, enabled women to explore prohibited territory under cover and to find an authoritative voice. Hence, the earliest art-historical writing by women often appeared in or took the form of guidebooks and travelogues, practical manuals, popular biographies and translations, or it occupied the private space of letters and diaries, or else it was fictionalised in novels and poetry, or rendered anonymous by the masculine voice and standardised house styles of the periodical press.

This chapter explores how women seized upon the opportunity to extend the acceptable womanly roles of teacher and guide and to make use of the literary forms that were condoned to write about art. It focuses on their travel guides and translations, both their literal rendition of foreign language art texts into English, and their figurative translation of the experience of viewing art into other literary and performative media, such as ekphrastic poetry and exhibition. Several recent studies of professional women writers in the nineteenth century have drawn attention to their cultural work as travellers and translators, and to their particular role in the economies of intellectual exchange, uncovering their formative influence on developing concepts of gender and modernity.[3] Here my interest is more specifically in the contribution of their travel writing and translation projects to nineteenth-century writing about art, and in further understanding the specificity of their engagement with the experience of art through these media and how that might be contextualised.

Travel writing

Travel books and guides came into vogue in the early nineteenth century with the opening up of Continental Europe following the defeat of Napoleon, the wider distribution of wealth, and the advent of the railway and the steamship, and women were quick to recognise and exploit both the literary and the commercial possibilities of the form. Guidebooks, letters and journals on the subject of travel and residences abroad were, indeed, the forms in which a number of women who were later to become known as art historians first established their credentials as writers. For instance, the well-travelled Maria Graham's earliest publications included her *Journal of a Residence in India* (1812), *Letters on India* (1814), *Three Months Passed in the Mountains East of Rome, during the year 1819* (1820), *Journal of a Residence in Chile* (1824) and *Journal of a Voyage to Brazil* (1824), while Elizabeth Rigby's writing career as an art historian and critic was likewise launched with a book of *Letters from the Shores of the Baltic* (1841) which, as we shall see, contained interesting material on art. And Anna Jameson's publishing career followed a similar trajectory, from the early tentative comments on art peppered through her *Diary of an Ennuyée* (1826), a book based on her Continental travels as a governess, through her more knowledgeable observations on contemporary German art, the German and Italian 'primitives', and women artists in *Visits and Sketches at Home and Abroad* (1834), to her guidebooks to public and private galleries and *Memoirs of the Early Italian Painters* of the early 1840s, and finally in the late 1840s and 1850s her most original and important work, the multi-volume study of iconography in the arts, *Sacred and Legendary Art*.

Women were more easily able to introduce passages of art commentary into the looser, more informal genres of the essay, the journal, sketches and letters, than to launch straight into comprehensive histories of art, and for writers such as Graham, Rigby and Jameson the experience of publishing in these forms early in their careers gave them a useful apprenticeship for their later more specialised art publication. And of course letters and journals were suitably modest vehicles for women, as were the other less formal modes of writing with which they identified. Visiting, sketching and diarising are quintessentially female activities, and early in the century it was no doubt politic to observe such generic decorum.

Nevertheless, although such generic choices were in a sense thrust upon women, it is also interesting to think about how women experimented with and re-made genres in order to write about the subjects that interested them. After all, if we accept that later writers, such as Vernon Lee, exercised a positive preference for writing about Renaissance art in the more fragmentary, suggestive and personal form of 'a series of impressions' rather than in the form of a grand narrative,[4] we should not dismiss the idea that women writing fifty years earlier might have been doing the same. Jameson's *Diary of an Ennuyée*, for instance, though widely criticised for, among other things, its confused generic identity, was an interesting experiment that instantly brought fame to its unknown and unconnected author. Originally published anonymously under the title *A Lady's Diary*, it is, as Judith Johnston observes, 'a strange mixture of fiction and non-fiction in imitation of de Staël's *Corinne*', in which '[t]he stilted fiction of the gothic love plot and the voice of its lachrymose heroine contrasts vividly with the non-fiction where the cheerful traveller, supposedly that same heroine, records with lively interest all she sees'.[5] An early example of how Jameson 'never failed to turn every journey to financial account by publishing her travel experiences',[6] the *Diary*'s hybrid form made it from the beginning a target for criticism: 'a guide-book and a romance form an incongruous mixture', complains the *Westminster Review*, 'and we certainly wish they could be separated in future'.[7] The *Diary* connects the genres of travel and romance, and it also makes explicit the link between travel writing and the feminine. Its deployment of a gothic romance fictional framing device may suggest that Jameson did not at this stage of her career feel authorised to publish a piece of straightforward travel literature or a guidebook, preferring to hide behind the fiction of a 'Lady's' diary, tried and tested territory for the woman writer. Her second travel book, however, *Visits and Sketches at Home and Abroad* (1834), is a markedly more confident and coherent piece of travel writing which continues to make use of different generic modes such as the dialogue and the journal, but bears the hallmark of her mature writing with its detailed focus on art works she has seen in the course of her journeys. That focus becomes still more defined and the genre of the guidebook more explicit in *A Handbook to the Public Galleries of Art in and Near London*, published by John Murray in 1842, a book that achieved some high-profile reviews in the press. By the mid 1840s she had established a reputation as both a travel writer and a guide on artistic subjects, and in so doing had taken control of the genres available to her and devised her own style of writing about art.

If for women like Jameson, Graham and Rigby the authoring of guidebooks was a stepping stone to higher forms of art criticism and history, for others it was their contribution to the generic definition of the guidebook upon which their reputation rested. Such a woman was Mariana Starke, an intriguing example of a woman who early saw a publishing opportunity for a popular pocket guidebook for the growing number of English travellers to the Continent. Having lived in Italy and published an account of her residence there as *Travels in Italy* in 1802, she went on to produce her best-selling *Information and Directions for Travellers on the Continent*, which went into many editions between 1820 and 1838. She carefully explains the innovative nature of her guide, which is intended 'to comprise, within the compass of One Portable Volume, all the information necessary for Travellers on the Continent of Europe, and the Island of Sicily'.[8] And she also makes clear the original research involved for her in gathering together both the cultural and the practical information necessary for the modern traveller, and in continually revising and updating her information. And so the seventh edition is described as 'Thoroughly Revised and Corrected with Considerable Additions, made during a recent expensive journey undertaken by the Author, with a view to render the work as perfect as possible', and the reader is assured of the personal commitment of the author, and the magnitude of her task:

> it was requisite to examine with exactness, and give a detail, calculated to be read upon the spot, of the ancient edifices, principal museums and galleries, public and private, in the above-mentioned countries. It was also requisite to copy all the most frequented routes from the post books lately published by Royal authority; and this has been the Author's employment during the last three years.[9]

Starke undertakes to summarise the views of European art specialists in her 'ample, and I hope correct Catalogues of the most valuable specimens of Architecture, Painting, and Sculpture, which adorn France, Germany, Italy, &c.', reinforcing 'the opinions of Nardini, Venuti, Winckelmann, and Visconti, on some of the most celebrated works of Art' by awarding the best of them, rather disconcertingly for the modern reader, one or more exclamation marks, in a way that anticipates Baedeker's system of stars.[10] But she also makes the point that her guide contains original material on the art treasures her readers will encounter on their journey. For example, we are told there exists '[n]o complete printed description of the sculpture, frescos, and oil-paintings in the Vatican, and private galleries at Rome', and no guide to Sicily, its history and antiquities. Her work, she states, endeavours 'to supply this deficiency'.[11]

The voice of the guidebooks is overtly feminine. In the introductory material to each successive volume the author speaks as a woman to the imagined concerns of her readers. The fifth edition, for example, carries an Advertisement at the beginning addressing English travellers' anxieties about the dangers of being accosted by 'disbanded soldiers, converted into banditti' in the South of France, the Alps and the Apennines, in which she assures her readers that '[h]ighway robberies, indeed, are quite as uncommon on the Continent at present, as they were formerly', and that 'English Travellers, even when going post, have rarely been robbed, unless owing to imprudence on their own part, or on that of their attendants'.[12] The Introduction to the same volume also explains that, as a woman who has twelve years' experience of nursing consumptive patients, 'during the greater part of which period my time and thoughts were chiefly occupied by endeavours to mitigate the sufferings of those most dear to me', she is well qualified to give advice to 'those of [her] Compatriots, who, in consequence of pulmonary complaints, are compelled to exchange their native climate for the mild temperature of Italy', and to endeavour 'to guard them against those serious inconveniences which too generally retard, and not infrequently prevent, the recovery of consumptive persons'.[13]

The feminine note that characterises the practical aspects of these volumes spills over into their treatment of art. The section on the Pisan Campo Santo is a good example. Travellers interested in tracing the revival of the arts are encouraged to begin their journey into Italy, and concurrently into Renaissance art, in Pisa, and specifically at its 'most beautiful Edifice', and the cradle of Italian art, the Campo Santo, which had by this point become, as Robyn Cooper has shown, a place of Romantic pilgrimage, and which Starke herself was to promote as a fashionable tourist destination.[14] Starke writes enthusiastically about the frescoes by early Italian painters that adorn its walls, foreshadowing the promotion of the so-called Primitives by women such as Maria Callcott and Anna Jameson, who were themselves in the vanguard of Pre-Raphaelitism, and demonstrating her own independent and discerning judgement. Some twenty years before such early Italian fresco work came into vogue in England, and when it still represented a minority taste, she was writing for a popular readership about both the strengths and what she perceived to be the deficiencies of the Campo Santo frescos: 'It is remarkable that, among the immense number of countenances contained in these paintings, we scarce find two alike. The faces, generally speaking, are well done; the figures and drapery stiff; the perspective is bad; but the borders, which form the several compartments, are particularly elegant.'[15]

Most interestingly of all, though, given the guidebook format, she inserts into her descriptive catalogue of monuments and pictures and practical hints for travellers, on the grounds that it is 'descriptive of the Campo-Santo', a 'Sonnet to Grief' that she herself, after the style of Madame de Staël's Corinne, had felt moved to compose:

> STRUCTURE unmatch'd! which braves the lapse of time!
> Fit cradle of the reviving Arts to rear!
> Light, as the paper Nautilus, appear
> Thy arches, of Pisano's works the prime.
> Famed Campo-Santo! Where the mighty Dead
> Of elder days, in Parian marble sleep,
> Say, who is she, that ever seems to keep
> Watch o'er thy precincts; save when mortal tread
> Invades the awful stillness of the scene?
> Then struggling to suppress the heavy sigh,
> And brushing the big tear-drop from her eye,
> She veils her face – and glides yon tombs between.
> 'Tis GRIEF! – and by that thick veil the Maid I know,
> Moisten'd with tears which never cease to flow.[16]

The veiled and weeping woman, watching over this cradle of the arts, and the sympathetic female travel guide, looking after the needs of her inexperienced, fearful and perhaps sickly charges, and at the same time overseeing and conducting them through the great cultural monuments of the mighty Dead, seem uncannily connected. Both the poet and her subject are defined by their eyes, sites of empathetic encounter which signify both vision and affect, looking at art and being moved to tears by it, and, in this poem, interpolated so fancifully into the matter-of-fact guidebook prose, are ineluctably feminine.[17]

Although Mariana Starke does not feature in Elizabeth Rigby's 1845 article on 'Lady Travellers' for the *Quarterly Review*, it was no doubt writing such as hers, as well as the twelve volumes of travel literature under review, that led Rigby to remark on the connections between visuality and the feminine in English women's travel literature. Writing anonymously, and adopting a male voice, she begins:

> That there are peculiar powers inherent in ladies' eyes, this number of the Quarterly Review was not required to establish; but one in particular, of which we reap all the benefit without paying the penalty, we must in common gratitude be allowed to point out. We mean that power of observation which so long as it remains at home counting canvass stitches by the fireside, we are apt to consider no shrewder than our own, but which once

removed from the familiar scene; and returned to us in the shape of letters or books, seldom fails to prove its superiority.[18]

Women's eyes do, it seems to the author, have peculiar – or at least different, and superior – observational powers from men's, that make their travel writing as different from men's as women's letters are, 'overflowing', as they do 'with those close and lively details which show not only that observing eyes have been at work, but one pair of bright eyes in particular'.[19] And since 'every country with any pretensions to civilization has a twofold aspect, addressed to two different modes of perception, and seldom visible simultaneously to both', that is 'a home life as well as a public life, and the first quite necessary to interpret the last', then every country 'to be fairly understood requires reporters from both sexes'.[20] Although Rigby apparently here delegates the female eye to the domestic and the male to the public sphere, in a familiar rehearsal of the dominant separate spheres ideology, her female observer is notably abroad, away from the hearth. Furthermore, the 'marriage' of these two ways of seeing that she envisages and recommends captures, not a hierarchically gendered visual order after the model of that patriarchal Victorian institution, but what she describes as the essential '*domesticity* of the English character'.[21] In other words, 'ladies' eyes', women's particular modes of perception, are made to define a fundamental quality of Englishness, and of English ways of seeing.

Although in this article she was anonymously reviewing a dozen travel narratives written by women, Elizabeth Rigby's interest in lady travellers was a personal one, for she herself had a few years previously published, also anonymously, a book comprised of letters written during an extended visit to her married sister in Reval in Russia (now Tallinn, Estonia) from 1838 to 1841.[22] As for so many women, the epistolary form and the requirement of the travel genre to describe wonders seen gave Rigby the opportunity she needed to publish her first critical writing about art, and *Letters from the Shores of the Baltic*, published in 1841, contains some nice passages of commentary on the arts in the region, in which we see the seeds of her later writing as a recognised authority on art. For example, her second letter describes the work of the Danish artist Thorvaldsen in Copenhagen, noting especially the new Frauen-Kirche, his figures of the twelve apostles, and the altarpiece, a bas-relief of Christ. Thirty-four years later she was to publish an article on the 'Life and Works of Thorvaldsen' in the *Edinburgh Review*.[23]

But while publishing these letters from the Baltic did enable Rigby to serve a kind of critical apprenticeship, her chosen form also determined and delimited what she was able to say. This is something she reflects upon in her fourth letter, where she tries to convey both her experience of visiting the Hermitage and her frustration at having to encapsulate that experience within the confines of a letter:

> The attempt to describe in one letter a building groaning with the accumulated collections of an ambitious, unsparing, absolute, and, in some few instances, discriminating imperial dynasty – one which would require visits of weeks in succession, and engross a volume of description – would be as vain as to pretend to comprise the British Museum in a few pages. For a detail of the far-famed Hermitage, fitting and well-named retreat for such an imperial anchorite as Catherine II, I must refer you to works of great length already devoted exclusively to it, without the aid of which my own superficial view would have been of little avail.

The description that follows recalls Foucault's characterisation of the museum as 'heterotopia', that is, a site 'capable of juxtaposing in a single real space several spaces, several sites that are in themselves incompatible'.[24] Rigby dwells on the 'positive labour of viewing' a sightseer is obliged to 'undergo' in order to appreciate such a palace, and the 'powers of attention' it demands:

> after running through forty magnificent and glittering apartments, beyond the first ten of which the powers of attention can no longer possibly be commanded, the miserable sight-seer returns with a head swimming with the colours and forms of every school, through which the delicious Alba Madonna, by Raphael; the pale, fast-worn Christ, by Leonardo da Vinci – a whole succession of valuable lights, by Rembrandt – a never-to-be-forgotten Pordenone – and, for the sake of nationality, the Infant Hercules strangling the Serpent, by our Sir Joshua, though not among the most attractive of his productions, are dimly struggling; while Dresden Jars and Malachite vases – heads of Russian marshals and bodies of Thibet idols – golden trees, peacocks, owls, and mushrooms; the grown-up playthings of a semi-barbaric court; portfolios of first-rate prints – cases of gems and cameos, and whole swarms of natural history, are jostling each other in hopeless confusion; all centring in the enchanting vista of Raphael's exquisite Loggie, of which a perfect fac-simile here exists, and which alone is more than enough for the time I spent there. How then can I draw light out of this chaos? No; the Hermitage must be left to those who have given, or can give, it all the requisite time.[25]

The breathlessness of Rigby's account of hurtling through the accumulated splendours of this extraordinarily packed museum space captures the chaotic excess of the cultural encounter as she experiences it. Like the edifice itself, positively bursting at the seams with its extravagantly promiscuous imperialist collection, the monumentally long sentence strains to govern and contain the cumulative detail of her description of this 'barbaric' display of paintings, statuary, vases, knick-knacks, portfolios of prints, cases of gems and swarms of natural history specimens. Furthermore – and also, for all its size and plenitude, like the museum – the letter gives us not a comprehensive 'volume of description', or one of the 'works of great length' to which she refers, but a synecdochal sample of random items 'jostling each other in hopeless confusion'.

For some women, the impetus for writing a guidebook seems to have come out of a desire to bring such chaotic confusion to order. Anna Jameson, for instance, explains that she published her *Memoirs of Early Italian Painters and of the Progress of Painting in Italy* (1859) in order 'to enlarge [the] sphere of rational pleasure in the contemplation of works of art', while Kate Thompson neatly sets out the well-ordered plan for her *Handbook to the Public Picture Galleries of Europe* (1877) in the Preface, where she promises an examination of all the major and most of the minor European public galleries, a brief historical sketch of each of the European schools of art, chronological tables of every celebrated painter, accurate attribution, and accurate reference to the catalogue numbers attached to pictures.[26] Neither Jameson nor Thompson makes claims for her work as constituting a significant critical contribution in itself. Rather, they see themselves as providing handbooks to aid the appreciation of art by others, emphasising the womanly educational function of the guide, its role in leading the young and the inexperienced through the moral and intellectual complexities with which the gallery confronts them, and in tidying up the heterotopic confusions of art's history equally with its sites of display, like an orderly housewife or an enthusiastic nanny. Jameson describes 'this little work', her 'little book', as 'a companion for the young', and Thompson's Preface is full of the kind of disclaimers that are so typical of such nineteenth-century writing by women: on the advice of her father, we are told, she began the 'little exercise' of making notes on works they looked at together and gathering information about them purely for her own 'information and profit'; a male friend found her to have 'collected materials for a small manual which might be of some service, at all events to the untravelled tourist'; she remains 'greatly indebted' to her father, and regrets that 'some few clerical errors may have crept in' to her 'little work'. Thompson specifically draws our attention to the fact that, although she has carefully examined every painting of which she writes, she has 'not felt [herself] qualified to enter into the region of Art criticism, and [has] not aspired to do so'. She does, however, add rather apologetically, in spite of herself, 'Still it has not been found possible to see and compare so many fine works without occasionally expressing some sort of opinion here and there.'[27]

Writing her own guidebooks three decades later, to the paintings in the principal Florentine galleries and churches and minor museums, Maud Cruttwell is notably bolder in her claims to cultural authority. She unapologetically describes her enterprise as a 'Critical Catalogue' both 'for use in the Galleries' and 'as a book of reference for the student'.[28] She is critical not only of the art works she describes but also of the very genre of the guidebook. 'The descriptions usually given in guide-books, catalogues, and even in critical works are apt', she complains, 'to be most wearisome and useless, by reason of too much detail. If the reader is unacquainted with the painting no amount of such minute descriptions will enable him to visualise it. If he is acquainted with it they are superfluous.' She herself determines 'to draw attention to the general effect, to peculiarities of composition, of atmospheric effect, and of colour, and to such special and characteristic features as might escape notice'.[29] She throws up her hands at the disorderly state of the Italian numbering system, and arranges her catalogue in an order that maximises the visitor's ease of viewing: 'Owing to constant changes of place the numbering of the pictures is in so chaotic a state that any sort of numerical sequence has been necessarily abandoned, even by the official guides. Advantage has been taken of this disorder to begin each room with the wall on which the eye naturally falls on entry.'[30] Authority is once more vested in the woman's eyes. The scholarly work for Cruttwell's guides is, we are firmly told, her own. No self-deprecatingly ladylike or nursemaid volume this! Rather it is the critical and scholarly study of a professional art historian. Even the quotations from Vasari that weave through the volume are, she informs us, selected and translated by her.[31]

Translation and ekphrasis

Translation was of course itself another of those permissible forms of public expression that enabled women to gain access to the world of letters. George Eliot was, for example, known as the translator in 1846 of David Friedrich Strauss's *Das Leben Jesu* and in 1854 of Feuerbach's *Das Wesen des Christenhums* before she achieved fame as a novelist, and Harriet Martineau published her influential condensed translation of Auguste Comte's *Philosophie positive* in 1852–3. Specifically, translation was for many women the means of entering the field of art criticism and history in the early nineteenth century. Women were responsible for publishing English editions of important Italian, French and German art-historical texts: for instance, Elizabeth Rigby/Eastlake's translations of Passavant (1836) and Waagen (1853, 1857) referred to in Chapter 1; Mary Merrifield's translation of Cennino Cennini's recently discovered fifteenth-century *Treatise on Painting* in 1844, followed in 1849 by her two-volume collection *Original Treatises*; Margaret Hutton's anonymous translation of Kugler's *Handbook of the History of Painting* in 1842, updated by Elizabeth Eastlake in 1851; Mrs Jonathan Foster's translation of Vasari's *Lives* (1850–2), which went into a new edition in 1867; Fanny Elizabeth Bunnett's translation of Wilhelm Lübke's *History of Art* (1868); Mrs A. H. Clough's translation of Jacob Burckhardt's *The Cicerone; or, Art Guide to Painting in Italy, for the Use of Travellers* (1873); and Mrs Charles Heaton's edition, from the German, of Julius Meyer's *Antonio Allegri da Correggio* (1876). The importance of such work (and this is but a sample) should not be underestimated, for not only were these women responsible for bringing some of the most influential of Continental writing on art to the Anglophone world but also, as Sherry Simon points out, 'translation frames and directs ongoing processes of intellectual transmission … translators are involved in the materials through which they work; they are fully invested in the process of transfer'.[32]

Women were also, though, deeply engaged in 'translation' in a more metaphorical sense, and Simon's observation applies equally to this more figurative understanding of the term. In her critical study of Anna Jameson, Judith Johnston makes a case for the importance of the activity of translation thus broadly conceived in Jameson's work, noting that during a winter stay in Toronto in 1837 she began her serious study of German, and began 'to practise forms of translation, which included criticism and interpretation'.[33] Her 'translations' of German art and literature, including, for example, a fascinating response to Adam Oehlenschläger's play *Correggio* that is discussed by Johnston, were to make up the 'winter' section of her travel book *Winter Studies and Summer Rambles in Canada*, which appeared in 1838 and was written explicitly for Englishwomen. Not only did Jameson go on to translate the plays of Princess Amelia of Saxony from German to English but, as Johnston suggests, the idea of translation, more figuratively conceived, would inform her subsequent writing, not least her guides to and studies of art. In her preface to the first collected edition of her *Memoirs of Early Italian Painters and of the Progress of Painting in Italy* (1859), she reflects on how her work involves translation between words and images, musing indeed on the transactional nature of the verbal and the visual in the interpretation of art. 'We should be able to read a picture as we read a book', she declares: 'A gallery of pictures may be compared with a well-furnished library; and I have sometimes thought that it would be a good thing if we could arrange a collection of pictures as we arrange a collection of books', that is, by subject. She goes on to draw an extensive parallel between a library and a picture gallery in which the latter is organised according to the same principles as the former. It is through the imaginative translation of the visual into the verbal that Jameson hopes to stimulate 'comparative and discriminating reflections' and 'enlarge [the] sphere of rational pleasure in the contemplation of works of art'.[34]

Many other women were, like Jameson, involved in acts of translation that, though they sometimes included, went beyond the linguistic; for example in 'translating' specialist information for educational purposes or for a popular readership, or simply for the untravelled. For Mary Merrifield, this meant that not only did she translate Italian treatises on fresco technique into English, but she also published *Practical Directions for Portrait Painting in Watercolours* in 1851, and a *Handbook of Light and Shade, with especial reference to Model Drawing* in 1855, and in 1857 published a guidebook to Brighton, all of which depended on the translation of expert knowledge from specialist into lay language. Others were similarly involved in the transmission and dissemination of knowledge to the general reader, or specifically to women, children or the working classes, from Mariana Starke with her guidebooks for travellers in the 1820s, Maria Callcott's *Essays Towards the History of Painting* (1834) and Anna Jameson's *Winter Studies and Summer Rambles* (1838) written for a female readership, to Clementina (Kit) Anstruther-Thomson's late-nineteenth-century lectures on aesthetics at Toynbee Hall and gallery tours for the working classes.[35]

The translation of a piece of writing from one language into another, as it is commonly understood, constitutes, as André Lefevere notes, 'only one type of text that makes an "image" of another text. Other types would be criticism, historiography, commentary and anthologizing.'[36] His point is most relevant to this study, of course, and is peculiarly resonant where the text being translated is itself an image. The concept of 'translation' is a useful one when thinking about the rhetorical act of interpreting visual images and, within that, about the different languages and forms such rhetoric might take. For what Richard Stein in his study of literary representations of the fine arts in the nineteenth century has called the 'ritual of interpretation'[37] must always involve 'translation': of the visual to the verbal, or the aural, or indeed into other visual representations, whether pictures, sculptures, performance or dance. In his essay 'The Task of the Translator', Walter Benjamin describes the activity of translation itself in strikingly visual terms, as 'transparent': 'it does not cover the original, does not block its light, but allows the pure language, as though reinforced by its own medium, to shine upon the original all the more fully'.[38] One of the things I wish to explore in this chapter is the way the image, to continue Benjamin's compelling metaphor, is refracted in different discourses and different generic forms. However, translation is a practice that raises questions of origin, power and difference, and I am therefore also interested in the extent to which such discourses and genres are not, as Sarat Maharaj puts it, like 'stacking panes of glass one on top of another, a matter of sheer transparency', but mediated by culture, and particularly I am concerned with how they are intersected by gender.[39]

Translation has become an eloquent metaphorical concept for cultural studies theorists addressing, like Maharaj, the question of 'The Untranslatability of the Other', and the dilemma of those, like migrants and women, who inhabit ambiguous interstitial or marginal spaces in relation to the dominant culture, and struggle between two languages. For Simon, 'Translation, as a tangible representation of a secondary or mediated relationship to reality, has come to stand for the difficulties of access to language, of a sense of exclusion from … the authoritative codes of Western culture.'[40] There is plenty of evidence in the work of female art historians in the nineteenth century to support the view that they regarded themselves as metaphorically 'foreign', as writing from difference. Speaking from the margins of the emerging profession, they do indeed seem well equipped for the activity of translation as Benjamin, writing (albeit metaphorically, here deploying the aural metaphor of an echo and its reverberations) of the actual translinguistic process, suggestively views it:

> Unlike a work of literature, translation does not find itself in the center of the language forest but on the outside facing the wooded ridge; it calls into it without entering, aiming at that single spot where the echo is able to give, in its own language, the reverberation of the work in the alien one.[41]

Sherry Simon certainly finds that the gendering of translation as a feminine activity is 'a persistent historical trope':

> 'Woman' and 'translator' have been relegated to the same position of discursive inferiority. The hierarchical authority of the original over the reproduction is linked with imagery of masculine and feminine; the original

> is considered the strong generative male, the translation the weaker and derivative female ... the language used to describe translating dips liberally into the vocabulary of sexism, drawing on images of dominance and inferiority, fidelity and libertinage.[42]

However, this account of the ways in which translation has been gendered historically is insufficiently nuanced to describe some forms of translation, such as ekphrasis, a classical and Renaissance poetic trope which enjoyed a revival in the nineteenth century when the 'sister arts' talked to each other with new dialogic vigour. James Heffernan, for instance, sees ekphrasis in somewhat different gendered terms, as a contest between the power of the feminine image which, Medusa-like, can freeze, stupefy and imprison the male observer, and the controlling interpretative authority of masculine language, in which art criticism speaks for, and regulates, the silent picture.[43]

This model presents an interesting dilemma for the female art historian, or indeed for any woman writing about art objects, for it supposes a gender economy in which not only the gaze but also the discourse of art criticism is masculine. However, as we have seen in other areas of their writing about art, women were resourceful and strategic in circumventing the masculine prerogative of art criticism, and in negotiating the discourses and genres available to them. There are examples throughout the century of female ekphrastic poetry that trouble the unproblematised notion of the male gaze and the masculine commentator equally with the petrifying look of the Medusan feminine image. Early in the period, for example, in L.E.L.'s 'Poetical Sketches of Modern Pictures' of 1823, a collection of twelve poems on paintings, the poet indulges her passion for pictures as 'A world for mind to revel', confessing 'I love / To give a history to every face, to think, – /As I thought with the painter, – as I knew / What his high communing had been'.[44] True to her word, she translates for the reader the narratives embodied in the genre paintings she describes, often speaking to and for their female subjects, identifying with and ventriloquising their imagined states of mind. Her poem on Newton's *A Girl at Her Devotions*, for example, closes with a frank acknowledgement that the empathetic understanding by the female poet of the young girl's feelings supersedes what is actually there in the painting itself: 'now none are nigh / To mock with curious or with careless eye, ... she may dwell / On feelings which that picture may not tell'.[45]

The idea that a sensitive woman looking at a picture may 'tell' its innermost meaning in a way that is denied those with merely 'curious or with careless eye' and even, it is suggested, goes beyond the understanding of the artist who painted it, informs other poetry about art by women writing throughout the century. Although Christina Rossetti's poem 'In an Artist's Studio' (1856) is not strictly an ekphrastic poem, it too, and more overtly, unsettles the traditional ekphrastic gender roles identified by Heffernan, and indeed the archetypically masculine gaze embodied in her brother Dante Gabriel Rossetti's paintings. The poem is not about one picture but a composite of all the pictures the Pre-Raphaelite artist painted of his idealised 'Woman', who is herself a composite of his lovers and models (Elizabeth Siddall, Jane Morris, Fanny Cornforth, Emma Brown), for 'One face looks out from all his canvases', and 'every canvas means / The same one meaning'. 'In an Artist's Studio' foreshadows Deborah Cherry and Griselda Pollock's work (building on Elizabeth Cowie's important 1978 article 'Woman as Sign') on Dante Gabriel Rossetti's pictures, and Pollock's 'photo-essay' on 'signs of femininity' in his 'portraiture', which demonstrates the interchangeableness of his subjects, and her contention that his female faces are not, in fact, portraits at all. Christina Rossetti, looking for the woman of her brother's canvases, seems to '[find] her hidden just behind those screens'; but actually, the final line of the sonnet, acknowledging that the face on the canvas is 'Not as she is, but as she fills his dreams', anticipates Cherry's and Pollock's argument that the signified of the 'sign' of woman is not 'a woman, or even Woman', but 'masculine creativity'.[46] The poet recognises the all-consuming, vampire gaze of the male artist, who 'feeds upon her face by day and night', but recuperates, by way of her own critical gaze, female vision, registering the fact that the woman of his painting 'with true kind eyes looks back on him'. This is, finally, a poem about women looking, an ekphrastic translation that brings into focus the powerful male creator of the female image, but which finally asserts the interpretative authority of the female observer who speaks for the silent picture and the 'hidden' woman it contains.

This is the power that the ekphrastic poet arrogates to herself in other poems about pictures from this period. The poet Emily Pfeiffer (1827–90), for example, author of a collection of political and artistic commentaries based on her travels in 1884 to Eastern Europe, Asia and the US, *Flying Leaves from East and West* (1885), and known too for her essays and journalism on the social position of women, published as *Women and Work* in 1887, also wrote poetry about paintings. For example, she published a pair of ekphrastic sonnets on two paintings depicting Mary, the mother of Christ, by Fra Angelico in San Marco. The first of these, under the title 'The Joy of Joys', responds to the radiant figure of the Madonna della

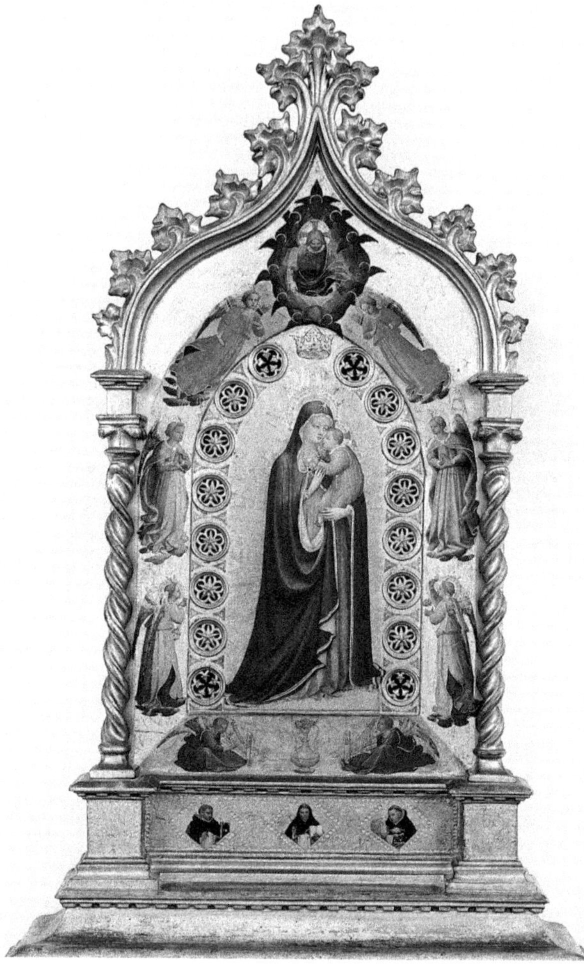

Fig. 6. Fra Angelico, *Madonna della Stella* (*c.* 1424)

Stella (*c.* 1424, Fig. 6), described by Maud Cruttwell as a 'small miniature-like painting of great beauty':[47]

> THOU standest within thy tabernacle, crowned,
> Rapt from the world's vain pleasures and turmoil,
> While, filled with blessing, and sweet hourly toil,
> In lasting service thy meek hands are bound;
> Nor on thy hands alone love's chains are wound,–
> They bind thy soul, whose airier flight they foil,

And bring thee home again with fond recoil,
When thou too far wouldest leave familiar ground.

But thou who givest the nectar of thy veins
In self-surrender, what were costliest toys
Of man's creation, to the heaven-sent gains,
Which, holding spirit and flesh in equipoise,
Keep thee suspended in thy flower-soft chains,
And yield to thee alone the joy of joys![48]

The second sonnet focuses on a detail of the Mater Dolorosa within a larger Crucifixion scene (Fig. 7), and is entitled 'The Sorrow of Sorrows':

WOMAN, those hands are bare that were love's throne,
On alien props thy helpless arms are spread;
Thy hope is mocked at, and thy glory fled,
Thy labour nought; love could not make thine own
Him, who was of thy flesh and of thy bone;
By woman's tears is no man's doom withstead;
Prayer could not ransom that devoted head;
Grief cannot pierce death's silence with its moan.

Thou – sainted mother of a son divine –
Whose lips are guarded by thy chastened will,
The blind, brute anguish marked thee with its sign
Before love crucified beheld thee still –
Indrawn – as one who travails with a birth,
Vast as the shadow which o'erwhelms the earth.[49]

Interestingly Pfeiffer's paired sonnets, printed on facing pages, make a diptych of the two Madonnas, who figure in two entirely different and physically separated paintings: 'The Joy of Joys' Virgin is based on the poet's response to the exquisitely delicate tempera on wood painting that was at that time hung in Fra Angelico's own cell on the first floor of the monastery; 'The Sorrow of Sorrows' focuses on a small group around Mary, grief-stricken, at the foot of the Cross, which is part of a large Crucifixion scene in the more public space of the Chapter House at ground level in the main cloister. It is Pfeiffer who connects them by drawing attention to the hands of the Madonna in each, bound in 'The Joy of Joys' as 'love's throne', empty and bare in 'The Sorrow of Sorrows', where her 'helpless arms are spread', 'On alien props'. In her reading of these pictures, Pfeiffer remakes them; for while Fra Angelico has turned readers (of the Bible) into spectators, she takes charge of the image again, translates it into words, and returns it to the reader as a newly conceived altarpiece.

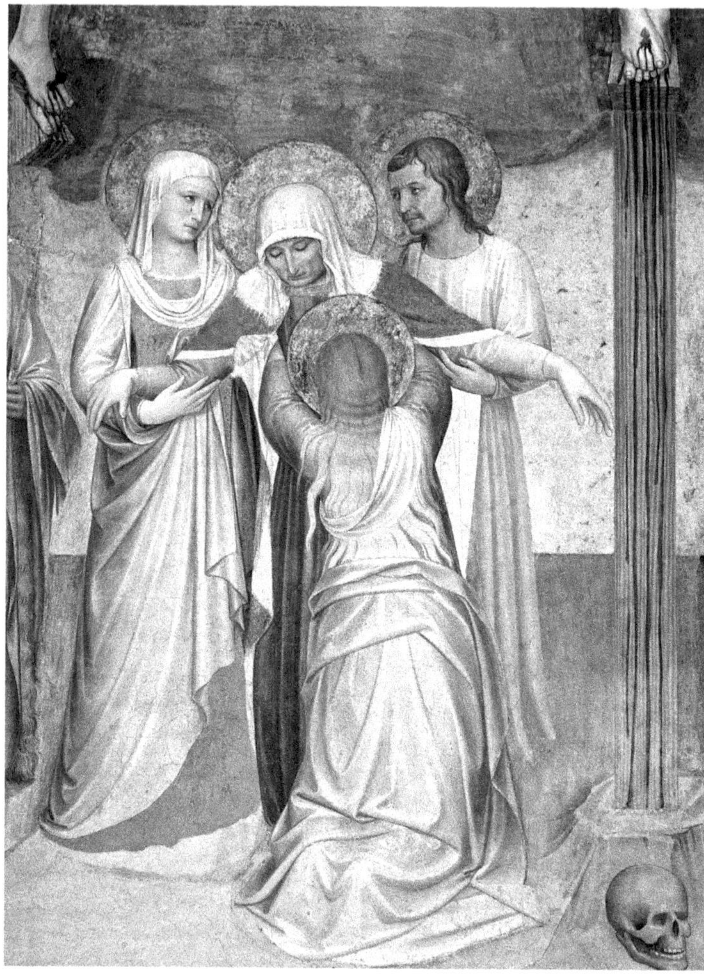

Fig. 7. Fra Angelico, *The Crucifixion*, detail of the Virgin and attendants from the Chapter House (1441–2)

Pfeiffer's poems are alive to the gender politics of spectatorship. Fra Angelico's images of the Holy Mother were intended for private contemplation – the first, in particular, for the solitary contemplation of the monk in his cell; they were not meant for women's eyes to behold. Today they can be accessed by women, and Pfeiffer emphasises her own first-hand experience of them. Both sonnets are prefaced by a note that explicitly places the poet herself before the frescos in the Dominican monastery.

'The Joy of Joys' was composed, we are told, '[i]n face of the picture of the radiant Madonna and Child, by Fra Angelico, in his cell at San Marco'; 'The Sorrow of Sorrows', '[i]n face of the Mater Dolorosa in the fresco of the Crucifixion, in the Chapter room, by the same'. Yet, as Pfeiffer was likely aware, only a few years previously women were denied access to the interior of the monastery and unable to view the paintings that adorned it. When George Eliot (whom Pfeiffer admired, describing her in her elegiac poem 'The Lost Light' written after the novelist's death as her 'lost queen and captain')[50] visited San Marco as part of her research for *Romola* in 1860, she was not allowed, as a woman, to enter the inner sanctum of the building and view the subject of 'The Joy of Joys', nor was she given access to the cell that had been occupied by Savonarola, who is such an important figure in her novel. Instead she had to rely on notes taken on her behalf by her partner George Henry Lewes for her own description of the interior of the monastery. Eliot was, though, permitted to enter the Chapter House, where she saw Fra Angelico's large Crucifixion, which she too admired enormously, singling out for special praise, as Pfeiffer was later to do, the group of grieving women at the foot of the Cross. She wrote in her journal, 'The frescoes I cared for most in all Florence were the few of Fra Angelico's that a donna was allowed to see in the Convent of San Marco. In the Chapter-house, now used as a guardroom, is a large crucifixion, with the inimitable group of the fainting mother, upheld by St. John and the younger Mary, and clasped round by the kneeling Magdalen.'[51]

Eliot alludes to her female experience of exclusion from the cells, as well as to the painting in the Chapter House, in *Romola* to reinforce the heroine's own grief at the deathbed of her brother Dino, a Dominican monk. Romola, we are told, 'was conducted to the door of the chapter-house in the outer cloister, whither the invalid had been conveyed; no woman being allowed admission beyond this precinct'. As she tends her brother she is 'just conscious that in the background there was a crucified form rising high and pale on the frescoed wall, and pale faces of sorrow looking out from it below'. As the scene progresses, 'the pale faces of sorrow in the fresco on the opposite wall seemed to have come nearer, and to make one company with the pale face on the bed'.[52] In another chapter, Romola's own pale face is explicitly compared by one of the characters with 'that fainting Madonna of Fra Giovanni's'.[53] The tension between time- and space-based media in Eliot's narrative technique here gestures back to early Italian fresco series that tell biblical stories in panels that the viewer must put together, like a cartoon, and also creates a proto-cinematic effect that anticipates montage. A still image is engaged by her at once to conjure an authentic cinquecento scene in a particular time and place, and to situate the heroine both in a history of suffering women stretching back to the Madonna and in the evolving history of the Renaissance, at the very centre of the conflicting paradigms represented by the old medieval religious order and modern humanism.

Romola was published in serial parts in the *Cornhill Magazine* in 1863, and illustrated by one of the up-and-coming historical painters of the day, Frederic Leighton, who had established his reputation in the previous decade with numerous canvases depicting Italian Renaissance scenes. Yet as we have seen, visualisation was an important dimension of Eliot's own fictional arsenal. She was later to write in her notebook about what she hoped to achieve through 'the exercise of a veracious imagination in historical picturing', declaring: 'I want something different from the abstract treatment which belongs to grave history from a doctrinal point of view, and something different from the schemed picturesqueness of ordinary historical fiction. I want brief, severely conscientious reproductions, in their concrete incidents, of pregnant movements in the past.'[54] Eliot frequently in her fiction strategically reproduces actual art works, in all their concrete materiality, in order to conjure an intensified historical moment in the way she describes here, integrating art into her historical methodology in a way that is quite distinct from either 'grave history' or frivolous and banal picturesqueness and which chimes with other kinds of imaginative engagement with art by women in this period beyond the parameters of formal art history 'from a doctrinal point of view'. Indeed, her very phrasing here resonates with what other female 'translators' were trying to do that was distinctive in their contra-doctrinal essays into art criticism and history.

Sight and Song

Walter Benjamin describes 'translation' as occupying a position 'midway between poetry and doctrine', offering an 'interlinear version, in which literalness and freedom are united', whose meaning lies, indeed, 'between the lines',[55] and this is a formulation that seems remarkably apt for some of the women who were engaged in ekphrastic translation in the nineteenth century, such as Katharine Bradley and Edith Cooper, writing as Michael Field, whose volume *Sight and Song* (1892) represents one of the most comprehensive attempts in the period to render art into poetry. 'Doctrine' was, as it happens, the name by which the Fields, as they were affectionately dubbed by their friends, called Bernard Berenson in their hundreds of letters to him and his partner Mary Costelloe. 'Dear Doctrine', Katharine Bradley begins a letter to Berenson on 15 October 1892, for example, shortly after *Sight and Song* was published: 'We are building a Bacchic altar in the study: we want you to help.'[56] A few weeks later she writes 'lovingly' to Mary with the advice: 'when you want to club the Doctrine you will find an excellent diagram of method in Mantegna, Grosvenor Gallery Catalogue drawings … we gloat over the fine, free swing of the maenads' clubs!!!'[57] The Fields had first met Berenson, and through him Mary Costelloe, in 1891, and they quickly developed an intense friendship built around their shared passion for art, notwithstanding their mutual acknowledgement of Berenson's superior expertise. Indeed, they describe *Sight and Song* in their journal as 'too wholly due to our friendship with Bernard'.[58] And yet we see in their correspondence a dialogic exchange between 'the poets', as the Fields often refer to themselves, and 'the Doctrine' that reflects the particular nature of their discursively poised translational aesthetic, and Berenson was later to pay tribute to their work in his own *Florentine Painters of the Renaissance* (1896).[59]

Sight and Song was based on the poets' response to a series of paintings in British and Continental public galleries. Bradley and Cooper – aunt and niece, devoted lovers – had already made their name as Michael Field with a volume published in 1889 entitled *Long Ago*, comprising translations and elaborations of the Sapphic fragments, an intriguing and (for the times) audaciously explicit celebration of love between women. The aim of their new collection of ekphrastic poems was, as they explained in the Preface to *Sight and Song*, 'to translate into verse what the lines and colours of certain chosen pictures sing in themselves'.[60] The synaesthetic complexity of Michael Field's language here suggests the multidimensional sensory experience of looking at and responding to visual art works, something the women try to capture in the various kinds of writing they undertake around the production of this volume – their journal and their letters, as well as the poems themselves – in their attempt to provide such a translation. *Sight and Song*, specifically identified as a translation, continues the project of *Long Ago* in the sense both of articulating their lesbian experience and of locating them in a cultural tradition, only that experience is here specifically associated with visual hermeneutics and with the circulation of the verbal and the visual, and the cultural connections they make are not with a classical lesbian heritage but with recent and contemporary aestheticians and writers on art.

Sight and Song is an exploration of lesbian sexuality in the field of vision. Michael Field's is not the unified monocular gaze of the heterosexual male, as masculine spectatorship is often constructed, but the binocular look of two women, enacting lesbian desire but writing as a man. The persona of Michael Field constitutes a space, a field indeed, of cultural encounter, enabling creative translations between art forms and the juxtaposition of subjectivities (Bradley and Cooper described their collaborative writing as 'like mosaic work – the mingled, various product of our two brains'[61]). Looking at art, in Michael Field's poetry, evokes the three-dimensional stereoscopic gaze that had so exercised nineteenth-century optical scientists since the 1830s. The binocular gaze, that comes from almost, but not quite, one viewpoint, enacts a specular proximity that has particular metaphorical resonance for the shared visual experience of same-sex lovers. The volume articulates a dynamic stereoscopic gaze intersected by lesbian desire, a gaze of gays, a way of looking at art – collaboratively, and under a single assumed male name that they share (Katharine is privately 'Michael', Edith 'Field') – that enables a decentring of the observing subject and the radical destabilisation of the gender binary.

Sight and Song was published in an ornamental limited edition in 1892. It comprises thirty-one poems on thirty-one pictures (by artists such as Watteau, Correggio, Leonardo da Vinci, Botticelli, Tintoretto and Giorgione) located in both British collections (the National Gallery, Hampton Court, the Burlington) and Continental museums (the Louvre, the Ducal Palace and the Accademia in Venice, the Uffizi and the Accademia in Florence, the Accademia at Bologna, the Campo Santo at Pisa, the Städel'sche Institut at Frankfurt, the Grand Duke's Palace at Weimar, the Dresden Gallery). The book was not illustrated, and although some of the paintings would have been familiar to their readers, others were not widely known, and not easily accessible. Therefore the reader would for the most part have been encountering the pictures, perhaps for the first time, via the medium of the poems. The volume takes its place in a genealogy of ekphrastic writing which goes back to classical times, was strong in the Renaissance and enjoyed a revival in the nineteenth century when the 'sister arts' talked to each other with a new dialogic vigour. While each poem speaks to an individual work of art, the entire collection amounts to an imagined gallery, *une musée imaginaire*, a veritable 'museum of words' (to invoke James Heffernan's suggestive phrase).[62]

The poem that opens *Sight and Song*, on Watteau's *L'Indifférent* in the Louvre, provides a good introduction to the mode of the volume as a whole. It responds to a painting of a boy who, gaily costumed, centrally positioned and with arms outstretched, fills the canvas. Martha Vicinus has written about the troublingly indeterminate figure of the adolescent boy in *fin-de-siècle* writing, that 'handsome, liminal creature [who] could absorb and reflect a variety of sexual desires and emotional needs' and whose 'protean nature displayed a double desire', in ways that throw light on its positioning as the first poem in the volume.[63] Edith Cooper, with her short hair and boyish looks, and her 'protean nature', was conscious of her own adolescent appeal. In a journal entry, for example, she likens herself to Antinous, the beautiful boy beloved by the Roman Emperor Hadrian, and Katharine often refers to her 'Henry' as a boy.[64] Furthermore, both poets identify with 'indifference' itself at the end of their celebrated poetic manifesto 'It was deep April', published the following year in 1893, in which they resolve to be 'Poets and lovers evermore', when they proudly proclaim themselves to be 'Indifferent to heaven and hell'.[65] In Michael Field's encounter with Watteau's painting, the eroticism of the double viewers' gaze is met by the indifference of the dancing boy: 'in vain we woo'. The autonomy of the art object is expressed in sexual terms, as this in-between, adolescent boy-man, this 'gay youngster' with the round eyes, refuses to respond to the inviting gaze of the man/woman, single/double viewer with a 'glance', even though 'old enough for manhood's bliss' (*Sight and Song* pp. 1–2). Norman Bryson has written about the way in which the glance subverts the magisterial authority of the gaze, about how: 'Against the Gaze, the Glance proposes desire, proposes the body, in the *durée* of its practical activity: in the freezing of syntagmatic motion, desire, and the body, the desire of the body, are exactly the terms which the tradition seeks to suppress.'[66] The potency of the glance is most forcefully conveyed in Michael Field's poem on Leonardo's *La Gioconda*, which begins with Mona Lisa's iconic 'Historic, side-long, implicating eyes' (*Sight and Song* p. 8), and in which the gaze of the man/women poet/viewers is subverted by the glance of the predatory smiling woman who waits for her prey. Under her sidelong scrutiny, the lips, the sexualised breasts, 'where twilight touches ripeness amorously' (p. 8), arrest the eye and disperse the gaze, insisting upon 'the desire of the body' that, according to Bryson, 'the tradition seeks to suppress'. But in the poem on Watteau's boy the dancer withholds his glance, and thereby withholds joy, so absorbed in the rhythms of his dance is he. The gaze of the poets, writing from difference, and themselves inhabiting an interstitial sexual and authorial identity, encounters only indifference.

Michael Field is similarly drawn to paintings of St Sebastian, writing poems on both Correggio's and Antonello da Messina's paintings in the Dresden Gallery of the saint who is described by Bradley and Cooper in their journal as 'half a pagan and was a shepherd boy before he knew of Christ and martyrdom'.[67] The poem on Correggio's *Saint Sebastian* begins:

> Bound by thy hands, but with respect unto thine eyes how free –
> Fixed on Madonna, seeing all that they were born to see!
> (*Sight and Song* 32)

The poem seems to be all about the erotically charged look.

> The Child thine upward face hath sighted,
> Still and delighted; (32)

The poets write in their journal, rather disconcertingly, about how Sebastian's 'face plays with the child'.[68] Here, Sebastian is seductively described as 'Caught in the play of Heaven's divine advances' (p. 32):

> While cherubs straggle on the clouds of luminous, curled fire
> The Babe looks through them, far below, on thee with soft desire.
> Most clear of bond must they be reckoned –
> No joy is second
> To theirs whose eyes by other eyes are beckoned. (33)

Michael Field imaginatively enters the poem, emphasising the enjoyment of the mutual desiring gaze, and identifying with the visual connection between Sebastian and the Christ child – 'Oh, bliss when with mute rites two souls are plighted!' (p. 32). The poem concludes by moving out of the pictorial space of the canvas to the first-person voice of the desiring poet/viewer:

> Oh might my eyes, so without measure,
> Feed on their treasure,
> The world with thong and dart might do its pleasure! (33)

It is a complex piece of visual articulation whereby the poet/viewer and, through him/her/them, the reader, in their own visual triangle, are made party to the triangulated desiring gaze of Sebastian, the Madonna and the Christ child.

Da Messina's *Saint Sebastian* is also depicted as sexually desirable: 'Sound in muscle is the boy' (p. 74), 'Naked, almost firm as sculpture, is his form' (p. 72), and his 'massive' mouth (p. 73) and long, flowing chestnut locks contribute to the orientalised and eroticised scene, in which

> Arch and chimney rise aloft into the air:
> On the balconies are hung forth carpets rare
> Of an Eastern, vivid red;
> Idle women lean
> Where the rugs are spread,
> Each with an indifferent mien. (71)

Michael Field responds here, again, to indifference, but also to a figure who was even then a male homosexual icon, and Martha Vicinus remarks more generally on the lesbian poets' fascination with the tropes of male homosexuality.[69] But if the poets empathise here with the homoerotic Sebastian, elsewhere we find them identifying with pictorial representations of heterosexual lovers, such as Botticelli's *Venus and Mars* in the National Gallery.[70] In this famous post-coital scene it is of course the woman who looks, reversing a 'sleepwatching' tradition which more usually depicts a male watcher voyeuristically observing a female sleeper. This is not lost on Michael Field, who in the poem on the painting describes her posture in phallic terms ('She rears from off the ground / As if her body grew / triumphant as a stem / That hath received the rains, / Hath softly sunk with them, / And in an hour regains / Its height and settledness' (pp. 43–4)), and connects her sexual potency with her gaze:

> Yet are her eyes alert; they search and weigh
> The god, supine, who fell from her caress
> When love had had its sway. (44)

Hers is a powerful, scrutinising gaze. The poem closes with that look:

> Ironical she sees,
> Without regret, the work her kiss has done
> And lives a cold enchantress doomed to please
> Her victims one by one. (46)

Bartolomeo da Veneto's *Idealized Portrait of a Courtesan as Flora* (*c.* 1520–5) (Fig. 8), with its Medusan suggestiveness, is a painting that seems to invoke the trope of the 'cold enchantress' and her 'victims' even more compellingly, but Michael Field rereads the petrifying Medusa look in interesting ways. The poem from the first stresses the autonomy of the art object and of the woman who is its subject, who has been identified variously as Lucrezia Borgia, Flora and a courtesan. Like the figure in Watteau's *L'Indifférent*, she resists the viewer: 'her leftward smile endows / The gazer with no tidings from the face' (p. 27). The viewer is forced to conjecture by imagining beyond the painting itself:

> She saw her beauty often in the glass,
> Sharp on the dazzling surface, and she knew
> The haughty custom of her grace must pass:
> Though more persistent in all charm it grew
> As with a desperate joy her hair across her throat she drew
> In crinkled locks stiff as dead, yellow snakes …
> Until at last within her soul the resolution wakes

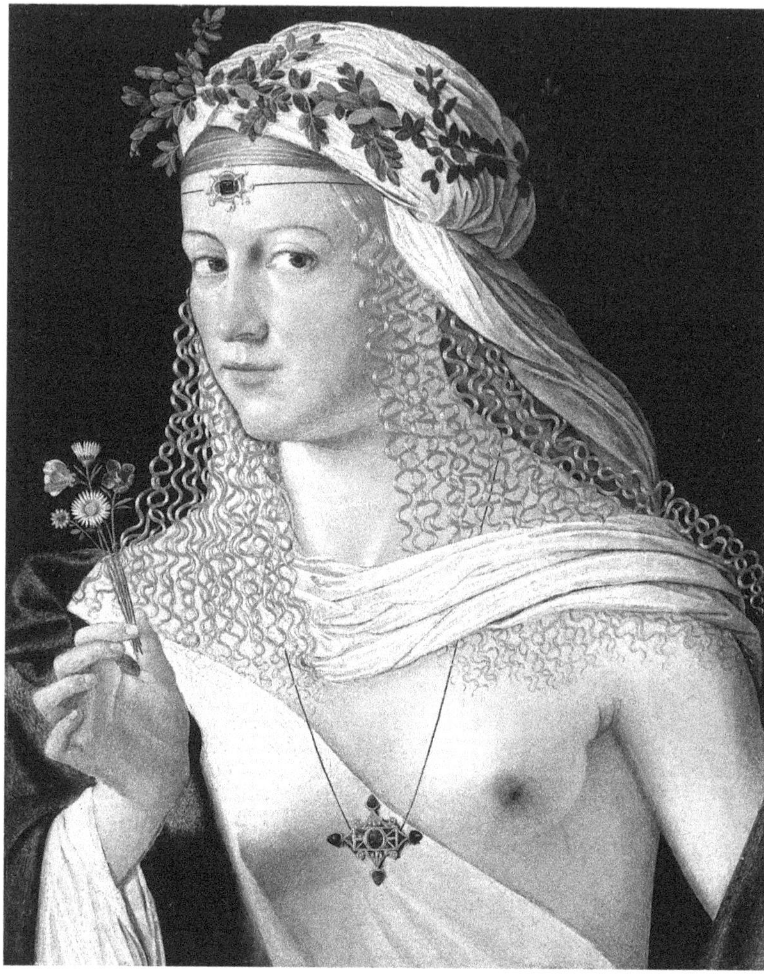

Fig. 8. Bartolomeo da Veneto, *Idealized Portrait of a Courtesan as Flora* (*c.* 1520–5)

She will be painted, she who is so strong
In loveliness, so fugitive in years:
Forth to the field she goes and questions long
Which flowers to choose of those the summer bears;
She plucks a violet larkspur, – then a columbine appears
Of perfect yellow, – daisies choicely wide;
These simple things with finest touch she gathers in her pride.

Next on her head, veiled with well-bleachen white
And bound across the brow with azure-blue,

She sets the box-tree leaf and coils it tight
In spiky wreath of green, immortal hue;
Then, to the prompting of her strange, emphatic insight true,
She bares one breast, half-freeing it of robe,
And hangs green-water gem and cord beside the naked globe.

So was she painted and for centuries
Has held the fading field-flowers in her hand
Austerely as a sign. (27–9)

Michael Field narrativises the woman's agency, by representing her not merely as the passive model for the painter's art, but as the active subject, the artist indeed, of her own self-creation. We see the sharp-edged beauty of the face in the glass grow into the illusionism of the painted image – the over-determined language of flowers, the fetishised hair, the bared breast resonating with the signs of sexuality in nineteenth-century painting as well as Renaissance – and we watch the observer of the image in the mirror transfer the labour of vision to the viewer of the painting, who is explicitly envisaged:

... O fearful eyes
And soft lips of the courtesan who planned
To give her fragile shapeliness to art, whose reason spanned
Her doom, who bade her beauty in its cold
And vacant eminence persist for all men to behold! (29)

She 'gave to art a fair, blank form, unverified by life' (p. 29), leaving it to the later viewer and ekphrastic poet, Michael Field, to vocalise the image and make a narrative for her, to give the pure image a history and a future. 'Her eyes are fresh', and she is able to '[conquer] death' (pp. 29–30), to transcend her mortal condition. However, her portrait signifies, not by its inherent meaning, but rather by its vacancy, an emptying out of meaning that the viewer of the painting must labour to re-inscribe.

For these viewers who are a man only in name, the woman with the bared breast and serpentine hair who looks out from the canvas is neither monstrous nor threatening. She is beautiful, and she has taken control of her own representation. She reasserts the female gaze. 'Michael Field', as a disembodied masculine sign, cannot be turned to stone, and Katharine Bradley and Edith Cooper do look directly at this Medusa figure. Michael Field explains in the Preface to *Sight and Song* the poets' 'effort to see things from their own centre, by suppressing the habitual centralisation of the visible in ourselves', as 'a process by which we eliminate our idiosyncrasies and obtain an impression clearer, less passive, more intimate' (vi). Their collaborative, triangulated lesbian gaze involves a negotiation of meaning; their processing of what is seen is a joint enterprise that decentres visual experience and, while still fundamentally impressionistic, and indeed 'intimate', reaches towards a kind of objectivity. In the 'mosaic [Field]work' of *Sight and Song*, I suggest, we encounter an intriguing late-nineteenth-century attempt to write about art that refuses to try to codify the way art is viewed, to regard aesthetic experience as a scientific or 'philosophico-theoretical' process, but instead develops a genuinely collaborative creative and critical practice that links the stereoscopic gaze unequivocally to desire between women.

In the Preface to *Sight and Song*, Michael Field reviews 'the method of art-study from which these poems arose', explaining that they aim 'to express not so much what these pictures are to the poet, but rather what poetry they objectively incarnate', an attempt that 'demands patient, continuous sight as pure as the gazer can refine it of theory, fancies, or his mere subjective enjoyment', before 'the inevitable force of individuality' and 'temperament' is allowed to 'have play' (v, vi). Like some other more prominent Victorian cultural commentators, such as Matthew Arnold (with his injunction to see the object 'as in itself it really is')[71] and John Ruskin (with his insistence on observing 'truth' with an 'innocent eye'),[72] Michael Field is here stating an objectivist aesthetic based on the idea of a 'pure' gaze. Yet of course, as Bryson observes, 'Between the subject and the world is inserted the entire sum of discourses which make up visuality, that cultural construct, and make visuality different from vision, the notion of unmediated visual experience. Between retina and world is inserted a *screen* of signs, a screen consisting of all the multiple discourses on vision built into the social arena.'[73] If a screen of signs intervenes between the 'pure' gaze of the observer and the art object – not least the formal discourse of Art History, and the construction of galleries and exhibition spaces that conspire to decontextualise and remove the image from the 'world' – then for the reader who approaches these paintings by way of Michael Field's 'translations' of them into verse the field of vision is, as it were, doubly mediated. Fieldwork becomes part of the screen. This is of course unavoidably the case whenever our experience of art is 'screened' by the art critic or historian in whose commentaries the ironic ambiguities of the term, denoting at once concealment, segregation and display, seem especially evident. But the particular scenario envisaged for the reader of *Sight and Song* seems to imply an even more complicated form of screen-play than usual because of the critical and erotic dynamic between the two women viewing art through each other that supervenes upon the aesthetic experience of the viewer of the painting in the gallery.

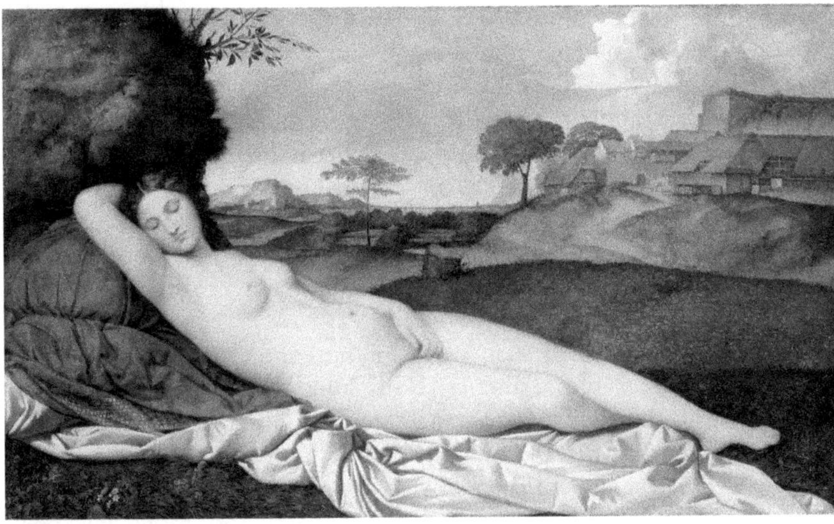

Fig. 9. Giorgione, *The Sleeping Venus* (*c.* 1510)

Michael Field's poem on Giorgione's *The Sleeping Venus* (Fig. 9) offers an interesting example of this double triangulation, of the two women observing the painting, and of the reader, the poem and the painting. Venus's body is lovingly described in terms of 'the verdant swell / Of a soft country flanked with mountain domes' (p. 98) that provides the *mise en-scène* of the painting. The Goddess of Love and Mother Earth are depicted as lying in a same-sex embrace. Like 'the Fields', indeed in the very bosom of the fields (and in fact described in a diary entry of 16 August 1891 as 'simple as our fields'),[74] they are united by the bond of their sex. The body of Venus, who has fallen asleep after pleasuring herself, is appreciatively described by the poet-lovers. 'No one watches her', they write.[75] And yet of course *they* watch her, and through them so do *we*. The operation of the gaze in this poem is problematised still further if we consider how the reader/viewer enters the meaning-making process. Sight and sexuality are metaphorically linked in this poem, as the sleeping Venus's closed eyes are compared to 'full buds that stay, / Through the tranquil, summer hours, / Closed although they might be flowers', and aligned with the 'red lips' that 'shut in / Gracious secrets', the 'oval space' of her face, and the 'ruddy pomegranate' of her mantle (pp. 102–3). Kathy Alexis Psomiades has remarked of eroticised images of women in the late nineteenth century: 'We tend to assume, unlike the Victorians themselves, that these images can only be consumed in one way, with the effect of strengthening the structures of heterosexual romance, whereas actually a range of different viewers might consume them in very different ways.'[76] Michael Field, as the single male persona of two lesbian spectators/poets, offers such a different model of visual consumption. Under this masculine signature, Venus is appropriated by the desiring lesbian gaze, in a way that seems parodic of the phallocentric observer/observed power dynamic, as a deity for same-sex love. Subverting the conventionally gendered economy of vision, this poem celebrates the scopophilic pleasure of women gazing upon the beauty of a woman's body in a paean to female sexuality. Lesbian sexuality is inscribed in the field of vision.

How are we to situate such work in the context of late-nineteenth-century art writing and aesthetics? Both John Ruskin and Walter Pater were known to the Fields and, as Ana Parejo Vadillo has explored in a fine article on *Sight and Song*, the aesthetic manifesto proclaimed in the Preface and the poems themselves engage with their respectively objectivist and impressionist visual aesthetics in fascinating ways. And, as we have seen, while they were most intensely engaged in their art studies the Fields met and engaged in an intense correspondence with Bernard Berenson, at the very time he himself was beginning work on his first book on Renaissance art, *The Venetian Painters of the Renaissance* (1894).[77] They shared with Berenson an interest in developing and modifying a Paterian sensorial epistemology, and shared the view that, as Berenson wrote, echoing the Fields, 'We realize objects when we perfectly translate them into terms of our own states, our own feelings.'[78] Like Berenson, they responded to the tactile, physiological and psychological qualities of paintings together, as lovers, and tried to translate their intensely felt experiences into words. It was the Berensons who introduced the Fields to other intellectual and personal networks, most notably their near neighbours on the outskirts of Florence, Vernon Lee and Clementina ('Kit') Anstruther-Thomson, who provide a fascinating parallel example of a collaborative engagement with art in which a lesbian erotics is (as it seems to the modern commentator) quite openly performed, and used as the basis for a gendered account of the gallery experience that provides another intriguing example of women's ekphrastic art-historical practice.

The early letters between the Fields and the Berensons (as they were to become) are full of references to their work for *Sight and Song*, which was then in preparation, and are interesting for what they reveal about their interest in the gender of art writing. Sometimes the poets have questions for their friends, deferring to their authority in artistic matters, or asking them, as residents in Italy, to check their facts for them. 'Can you tell me whether

Giorgione's Venus is a noon-tide picture', Katharine asks Mary: 'It seems to M. F. it is; but out on seeming! "the male conscience" – exclusion of fancy & all sentiment not truly of the picture as the drop of honey oozing from a plum – is our aim.'[79] Here, Michael Field explicitly identifies the stern objectivity promised by the Preface with masculinity, the gender of his *nom de plume*. Berenson himself, as the 'Doctrine', or the 'Connoisseur' as he is alternatively called, is the personification of this patriarchal 'male conscience' to which the poets ostensibly aspire. But elsewhere we are given a glimpse of the more overtly 'feminine' experience – invoking a womb-like space and a birthing – that gave rise to the poems, as when Katharine writes to Mary Costelloe: 'In Frankfurt we had much comfort. Twice we were in the quiet, warm gallery; Michael has written 3 poems on 3 of the pictures there. They are deeply poetic pictures at Frankfurt, nay more there are poems in them & one has only to stare & wait till they give up their secret.'[80]

The letters provide fascinating glimpses of the creative process as they worked on their volume. 'This has been a full month for poems, & one of peculiarly happy work', writes Katharine to Mary in February 1892: 'We have finished the Giorgione Venus. Scarcely a bit that has not been over painted. I mean scarcely a verse that is not quite other than it was in its first form.'[81] Such word-painting is a fundamental part of their translation of sight into song. In the same letter, she tells her friend:

> MF was determined to get in the Angel's scarlet shoes in the Giovanni Bellini – as the painter has got them in, painting them with great joy – and not feeling them incongruous in the midst of that tragedy and passion. The scarlet shoes are in the poem; indeed I do not think a detail of that Bellini is shirked.[82]

The Fields' recognition of the *punctum* of the painting, the 'bright, scarlet shoes', aligns the poet/spectator with the painter, who 'got them in, painting with great joy', suggesting the fluid circulation of the verbal and the visual. Sometimes, though, looking entirely displaces writing and song. Writing to Berenson to thank him for sending them a photographic reproduction of Botticelli's 'Spring', Michael writes 'before her eyes & mouth I am dumb. She really is most terribly alive – herself, herself through every pore of her skin … But I am laying down my pen to stare at her.'[83] And at other times their 'vital pleasure' in the photographs he has sent them is conveyed not in song but in dance. Edith writes to Mrs Costelloe in 1892:

> We look at them continually. We worked our poem on the Magdalen of Timoteo Viti entirely from memory & from the wretched little woodcut in Kugler. We dance with joy to see her again in the soft photograph.[84]

The journal kept by Katharine Bradley and Edith Cooper during the period of their tour of the Continental galleries that provided the images for *Sight and Song* includes numerous entries recording their physical and empathetic responses to art. Their visits to Charlemagne's tomb, for example, left a great impression, and they responded to it as corporeal visual subjects. Writing of their first visit, Edith comments on the Cupola of the tomb in highly sexualised language: 'One thrills as one notes the severe arcades round it and its swelling roof that tell of Italian workmanship in the barbarous North.'[85] On their second visit, their response is more overtly physical: 'we kiss – yes, again & again, lover-like the steps that lead up to it. They are charnel-steps, old, loosening, full of dust, but worth the pressure of one's lips of flesh.' Through kissing, they try to become one with the object, and enjoy a kind of carnal/charnel knowledge, as the fleshly living 'lips of flesh' meet the dead 'charnel-steps'. The tomb produces a bodily response that manifests itself in a physical act. Then there is an abrupt transition from the world of the senses to that of the intellect: 'Sudden thought! The M. S. of the 1st two acts of Otho wd lack consecration unless laid on the pale astounding marble that he trod.'[86] Katharine runs back and brings the manuscript so that this rite can be observed.

This episode does represent an elaborate performance ritual, and there are other examples in their journals where they demonstrate an awareness of their own performativity, of their own spectatorship being observed by others, of being the object of someone else's gaze. For example, when they are in Dresden they both fall ill, but go notwithstanding to see a performance of *Tannhäuser*, 'muffled up to the ears in wraps', where they are conscious of being '"the beheld of all beholders"'.[87] They enter the art work empathetically, and articulate their powerfully physiological engagement. Edith writes: '*Tannhäuser* is in me – its motives fold me. Its hero gives me finer pain than the disease at my throat.'[88] Impressions of art work themselves into their experience of *Tannhäuser* (the figures are described as 'veritably Rubenesque'), and their journal entry is full of visual references: 'the simple joy of the second scene … is such that it goes out in touch & seeking gaze'; 'the lust of the eye has a pure world to receive, a green one, with cool white lights'.[89]

Edith's condition worsened and became serious, enforcing a period in hospital. As she becomes more fevered, her physical sensitivity becomes the more pronounced: 'my throat beats in time to the clock & the clock is ostentatiously audible. It seems like the systole & diastole of phenomenal life at your ear. Its chirping noise as it throbs is a torture.'[90] The medicalised language of this intensely physical account of contraction and dilation recalls Lydgate's analogy, in connection with optical metaphor, in *Middlemarch*, his insistence that 'there must be a systole and diastole in all enquiry', and 'a man's mind must be continually expanding and shrinking between the whole human horizon and the horizon of an object-glass'.[91] In her fevered state, Edith sees her body detached from her mind, like the first-person narrator of Charlotte Perkins Gilman's *The Yellow Wallpaper* (1892).[92] If Edith becomes the object of her own fevered gaze, for Katharine the hospital room, with Edith at its centre, assumes the attributes of a painting as her lover begins to recover: 'The pallors of the Shades are changed into a Watteau picture, or one might say, the ghastly group brightens into the half-gay, half-ascetic pictures of Fra Angelico.'[93]

When she ventures back out to a gallery, to see the *Sistine Madonna*, again Edith is somewhat performative: 'I lie back in the cushions, feel an invalid for the time being, + love *her*' (apparently connecting Katharine and the Madonna).[94] Here too Edith is conscious of being the object of the gaze as well as the subject:

> The pain in my head is torture – noise seems to pass like a screw down my back & my legs are obstinately averse from movement – yet I enjoy immensely, I savour beauty with new fineness of appreciation. I am watched suspiciously by the people as I lie back under the Sistine Madonna in the black [crossed through] folds of my lace, haggard and half-fainting. Supported by art & sunlight I reach the Hôtel.[95]

This response, in the accents and vocabulary of physiological aesthetics, represents a fascinating intervention of the subjective into the experience of art. Immediately before this journal entry is an entry noting Correggio's *St Sebastian*, 'tied to the tree', with 'bound hands & liberated face'.[96] There seems to be a strong correlation between Edith's physical experience in the gallery and the interpretation of the painting. Edith, like Saint Sebastian, is 'bound', unable to move: 'my legs are obstinately averse from movement'. She, also, is suffering 'torture', and yet she too, like Sebastian, is able to gaze upon the beauty of the Madonna.

The *Sistine Madonna* was, to be sure, one of those works of art before which Victorian visitors did experience extreme physical and emotional reactions. For Anna Jameson, it is the only perfect realisation of the ideal of the Madonna in art: 'for there she stands – the transfigured woman, at once completely human and completely divine, an abstraction of power, purity, and love, poised on the empurpled air, and requiring no other support: looking out with her melancholy, loving mouth, her slightly dilated, sibylline eyes, quite through the universe to the end and consummation of all things'.[97] George Eliot and George Henry Lewes were completely overwhelmed when they first saw the painting while visiting Dresden in 1858. Eliot recalls how 'a sort of awe, as if I were suddenly in the living presence of some glorious being, made my heart swell too much for me to remain comfortably, and we hurried out of the room', while Lewes, returning two days later, gazed at it until he felt 'quite hysterical'.[98] Lewes was to become a key figure in the study of physiological aesthetics that developed as a branch of psychology and aesthetics in Britain in the 1870s. His books *The Physical Basis of Mind* (1877), *Mind as a Function of the Organism* (1879) and *The Study of Psychology* (1879), together with Grant Allen's *Physiological Aesthetics* (1877), were foundational psychological texts in a field that was greatly to interest women such as Vernon Lee and her companion/lover 'Kit' Anstruther-Thomson later in the century.[99]

Lee had met Anstruther-Thomson in 1887, and they had quickly developed an intense and passionate relationship that intersected their work in fascinating ways. During a visit to a gallery in 1894, Anstruther-Thomson became aware that her breathing was affected by the experience of looking at particular pictures, and, believing her to be a peculiarly sensitive subject, Lee encouraged her to keep a diary monitoring the different physiological sensations produced by looking at art. Lee herself brought her reading in contemporary psychology and aesthetics to this raw data, and their collaborative experimental work eventuated in a series of intriguing joint publications in the area of physiological aesthetics, beginning with the essay 'Beauty and Ugliness' which appeared in 1897. In this interestingly eccentric intervention into late nineteenth-century psychology, they elaborate an aesthetic of empathy, arguing that the contemplation of a beautiful thing – a painting, a building or a sculptural form – elicits a motor response in the viewer, who unconsciously imitates the formal properties of the object of vision and, as it were, projects their own bodily movements back onto it: 'the aesthetic seeing, the "realisation" of form, was connected' as Lee later wrote, 'with bodily conditions and motor phenomena' that included '"muscular strains"', '"sensations of direction" … and sensations of modification in the highly subtle apparatus for equilibrium', and 'sensations of altered respiration and circulation sufficient to account for massive conditions of organic well-being and the reverse'.[100]

The 'Anthropomorphic Aesthetics' developed by Lee and Anstruther-Thomson is, then, strikingly corporeal and subjective, dependent upon a 'projection of our inner experience into the forms which we see and realise'.[101] It counters the universal truth claims posited by empiricism with a strenuous affirmation of relativism, asserting the individual perspective of the observer in the field of vision. The situated and localised interpretative strategies it promotes, the ideas about the particularised and experiential nature of perception, make room for multiple versions of spectatorship, and so empower women's looking. Yet their insistence on the significance of difference in aesthetic perception is nowhere explicitly identified as sexed or gendered in their formal writing on psychological aesthetics. Theirs is an explicitly embodied, agential and perspectival model of seeing, and yet the material implications of such a corporeal aesthetic are not realised, and their generic observer is disconcertingly ungendered. Lee's empiricist individualism was, it might be argued, so ideologically bound to physiological organicism that gendering was foreclosed.[102] Intriguingly, her work on physiological aesthetics does not explicitly invoke the *sexed* body, but the very absence of gender in a discourse so insistently predicated on embodiment is arguably symptomatic of Lee's ideological positioning, and of the contemporary art-historical and physiological rhetoric available to her.

However, Diana Maltz has written about the public gallery tours staged by Lee and Anstruther-Thomson as 'lesbian exhibition',[103] and the empirical experimentation in physiological aesthetics out of which these pedagogical performances emerged do appear to have provided a form and context for the women to articulate a form of art appreciation that was marked by gender and sexuality in ways that their formal publications on physiological aesthetics interestingly were not. Kit's own body, through her performed physiological response, enacts a three-dimensional representation of the art work that, as it were, replicates the three-dimensional stereoscopic gaze of the two female observers. Kit and, through her, Lee offered a corporealised public display of aesthetic responsiveness more akin to modern performance art than to conventional object-based critical discourse. Under Lee's direction, she responded physically to art works, with her reputedly magnificent statuesque body, before friends or an eager audience of young women in the British Museum or the National Gallery, or the Vatican or the Uffizi. A friend who was unsympathetic to this mode of art appreciation, the composer Dame Ethel Smyth, records one occasion in the Vatican when Kit, having been solicited by Vernon to 'show us that bust!', apparently 'ejaculated, "Look at that Johnny! How he sings! … how he sings!"'[104] The 'singing quality' that Kit, and hence Vernon, were so captivated by offers a suggestive parallel with Michael Field's interest in the translation of sight into song, and their verbalisation of 'what the lines and colours of certain chosen pictures sing in themselves'. Although the image in the Fields' journal of the haggard invalid Edith sinking back on her cushions is inflected somewhat differently from contemporary descriptions of the strappingly amazonian Kit stretching and swaying and throwing out her chest before an ancient Greek urn, all these women, who were known to each other, explored the experience of art in a profoundly empathetic and corporeal way, and developed a discourse of the body that took many different forms.

In his review of *Sight and Song*, a young W. B. Yeats criticised 'the two ladies who hide themselves behind the pen-name of Michael Field' for merely offering 'translations' based on their observation and interpretation of pictures, for having 'preferred to work with the studious and interpretive side of the mind and write a guide-book to the picture galleries of Europe, instead of giving us a book full of the emotions and fancies which must be crowding in upon their minds perpetually'.[105] Yet this seems to miss the very point of their project, and to diminish the imaginative reappropriation of genres such as translations and guidebooks by women writing throughout the century who aspired to work 'between the lines' and against the grain of conventionally 'doctrinaire' art history. This chapter has only begun to suggest some of the ways that their translation and reinterpretation of art contributed to more diversely articulated and understood histories of art – for, after all, women re-viewed art in many different forms, including visual renditions of original works, as copyists and photographers and painters – but it does gesture to the wider field of women's critical engagement with art and to their creative and sometimes radical experimentation beyond the bounds of what is formally recognised as art history. This accords with Martin Jay's view that 'the scopic regime of modernity may best be understood as a contested terrain, rather than a harmoniously integrated complex of visual theories and practices', that it may, in fact, 'be characterized by a differentiation of visual sub-cultures'.[106] In the next chapter we will see that even their more orthodox art-historical writing redefined the discipline as it was being formulated, and tended to present a differently inflected view of art and its histories.

CHAPTER 4

Women's periods

In her influential article 'Did Women Have a Renaissance' (1977), feminist historian Joan Kelly takes the example of the Renaissance to interrogate the 'universalist' view of history, and to demonstrate the gendered nature of traditional periodisation. Examining the economic, political and cultural role of women in the Renaissance, and the ideological and social formations that shaped their lives, comparing in particular the regulation of female sexuality with that of male sexuality, she concludes that 'there was no renaissance for women – at least, not during the Renaissance'.[1] This chapter revisits the question of periodisation in relation to the histories women wrote about art. Which periods did female art historians choose to focus on, and why? Did they write the Middle Ages or the Renaissance or the Eighteenth Century in ways similar to their male counterpoints? Did they focus on the same works of art, find the same period characteristics, follow the same themes, share the same tastes and make the same kinds of judgements? Did they draw similar comparisons between the past and the present, and to the same ends? And did they include women in their histories, and take account of gender in their definitions of a period style; and if so, did they conclude, as Joan Kelly was to do a century later, that women experience the historical era they inhabit in ways that are so incomparable to the experience of men that they have become invisible in conventional accounts of the past? Women did not have a Renaissance, ergo they are not considered consequential enough to be included in histories of the Renaissance, and their role in the culture of the sixteenth century is effectively erased.

'What "history" looks like', observes Judith Lowder Newton in her article 'Feminism and the "New Historicism"', 'what is included as "history"' and 'what constitutes an historical period' is determined by 'the degree to which gender relations, gender struggle, women, and women's activities and power are seen as being within "history", are seen as having significant or causative relation to the political and economic realms traditionally associated with men'.[2] For understandable reasons, modern feminist historians have been reluctant to associate themselves with a nineteenth-century genealogy that is popularly identified with the ladylike 'Lives' and 'Memoirs' of what Natalie Davis has called 'women worthies',[3] and which appeared to collude with Victorian gender ideology in approving 'influence' as woman's preferred *modus operandi* and the advancement of 'civilisation' as her chief mission. And yet, despite the conservative tendencies of this particular sub-genre of writing, some Victorian women's history – particularly art history by women that disrupted and transgressed disciplinary, generic and period boundaries, enacted liminality, performed across amateur and professional, high and popular culture – was quite radically revisionist and played a significant part, I suggest, in redefining traditional notions of the historical and in authorising both the female historian and the female historical subject. This chapter will explore how their work on particular art-historical periods, such as the Middle Ages, the Renaissance and the eighteenth century, and on the cultural role of women in these periods focused the emergent feminism of Victorian writers such as Anna Jameson, Emilia Dilke, Vernon Lee and Julia Cartwright. In reviewing periodisation, I will consider the ways in which female art historians such as these pioneered aspects of the 'New' feminist historicism of which Newton writes, in beginning the task of demonstrating that 'dominant representations and hegemonic ideologies are [not] monolithic and anonymous', but rather 'composed of many voices', 'internally divided' and 'unstable'.[4] In their work masculine-identified periods were complicated and feminised; sometimes, indeed, conventional periodisation was disrupted altogether.

A feminised Renaissance

The process of enabling those diverse voices from the past to be heard, and revealing those ideological instabilities, began for Victorian women with the necessity of raising their own voices against the dominant historical and aesthetic orthodoxies of their own day. It is perhaps no accident that several of the women art historians who are my subject here had close and sometimes problematical professional associations with John Ruskin or Walter Pater, the two principal (often opposing) Victorian commentators on art – and some knew both – and that they felt the need at some point to disclaim publicly their mentors' views on art, its history and its appreciation. The art historian, critic, artist and trade unionist Emilia Dilke, for example, whose work had been directed by Ruskin in his usual autocratic way until about 1862, published two articles in 1869 and 1870 countering all that the eminent critic held most dear, before going on to write a book on the Renaissance, a period that he of course particularly and famously maligned. In her 1869 review article 'Art and Morality' for the *Westminster Review*, she roundly rejects the practice that Ruskin made famous of moralising art, arguing instead for the primacy of 'the organic pleasure belonging to the simple sense-impression' and 'the mental pleasure belonging to the associations of experience' in the appreciation of art.[5] To support her view of the irrelevance of morality to aesthetic pleasure, and thereby rubbing salt in the wound, Dilke cites the art of Renaissance Italy, not by any means, she insists, the product of morally uplifting times or of morally exemplary artists[6] (and indeed, as she argues elsewhere, in its later phases characterised by a certain insincerity in matters devotional)[7] and yet supremely beautiful. A year later, reviewing Ruskin's Oxford lectures in a signed article for the *Academy*, she develops further her critique of Ruskin's religio-aesthetic doctrine, asserting: 'Art is neither religious, nor irreligious; moral nor immoral; useful, nor useless.'[8] Ruskin was to write to Dilke many years later, after he had forgiven her, 'I thought you always one of my terriblest, unconquerablest, and antagonisticest … powers … When you sat studying Renaissance with me in the Bodleian, I supposed you to intend contradicting everything I had ever said about art-history or social science.'[9]

But that was exactly what Dilke and a number of other female art historians of the period did, particularly in their writings on the Middle Ages and the Renaissance. The art historian, aesthetician, essayist and fiction writer Vernon Lee, for example, describes 'the great English critic' as 'irrefutable when he is a poet, and irrational when he becomes a philosopher', and in her two books on the Italian Renaissance she criticises some of his most famous attacks on Renaissance culture. 'The Italians had seen the antique and had let themselves be seduced by it, despite their civilization and their religion', she writes; 'Let us only rejoice thereat.' Ruskin is simply 'wrong', she asserts, when he tells us that 'in its union with Antique art, the art of the followers of Giotto embraced death, and rotted away ever after'. On the contrary, 'the antique perfected the art of the Renaissance, it did not corrupt it'.[10] She mischievously reverses Ruskin's assessment of the Middle Ages and the Renaissance through reading the funerary sculpture of the two periods. Whereas he had admired the Christian humility of the medieval tomb and denounced Renaissance funerary monuments for manifesting corrupt pride, Lee responds:

> the sculptor's work was but the low relief on the church flags, the timidly carved, outlined, cross-legged knight or praying priest, flattened down on his pillow as if ashamed even of that amount of prominence, and in a hurry

> to be trodden down and obliterated into a few ghostly outlines. But to this humiliated prostrate image, to this flat thing doomed to obliteration, came the sculptor of the Renaissance, and bade the wafer-like simulacrum fill up, expand, raise itself, lift itself on its elbow, arise and take possession of the bed of state, the catafalque raised high above the crowd, draped with brocade, carved with rich devices of leaves and beasts of heraldry, roofed over with a dais, which is almost a triumphal arch, garlanded with fruits and flowers, upon which the illustrious dead were shown to the people; but made eternal, and of eternal magnificence, by the stone-cutter, and guarded, not for an hour by the liveried pages or chaunting monks, but by winged genii for all eternity.[11]

In her spirited riposte to those who 'call this a degradation, and say that it was the result of corrupt pride, this refusal to have the dear or illustrious dead scraped out any longer by the shoe-nails of every ruffian, rubbed out by the knees of every kitchen wench',[12] Lee recuperates an art form vilified by Ruskin on account of the corrupt cultural values it ostensibly embodied, and announces an alternative aesthetic. In so doing, she revises the prevailing definition and understanding of the Middle Ages and the Renaissance as historical periods.

Like Dilke, Vernon Lee rejects more generally Ruskin's critical practice of 'making the physical the mere reflexion of the moral'.[13] By contrast with Ruskin's typological aesthetic and his teleological view of history, his ethical and transcendentalist view that, as she describes it, 'the whole system of the beautiful is a system of moral emotions, moral selection, and moral appreciation; and that the aim and end of art is the expression of man's obedience to God's will',[14] she proposes an 'art-philosophy entirely unabstract, unsystematic, essentially personal'. Her own position, as we have seen, is that 'the aesthetic phenomenon is individual, and varies with every single individual form; and since it consists in the attribution of an individual and varying complexus of dynamic (and perhaps organic) conditions, it must always, in real experience, bear the character of the individual form by which it is elicited'.[15] Models of the observer as embodied, particularised and situated – such as Lee and Dilke develop – resist specular hegemony, and make a space for women to look at and write about art in their own ways.[16]

If Dilke was initially a disciple of Ruskin, then Lee's intellectual mentor was Walter Pater. But she, too, was to diverge significantly from her teacher to develop quite distinct fields of study, very different historiographical methodologies, and unique theories of perception that set her radically apart from the mainstream English aestheticism of which Pater was the acknowledged father, and which, as we have seen, she satirised in her novel *Miss Brown* (1884). And in Dilke's case also, for all her interest in the pleasures of art and her championing of the Renaissance, she did not desert Ruskin merely to transfer her loyalties to Pater. Although she came to admire his work in other fields, one of her severest reviews was of Pater's *Studies in the History of the Renaissance*, in which, as discussed in Chapter 1, she criticised the volume for being insufficiently historical.[17] In an article in the next number of the *Westminster*, titled 'The Use of Looking at Pictures', her commitment to historicism is pivotal to her argument. Even pictures that have lost their appeal for modern sensibilities, she maintains, 'have a historical value. They may help to show how people living in a different moral and intellectual sphere think and act, or thought and acted in past times.'[18]

Emilia Dilke was, then, drawn to historicism as a critical mode, again like Vernon Lee, by her appreciation of cultural relativism, specificity and difference, by her distaste, in fact, for 'monolothic and anonymous' representations of historical periods. Kali Israel has written extensively on the modern historicist rigour of Dilke's work, and what form it took:[19] on how, *pace* Joan Kelly, she made 'explicit connections between the organization of social and economic forms and the state of the arts through exhaustive research into the material culture and political relations of an era'.[20] She points out, moreover, that Dilke was alert to issues of social organisation that directly affected women, and 'studied the work of art … in secular, material, and public settings that included women as makers and thinkers as well as images'[21] – as cultural agents, in short. Dilke writes, for example, in 1871 about how the feminised art of the sixteenth-century French sculptor Germain Pilon 'correspond[ed] exactly to the tone and taste of the court which Catharine de Medicis had formed'.[22] And later, in her book *The Renaissance of Art in France* (1879), in which she identifies the '[e]mancipation of the individual' as 'the watchword of the sixteenth century', Dilke celebrates the fact that '[t]he Renaissance, in proclaiming honour to every manifestation of human energy, gave each a claim to be worthy of culture'. Amongst other things, '[m]en and women, princes, prelates, nobles, all were building, fashioning anew their habitations', which meant that '[e]very art which could administer to house-luxury was … suddenly stimulated'. And the 'refinements wrought into … every … art of life', in particular the decorative and popularising arts, even the arts and pleasures of the table, were, Dilke argues, 'enhanced by the presence of women at the Court'.[23]

Emilia Dilke regularly wrote on Italian Renaissance art in periodicals such as the *Academy* in addition to her pioneering work on the French

Renaissance for which she is best known, and for all the detailed specificity of her research materials and methodology, it may also be said that she developed ideas about a generic Continental Renaissance as a period that profoundly affected her sense of the possibilities of self-liberation through art and scholarship. Israel has, indeed, argued that, offering as it did 'a model of learning which might include women amongst its subjects and objects', the Renaissance mediated and legitimated her own intellectual emancipation.[24] I should like to take Israel's argument that Dilke, aware of the connections between modern life and the history of which she wrote, appropriated the Renaissance to authorise for nineteenth-century women the pleasures of intellectual and spiritual self-development into a broader arena,[25] to consider the uses of a reconceived Renaissance, and in particular its construction as a period when some women enjoyed a powerful cultural position, for other Victorian female artists and historians as well.

Emilia Dilke was a woman with a flair for the performative who assumed a series of identities in the course of her professional life (baptised Emily Francis Strong, she wrote as E. F. S. Pattison, and was known as Francis Pattison, while married to Mark Pattison, and became Emilia, later Lady, Dilke upon her marriage to Charles Dilke).[26] A portrait of her by Pauline Trevelyan and Laura Capel (Fig. 10) shows her in 1864 adopting a Renaissance style, wearing a green brocade period dress decorated with gold fleur-de-lys to signify the work on the French Renaissance for which she had already made her name and, with brush in hand, painting a panel of sunflowers.[27] It is a picture that memorialises her as both artist and historical scholar, one that suggests both her Renaissance lineage and her modernity.

It draws attention, like so many Victorian paintings, of course, whether academic or Pre-Raphaelite, to the place of the Renaissance in the genealogy of the present. A more famous example is Frederic Leighton's painting *Cimabue's Celebrated Madonna is carried in procession through the streets of Florence*, exhibited at the Royal Academy in 1855, which invites comparisons between the brilliant artists and discerning patrons of Renaissance Italy and those of his own day. More often, among female artists, the form is the portrait, and the painter is the model, as in Julia Margaret Cameron's photographs of the Pre-Raphaelite painter Marie Spartali (later Stillman) in the role of a series of learned historical women, and the painter's own self-portraits, where she is depicted in sixteenth-century dress (Fig. 11).[28] In such pictures, as Deborah Cherry argues, 'While the artist draws on the codes of Venetian art, already re-used by male artists such as D. G. Rossetti … the reference is not to Venetian courtesans but

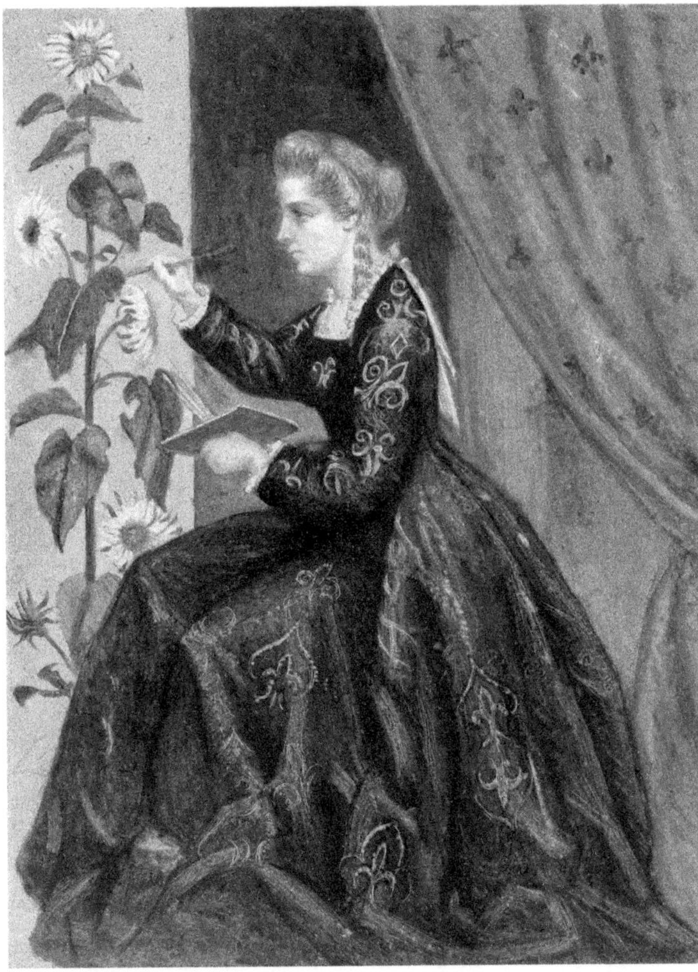

Fig. 10. Pauline, Lady Trevelyan (née Jermyn) and Laura Capel Lofft (later Lady Trevelyan), *Emilia Francis (née Strong), Lady Dilke* (*c.* 1864)

woman's achievements in the arts.'[29] In 1879, Spartali exhibited *Fiametta Singing* (Fig. 12) at the Grosvenor Gallery in London, a painting which Cherry observes represents 'an ideal of cultivated womanhood which was derived, as were the costumes, pictorial format with garden setting and the poem [by Boccaccio, translated by Rossetti, that accompanied it], from Renaissance Italy', and 'demarcates a particular space of and for femininity, representing women's pleasure in women's culture and articulating a

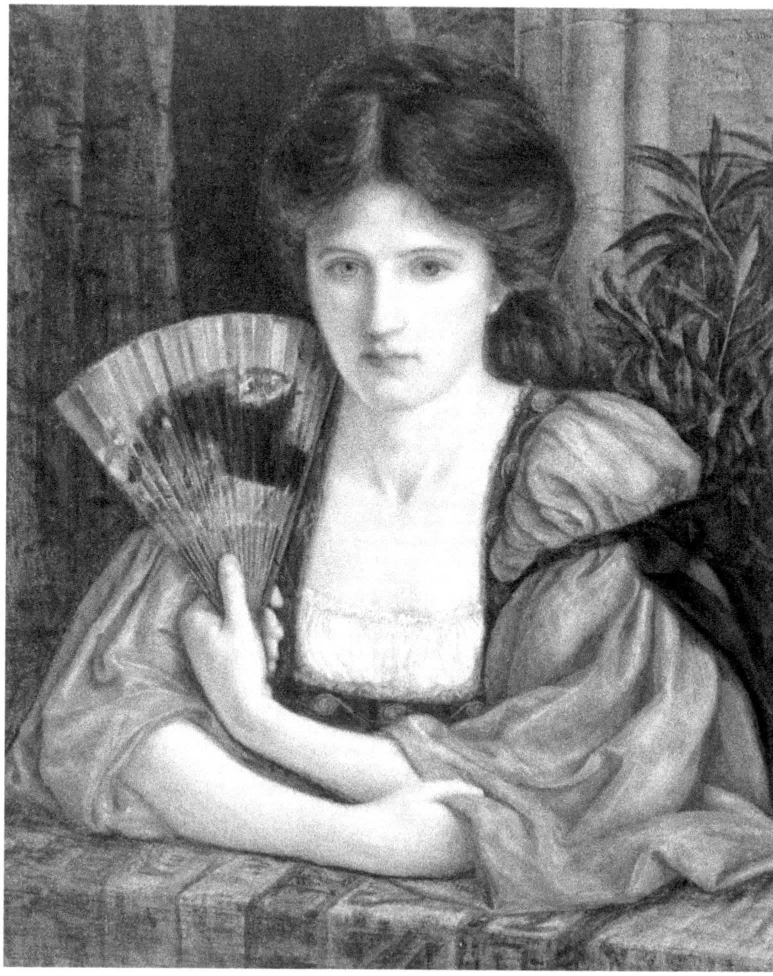

Fig. 11. Marie Spartali Stillman, *Self-Portrait* (1874)

continuum between production and consumption'.[30] It was by positioning themselves thus, and engaging in such feminised cultural exchanges, that some women artists and art historians found their own voice. However, although Victorian women artists such as Spartali frequently invoke Italian Renaissance subjects and styles, when they 'quote' Renaissance painters in their own work they are typically male artists. Evelyn De Morgan's Pre-Raphaelite *Flora* (1894) (Fig. 13), for example, was painted in Florence, and celebrates the city's early Renaissance artists, particularly Botticelli,

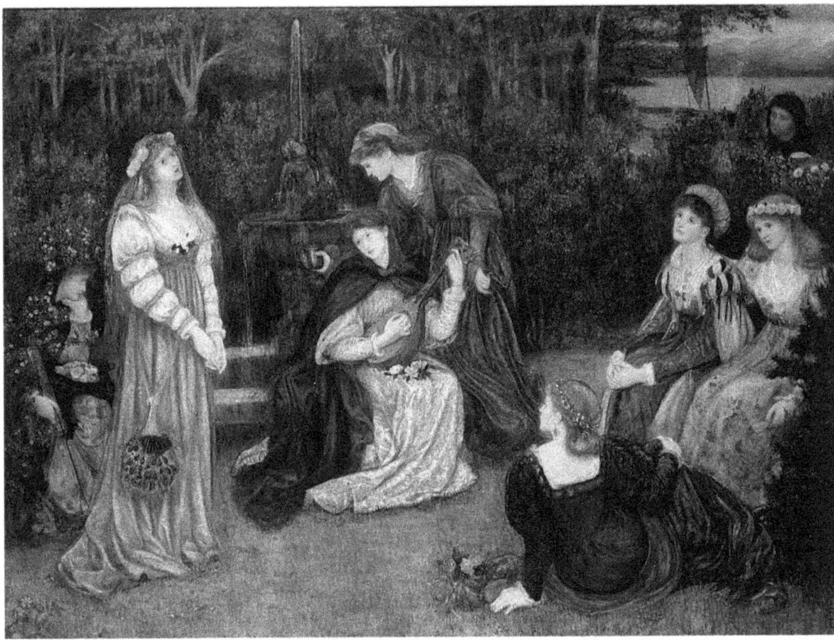

Fig. 12. Marie Spartali Stillman, *Fiametta Singing* (1879)

whose *Primavera* and *The Birth of Venus* provided models for De Morgan's single figure. The female artist claims her Renaissance heritage with this striking modern amalgam of two of its most famous iconic female figures, Venus and Spring, but it is a heritage founded on old 'Masters' rather than on the works of women artists of the Renaissance.

At the time when these women were active, of course, the work of the 'old mistresses' – as Griselda Pollock and Rozsika Parker have called them – was very little known.[31] One of the first British writers to publish on early Italian and Renaissance art – indeed, as we have seen, Adele Holcomb has dubbed her 'the first professional English art historian'[32] – Anna Jameson did show an awareness of female artists and emphasised feminine, even feminist, themes.[33] This widely read writer of popular histories of art and guidebooks published, for example, a book on Marian iconography, *Legends of the Madonna* (1852), as part of her series *Sacred and Legendary Art*, which was, as Holcomb points out, 'the first extensive study of the imagery of the Virgin' and 'the civilizing agency of feminine influence' it epitomised in the literature of art.[34] In her discussions of the representation in Renaissance art of both the Madonna and the Magdalen,

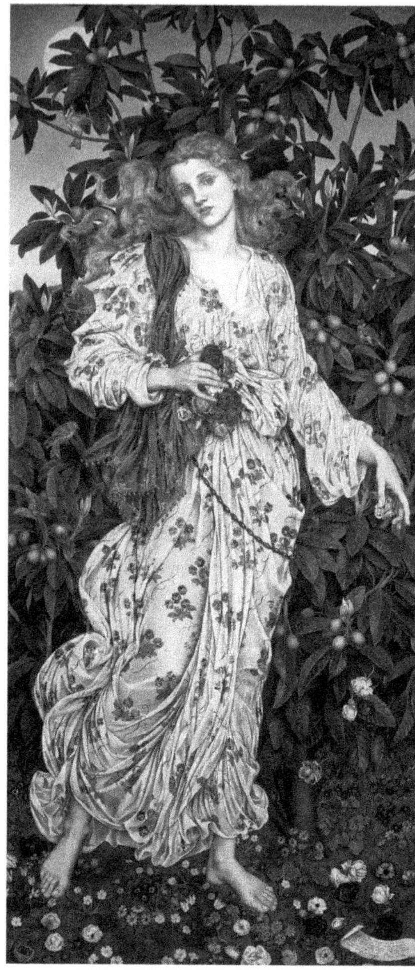

Fig. 13. Evelyn De Morgan, *Flora* (1894)

here and elsewhere, Jameson draws attention to the iconic resonances of such heroic female figures for contemporary women.

Twelve years earlier, she had written to her friend Ottilie von Goethe that she had begun work on a 'Biography of female Artists, and their social position philosophically and morally considered', a 'work of a far more important nature', she claimed, than any other on which she was engaged, and a project which she had 'been meditating for some years'.[35] Regrettably, this cherished project was never realised. Nevertheless, discussion of women

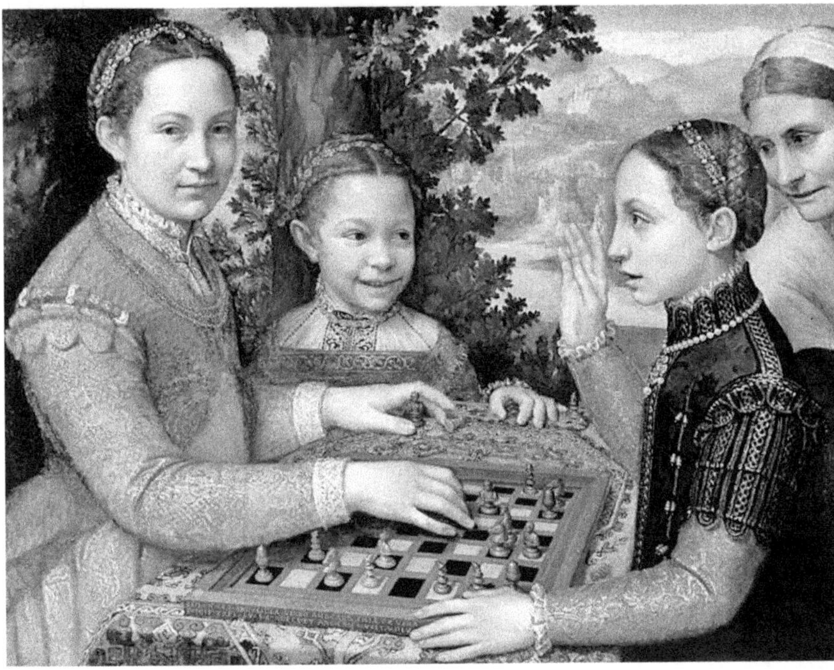

Fig. 14. Sofonisba Anguissola, *Game of Chess* (1555)

artists in her published work, tantalisingly brief though it is, gives some indication of the direction her projected book on female artists would have taken had it materialised. A section of her *Visits and Sketches at Home and Abroad* (1834), for example, refers to a number of women artists, among them several who were active in Renaissance Italy: the three Anguissola sisters, especially Sofonisba, whose 'most lovely works' are described by Jameson as 'glowing with life like those of Titian', and who painted some remarkable domestic interiors, among them a striking painting of her sisters playing chess (Fig. 14), a notably intellectual pastime for educated women;[36] Lavinia Fontana, who, according to Jameson, 'threw a look of sensibility into her most masculine heads';[37] the sixteenth-century Venetian painter Marietta Tintoretto who, 'when invited to the courts of Maximilian and Philip II, refused to leave her father';[38] the short-lived Baroque painter Elisabetta Sirani, of whom Jameson notes 'Madonnas and Magdalenes were her favourite subjects';[39] and the later seventeenth/eighteenth-century Venetian pastellist Rosalba Carriera.[40] All of these artists were, Jameson maintains, 'women of undoubted genius; for they each have a style apart, peculiar, and tinted by their individual character'.[41] But, she claims, they were '*feminine* painters', and thus unable to paint history: 'They succeeded best in feminine portraits, and when they painted history, they were only admirable in that class of subjects which came within the province of their sex; beyond that boundary they became *fade*, insipid, or exaggerated.'[42] As an example, she cites Elisabetta Sirani's *Annunciation*, which she considers 'exquisite', while her *Crucifixion* is declared 'feeble'.[43] Among women artists of the period, Jameson determines Artemisia Gentileschi to have 'most power', but she does not consider her to be a '*feminine*' painter, describing her as 'a gifted, but a profligate woman'.[44] (It is to Robert Browning's late poem 'Beatrice Signorini' that we must turn for a more interesting representation of that 'wonder of a woman' artist, 'Consummate Artemisia'.)[45] Jameson concludes her discussion of female artists by arguing that

> there is a walk of art in which women may attain perfection, and excel the other sex; as there is another from which they are excluded. You must change the physical organization of the race of women before we produce a Rubens or a Michael Angelo … I wish to combat in every way that oft-repeated, but most false compliment unthinkingly paid to women, that genius is of no sex; there may be equality of power, but in its quality and application there will and must be difference and distinction.[46]

Jameson's subscription to the ideological formulation that men and women occupy 'separate spheres' and her application of such gender codification to art identifies her as an early Victorian. Her lexicon anticipates Tennyson's more famous endorsement in *The Princess* (1847) of 'distinctive womanhood', and of '[n]or equal, nor unequal' relations between the sexes.[47] Nevertheless, Jameson's words about the 'physical organization of the race of women' also anticipate Virginia Woolf's comments a hundred years later about gender, genre and literary form, in *A Room of One's Own* (1929): about the 'man's sentence' that was 'unsuited for a woman's use'; about how 'the nerves that feed the brain would seem to differ in men and women'; about how '[t]he book has somehow to be adapted to the body' (although Virginia Woolf wholly rejected the idea of writing 'as a woman').[48] As well as noting an interest in women artists that was well ahead of her time, we can then detect an incipient feminism in Jameson's attempts to grapple with the gendered inflections of artistic production.

Historiography

It was not until later in the century that the role of women in the arts was given serious treatment by art historians, and then it was not the books dedicated to female painters as a separate and de-historicised category, like Elizabeth Ellet's *Women Artists in All Ages and Countries* (1859) or Ellen Clayton's *English Female Artists* (1876), that had the most interesting things to say about them, but rather those that assessed the cultural work of women in the context of particular historical periods and approaches. Vernon Lee, for example, underscores the difference between historical characters and events and the ways in which they have been mythologised in their fictional afterlives, including Renaissance women who were either demonised or rendered invisible. Thus she describes 'the wickedness of the Renaissance' as 'not a superhuman fury of lust and cruelty, like Victor Hugo's Lucrezia Borgia; but an indifferent, a characterless creature like the Lucrezia Borgia of history: passive to surrounding influences, blind to good and evil, infamous in the infamous Rome, among her father and brother's courtesans and cut-throats; grave and gracious in the grave and gracious Ferrara, among the Platonic poets and pacific courtiers of the court of the Estensi'.[49] She interests herself in lowly women as well as grand. 'The very first thing which strikes us', she notes, is that, because of the absence of the pernicious influence of feudalism in Italy, 'Tuscan peasants, for instance have real dignity, unlike the northern peasant'. She finds no greater contrast than when 'we compare the peasant woman described by Lorenzo [de Medici] with the female serf resuscitated by the genius of Michelet'.[50]

Lee was capable of writing cultural history that powerfully conveys the imbrication of art in the social, political and economic conditions of its production. In her chapter 'Mediaeval Love' in *Euphorion*, for example, she deconstructs the ideological contradictions of medieval courtly love poetry, situating it within feudal culture and pointing out 'that the very feeling which constitutes the virtuous love of modern poets is derived from the illegitimate loves of the Middle Ages'.[51] Emilia Dilke writes with a similarly astute awareness of gender and class formations. Writing of France under Richelieu in *Art in the Modern State*, she draws an analogy between the absolute state and the patriarchal family, observing:

> After the wasteful husbandry of the Renaissance, after its one-sided reclamation of individual liberty ... France had need to be reminded that the life of the state, like the life of the family, is founded on much renouncement of personal liberty, on much self-restraint and self-abnegation.[52]

According to Emilia Dilke, Vernon Lee and the late nineteenth-century art historian Julia Cartwright, it was during the period in between the exaggerated chivalries of the middle ages and the repressive regimes of the seventeenth century, in the Renaissance itself, that women enjoyed the most individual liberty and power, participating in the general emancipatory culture of the times. Lee found in the Renaissance the seeds of modernity:

> the germs of every modern thing, and much that was far more than a mere germ: it possessed the habit of equality before the law, of civic organization, of industry and commerce developed to immense and superb proportions. It possessed science, literature, and art; above all, that which at once produced and was produced by all these – thorough perception of what exists, through consciousness of our own freedom and powers: self-cognizance.[53]

Cartwright was fascinated by what this meant for cultured aristocratic women in the period. Like Dilke and Lee, she was notably alert to historiographical as well as to gender issues, and wrote in very clear-sighted and modern ways about history as representation. She draws attention, for instance, not only to the fact that our perspective on the past depends on which archival sources the historian uses, but also on the silences in the historical record, the interstitial stories that remain to be told. She points out, for example, that '[v]irtue goes quietly on her way, while vice is noisy and uproarious; the criminal forces himself upon the public attention, while the honest man does his duty in silence, and no one hears of him', and observes that '[t]his is especially the case with the women of the Renaissance'.[54] Her books take us from the masculine history of the public arena into the feminine private sphere:

> We see now, more clearly than ever before, what manner of men and women these Estes and Gonzagas, these Sforzas and Viscontis, were … We follow them from the battlefield and council chamber, from the chase and tournament, to the privacy of domestic life and the intimate scenes of the family circle.[55]

Julia Cartwright's concern is most certainly with the 'exceptional' historical women who, according to Joan Kelly, are typically the focus of early feminist studies: with Elizabeth Gonzaga, duchess of Urbino, and Isabella d'Este, marchioness of Mantua, both of whom are described as apt historical models for Castiglione's portrait of 'his ideal woman in the pages of the "Cortigiano"';[56] with Isabella's younger sister Beatrice d'Este, duchess of Milan, 'who, as the wife of Ludovico Sforza, reigned during six years over the most splendid court of Italy',[57] until her premature death; with Christina of Denmark, duchess of Milan and Lorraine, 'known to the world [only] by Holbein's famous portrait in the National Gallery' before Julia Cartwright devoted a book to her.[58] But if her subjects are indeed 'exceptional', unrepresentative women, Cartwright's work is nevertheless of great value in defamiliarising, by feminising, the Renaissance. Both her book on Isabella d'Este and that on Beatrice d'Este are audaciously subtitled 'A Study of the Renaissance', and both sisters are represented as active participants in the public life of their times. In the case of Beatrice, we are told, for example, of 'the important part which she played in political life at a critical moment of Italian history', as well as of 'the charm of her personality ... her love of music and poetry, and the fine taste which she inherited'.[59] We are shown her 'royally arrayed in brocade and jewels, standing up in the great council hall of Venice, to plead her husband's cause before the Doge and Senate', and later 'sharing her lord's counsels in court and camp, receiving king and emperor at Pavia or Vigevano'.[60] In the case of Isabella, Cartwright stresses her political, economic and cultural power, and also her typicality as a 'child of the Renaissance' whose 'thoughts and actions faithfully reflected the best traditions of the age'.[61] She elaborates on

> the character of a woman who was in a remarkable degree typical of the age in which she lived. Both in her faults and in her virtues, in her noble aims and generous ambitions, in the doubtful methods by which she strove to attain her ends, and in her easy toleration of vice and falsehood, Isabella d'Este was the child of her times.[62]

Given Cartwright's own work in the mediation of culture, her emphasis on the cultural role of these Renaissance women is of particular interest. We are told of Beatrice, for instance, that her 'genuine love of art and letters attracted the choicest spirits to their court, and exerted the most beneficial influence on the thought of the day', and that 'with her death, the whole Milanese state, that fabric which Ludovico Sforza had built up at such infinite cost and pains, crumbles into ruin ... Artists and poets, knights and scholars ... were driven out.'[63] Isabella's role as a patron, scholar and critic is emphasised still more. Cartwright writes:

> it is above all as a patron of art and letters that Isabella d'Este will be remembered. In this respect she deserves a place with the most enlightened princes of the Renaissance, with Lorenzo dei Medici and Ludovico Sforza. A true child of her age, Isabella combined a passionate love of beauty and the most profound reverence for antiquity with the finest critical taste ... She wrote endless letters, and gave the artists in her employment the most elaborate and minute instructions. Braghirolli counted as many as forty letters on the subject of a single picture painted by Giovanni Bellini, and no less than fifty-three on a painting entrusted to Perugino.[64]

It was clearly tempting for some Victorian women writers and intellectuals of fine, well-educated critical taste like Cartwright, who themselves

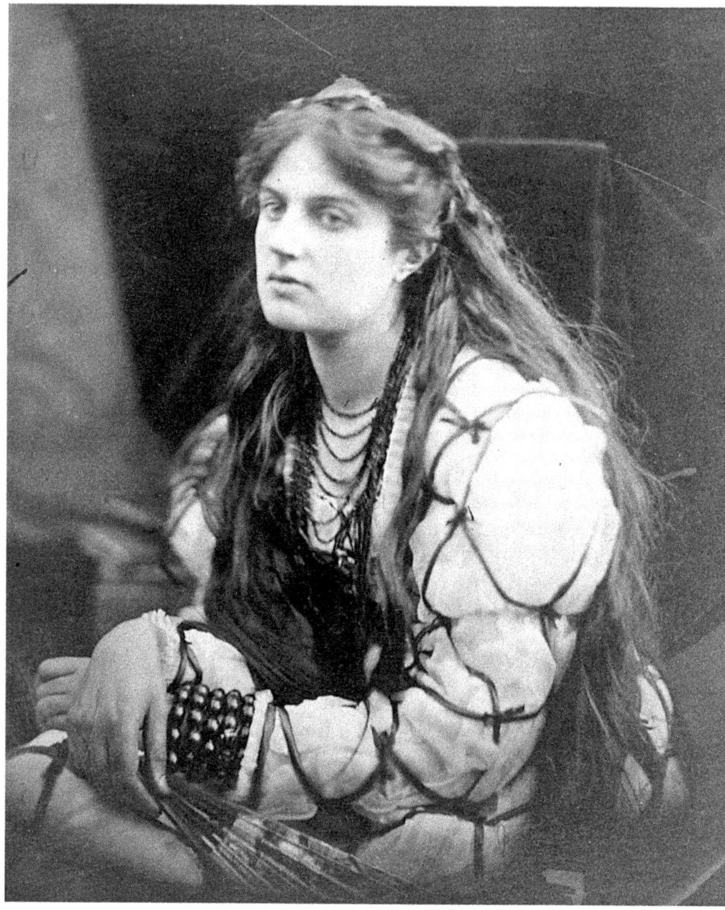

Fig. 15. Julia Margaret Cameron, *Hypatia* (1868)

revered past cultures and engaged in enlightened scholarship, to look to the past for models to legitimate their own artistic and scholarly aspirations. Cartwright was not the only woman to find such a model in Isabella d'Este. Thirty-five years before her history was published, Julia Margaret Cameron had in 1868 photographed the painter Marie Spartali dressed 'in character' as the neo-Platonic scholar, teacher and orator Hypatia (Fig. 15). As Deborah Cherry notes, 'The image consciously recalls the portrait of Isabella d'Este at Hampton Court, now attributed to Giulio Romano, not only in its presentation of the figure and three-quarter length format, but in the sumptuous dress adorned with ribbon decoration, bows pinned at the intersections, which belonged to the artist herself.'[65] Spartali, then, like Emilia Dilke, developed a personal style after the Renaissance women who inspired and were the subjects of her own art, and this was for her a distinctively feminine way of entering into the period.

It could certainly not be said of Vernon Lee, who preferred a severely tailored masculine style, that she adopted the feminine dress of a historical period as a way of inhabiting it culturally and intellectually; nevertheless, she did develop a very distinctive mode of accessing the periods of which she wrote, and a highly idiosyncratic methodology which marks out her own form of cultural history from other examples among her contemporaries. Furthermore, although she does use the metaphor of dress to describe her own historiographical practice, it is a fugitive Renaissance period garbed in 'rags and tatters' that she invokes. Careful to distinguish her enterprise in *Euphorion* from that of the conventional historian, she declares:

> The Renaissance has been to me ... not so much a series of studies as a series of impressions. I have not mastered the history and literature of the Renaissance (first-hand or second-hand, perfectly or imperfectly), abstract and exact, and then sought out the places and things which would make that abstraction somewhat more concrete in my mind; I have seen the concrete things, and what I might call the concrete realities of thought and feeling left behind by the Renaissance, and then tried to obtain from books some notion of the original shape and manner of wearing these relics, rags and tatters of a past civilization.[66]

She explicitly compares her historiographical approach with Impressionist painting, 'the only truly realistic art', at the same time acknowledging: 'I do not pretend that in question of history we can proceed along the principles of modern landscape painting':

> Yet it is nevertheless certain that the past, to the people who were in it, was not a miraculous map or other marvellous diagram constructed on the principle of getting at the actualities of things by analysis; that it must have been, to its inhabitants, but a series of constantly varied perspectives and constantly varied schemes of colour, according to the position of each individual, and the light in which that individual viewed it ... since it is not given to us to reproduce those of the near spectator in a region which we can never enter, we may yet sometimes console ourselves for the too melancholy abstractions and averageness of scientific representation, by painting that distant historic country as distant indeed, but as its far-off hill ranges and shimmering plains really appear in their combination of form and

colour, from the height of an individual interest of our own, and beneath the light of our individual character. We see only very little at a time, and that little is not what it appeared to the men of the past; but we see at least, if not the same things, yet in the same manner in which they saw, as we see from the standpoints of personal interest and in the light of personal temper.[67]

Drawing on the metaphor of contemporary impressionist landscape painting, Lee in this way authorises a view of the past that is avowedly subjective and partial, peculiar to herself, informed by 'currents of thought and feeling in myself'.[68] Born Violet Paget in 1856, she had adopted the sexually indeterminate name Vernon Lee when at the age of twenty-one she began to publish in the British periodical press because, as she wrote to a friend, 'I am sure that no one reads a woman's writing on art, history or aesthetics with anything but unmitigated contempt.'[69] She lived, as we have seen, as an expatriate Englishwoman in Italy, and wrote prolifically under this strategically androgynous pseudonym on art, aesthetics, literature, history and place in generically adventurous forms throughout the last two decades of the nineteenth century and into the twentieth. In Italy she was surrounded by the past eras of which she wrote, but she was sceptical about the possibility of historical encounters with the 'real' past:

It seems as if all were astoundingly real, as if, by some magic, we were actually going to mix in the life of the past. But it is in reality but a mere delusion, a deceit like those dioramas which we have all been into as children ... So also with these seeming realities of Renaissance life ... we can see, or think we see, most plainly the streets and paths, the faces and movements of that Renaissance world; but when we try to penetrate into it, we shall find that there is but a slip of solid ground beneath us, that all around us is but canvas and painted walls, perspectived and lit up by our fancy; and that when we try to approach to touch one of those seemingly so real men and women, our eyes find only daubs of paint, our hands meet only flat and chilly stucco. Turn we to our books, and seek therein the spell whereby to make this simulacrum real; and I think the plaster will still remain plaster, the stones still remain stone.[70]

Such writing strikes a very different note from the confident empiricist histories that we associate with the nineteenth century, suggesting, and indeed enacting, alternative ways of engaging with the past, given the impossibility of a masculinist 'penetrating into' the Renaissance. Like Michael Field, conjuring the Renaissance woman who inhabits an extra-picture space somewhere between Bartolomeo da Veneto's painted canvas and the world it depicts, Vernon Lee enters the imaginative spaces between the historically authentic Renaissance and its simulacra, the 'daubs of paint' on the 'flat and chilly stucco', accessing the period through its visual remains, yet understanding that her own history is but a construction of the past, based on fragments that are themselves mere representations.

It is impossible to have a real dialogue with the Middle Ages or the Renaissance, Lee declares: 'We must never hope to evoke any spectres which can talk with us as we with them … They are all faces, those which meet us in the pages of chronicles and the frames of pictures: they are painted records of the past – we may understand them by scanning well their features, but they cannot understand, they cannot perceive us.'[71] These periods are out of reach. However, catching hold of the eighteenth century had been quite a different matter for a cultural historian so attuned to the spirit of place and the aura of material objects. As she brought to a close her first book *Studies of the Eighteenth Century in Italy*, published four years before *Euphorion* in 1880 when she was just twenty-four, Vernon Lee described why it was a matter of urgency to write about eighteenth-century scholarship at that particular moment. It is a pivotal time, she points out, when '[t]he men and things of the Italian eighteenth century have not yet been exhumed and examined and criticised and classified; they have not yet been arranged, properly furbished and restored, like so many waxwork dolls decked in crumbling silk and lace, like so many pretty, quaint, or preposterous nicknacks in the glass cases of our historical museum'. They remain still, but only for a very short time, just within imaginative reach:

> An old book of cantatas of Porpora, an old volume of plays of Carlo Gozzi, does not affect us in the same manner as a darkened canvas of Titian or a yellowed folio of Shakespeare; these latter have passed through too many hands, been looked at by too many eyes, they retain the personality of none of their owners. But the volume of Gozzi's plays was probably touched last by hands which had clapped applause to Truffaldino-Sacchi or Pantalone-Darbes; the notes in the book of cantatas may last have been glanced over by singers who had learned to sing them from Porpora himself.[72]

We have never known the people of the eighteenth century, she says, 'but we have met occasionally men and women who have': the lady 'whose hand, which pressed ours, had pressed the hand of Fanny Burney', and the old musician 'who had sung with boyish voice to Cimarosa and Paisiello those airs which he hummed over for us in faint and husky tones'.[73] It is this intense desire for tactile contact with a past world about to move beyond her grasp, for the faintest echo of performances which can never again be heard, before its men and women are 'exhumed, restored, put into glass cases and exhibited mummy-fashion in our historical museums',[74] that defines the particular quality of Lee's approach to the eighteenth century.

Her engagement with her material is highly personal and performative. She was later to write of her 'unaccountable passion', as a child, 'for the people and things of the eighteenth century, and more particularly of the eighteenth century in Italy': 'How it arose would be difficult to explain; perhaps mainly from the delight which I received from the melodies of Mozart and Gluck, picked out with three fingers on the piano. I followed those sounds; I pursued them, and I found myself in the midst of the Italian eighteenth century.' Stressing that she means this 'literally', she adds: 'I really did find my way into that period, and really did live in it.'[75] *Studies of the Eighteenth Century in Italy* is the intriguing product of this Orlando-like excursion, and is fascinating among other things for its ficto-historical negotiations of the present and the past, the real and the imaginary.

Although well researched and scholarly, *Studies of the Eighteenth Century in Italy* is consciously subjective and fanciful, and avowedly partial. Her subject is carefully circumscribed, her focus not 'the universal character of the century itself', a character which she finds to be 'far more spontaneous and strongly marked in other countries' than in Italy,[76] but rather the art forms that were national in their origins and characteristics, and had their roots deep in Italian history and civilisation; namely the musical, dramatic, performing and associated visual arts of the period. This is a history of the arts, and also the exploration of an innovative historical methodology. As scholarly and well researched, and also as culturally mediated, as Lee's study undoubtedly is, she represents herself not as an antiquarian or a literary historian or a music critic or a critical theorist but as 'an aesthetician',[77] one who knows Italy intimately, and whose understanding of its eighteenth-century art and life is felt on the pulses. She performs aestheticism as she was later, in her collaborative work with Clementina Anstruther-Thomson, to perform, through her co-author, and theorise a corporealised spectatorship of art. We are invited to picture her wandering through the streets and rediscovering an eighteenth century that is more authentic because its traces, fragments of a world that has not quite passed away, may still be found in a kind of metonymics of history; may be found in dusty volumes rummaged from market stalls, like Browning's 'old yellow book' that became the basis of *The Ring and the Book*, or in forgotten little archives; in sudden encounters with faded portraits; in the street theatre and puppet shows which are all that remain of a rich indigenous heritage; and in neglected gardens and ramshackle rooms that once were the venues of august cultural gatherings.

Throughout her life, Vernon Lee was obsessed with the idea of the 'genius loci', the way history is embodied in place, and in this early volume places are invested with the spirit of the past, and made into sites of intensified experience and meaning. Thus, the first chapter, 'The Arcadian Academy', begins with an account of how she first visited the decaying Bosco Parrasio, in Rome, 'once the meeting place of the Arcadians, and now the only remnant of their possessions', and how she 'returned often and often to spend the burning afternoons in the shady garden, or in the cool, dismantled rooms, going home at sunset, carrying away bunches of flowers, ... sketches ... and above all, vague impressions, quaint and sentimental, of the long-deceased and long-forgotten world of the last century'.[78] And again at the end of the chapter, she returns us to the desolate remains of the villa, where '[a]s we stand once more ... we feel even more powerfully than before how deep a gulf separates us from those times, so near to our own, yet so forgotten, when the Academy of the Arcadi represented the whole literary life of Italy'.[79] The following chapter, 'The Musical Life', is similarly framed by her visit to the home of the old Philharmonic Academy in Bologna. And her description of how she 'stumbled one day' upon the Paduan house and garden of the formerly great but now forgotten singer Pacchierotti becomes the occasion for summoning a fanciful memory 'that we ourselves must once, vaguely and distantly, have heard that weirdly sweet voice, those subtle, pathetic intonations'.[80]

Vernon Lee does not focus on the visual arts in this volume; indeed, she sweepingly claims that in the eighteenth century '[t]he plastic arts were dead everywhere, and had not yet been galvanised by criticism into a spectral semblance of life'.[81] Nevertheless, there are many points in the text when she herself galvanises paintings into 'a spectral semblance of life', and the visual is so interwoven into her methodology and so fundamental to her critical representation of the eighteenth century in Italy that her *Studies*, as her choice of title implies, may be said to constitute a cultural history of this period that embraces all the arts, which are seen to be closely integrated. At all of the sacred sites she haunts, she is in turn haunted by the shades of the dead, in the form of their portraits. A 'crowd of *rococo* figures', 'time-stained portraits of long-forgotten men and women', look down from the mildewed walls of the Arcadian Academy like an 'assembly of literary ghosts, their gala dresses and gala looks fading away in oblivion'.[82] At the once vibrant centre of Italy's music in Bologna, she finds 'a crowd of dead musicians, members of the once-famous Philharmonic Academy, in purple and lilac, and brocade and powder, who look down upon us from the walls'.[83] A dusty portrait of Pacchierotti hangs in the darkened lumber room of his former home, on the basis of whose faded romantic suggestiveness Lee conjures the spectral traces of a man who 'must have been an intense instance of that highly-wrought sentimental idealism which arose, delicate and diaphanous, in opposition to the hard, materialistic rationalism of the eighteenth century'.[84] Her lexicon, here and elsewhere, strikingly echoes Pater's when, as he does in his essay on Winckelmann, for example, she seeks to articulate an alternative, feminised vision of the period.

The pictures of which Lee writes do not always have such fantastic and ghostly resonances. Sometimes, as in the case of the self-portrait of the beautiful and talented painter Faustina Maratti that Lee finds in the Arcadian Academy, a painting can enable her to resurrect the individual subject in such a way as to 'make one understand', in the instance of Faustina, why she was so admired by 'the most eminent men of Italy'.[85] A portrait of Metastasio is subject to a relentlessly physiological reading in which every detail of his anatomy and posture is made suggestive of his character;[86] while a 'beautiful bust' and a 'smutty portrait' of Corilla Olimpica, which attest, among other things, to the 'squinting eye, which was supposed to make the immediate conquest of anyone upon whom she chose to fix it while in the enthusiasm of improvising', are mobilised by Lee to bring this extraordinary, talented and scandalous *improvvisatore* to life.[87] Sometimes paintings are made to provide the basis for an imagined scenario, as when the concert pictures of Niccolò Abati and Leonello Spada are invoked to bring to life a scene of players and singers on stage sitting around the harpsichord; Lee recalls one such picture in which 'a musician has left the harpsichord and is pacing the boards, plumed hat in hand, with solemn gesture', and wonders, 'Is he reciting, or is he singing? Is this a rudimentary opera or merely a play interlarded with concerts?' thus dramatising the pivotal moment of the birth of the opera as she has been describing it.[88] Elsewhere a painting performs the function of naturalising the interpolation of a story into the larger narrative, as when a picture at the Bosco Parrasio of Perfetti in his many-coloured costume enables an account of how he was awarded the crown worn by Petrarch.[89] Or, as in the case of the different styles of portraits and prints depicting the singer Farinelli, the visual evidence is deployed to complicate both character and ideas of historical and painterly representation.[90]

Lee regularly gives vent to her frustration at being unable to make aural reconstructions of eighteenth-century music. And so of Gasparo Pacchierotti she writes, '[W]e feel an indefinable sense of dissatisfaction, a wistful, dreary sense of envy for what did not fall to our lot, and of pain at the thought that all that feeling, all that imagination, all that careful culture, has left no trace behind it. In turning over the leaves of memoirs and music-books we try, we strain as it were, to obtain an echo of that superbly wasted vocal genius.'[91] But her visual imagination never lets her down. She sees the singers and the performances that she cannot hear. And so she writes, 'We may picture to ourselves those musical gatherings in the Bulgarellis' house.' And picture them she does, in very great detail, and the figures who attend them, such as the 'energetic yet almost regal' singer, the Romanina: 'Yes, we can see her moving about in her rustling brocade and trailing velvet, going from the great singer lolling about the harpsichord, his fat sentimental face half hid in his curly wig and lace frill, one fat bejewelled hand thrust into his satin doublet, the other playing with his music roll … from him to some obscure fair-haired young man'.[92]

Lee is clearly entranced by the eighteenth century as spectacle, as her many luscious descriptions of carnival and other theatrical pleasures attest. Furthermore, her own representation of the period is highly staged – a piece of theatre, like the extravagant operas and shows she invokes for her readers. In her introduction to a later work, *Althea* (1894), she refers to her '*dramatis personae*', and to the need occasionally 'to copy from other showmen's boxes a spiritual puppet for which I had no model'.[93] Like the illusion-generating optical gadgetry that proliferated in the nineteenth century, Lee's prose deceives the eye through a series of animating special effects. Like the showman with whom she identifies, she translates the two-dimensional page into a believable three-dimensional living world, then draws attention to the trickery, as she returns us to the solid reality of the book. 'Is it a reality?' she asks. 'Has Menego rowed us over the lagoon? … Have we really witnessed this incident of fishing life on the Adriatic?' 'No,' she confesses, 'we have only laid down a little musty volume, at the place marked "Le Baruffe Chizzotte".'[94] The historian of film, Tom Gunning, has written of a formative technology of 'attraction' at work in the development in the late 1880s and 1890s of a modernised mass visual culture. His discussion of the strategies of early film throws light on Lee's tactics for engaging the attention of her audience: 'From comedians smirking at the camera, to the constant bowing and gesturing of conjurers in magic films, this is a cinema that displays its visibility, willing to rupture a self-enclosed fictional world for a chance to solicit the attention of the spectator.'[95] Lee's writing manifests the kinds of devices and theatricalities identified by Gunning. And so while her principal strategy is to persuade us of the authenticity of the eighteenth century she brings before us (by, for example, imaginatively entering the experiences of a historical figure such as Dr Charles Burney, retracing his 1770 musical tour through France and Italy, and embellishing the account in his journal with the kind of small detail that creates a 'reality effect'), she regularly disrupts and destabilises the effect of the real she has so carefully constructed by exposing its textuality and fictiveness.

Pietro Metastasio, Carlo Goldoni and Carlo Gozzi are Lee's exemplary writers, and she draws on portraits, letters, journals and memoirs as well as their creative works to offer personal and speculative accounts of their lives and careers. She was interested in them, as she was in the painters and musicians of the period, not only as artists, who belonged to 'the unchangeable eternal world of the grand and lovely ideal', but also as men, who belonged to 'the ephemeral world of quaint and ludicrous reality'.[96] Hard though it may be to find a copy of Gozzi's plays a hundred years after his death, and to reconstruct their performance, they do survive in a material form, as that ephemeral world does not. Lee was more fascinated still by the Italian art of the eighteenth century that had no material existence, and that was itself fundamentally ephemeral, in particular the art of the extemporary poet and the singer. Lee laments 'the genius spent in an extemporised vocal ornament which was never transmitted to paper, in the delivery of a few notes which lasted but a second; the genius squandered in the most evanescent performance, the memory of which died with those who had heard it'.[97]

Lee is determined that the other usual casualties of the historical record, women, will not likewise disappear without trace. Nor do we only hear of the powerful women who played a significant role in eighteenth-century cultural and political life: of Maria Theresa herself, in the Imperial Palace at Vienna; of the Grand-Duchess Dowager of Tuscany, Violante Beatrice of Bavaria, who in 1725 summoned the *improvvisatore* Perfetti to Rome, where he was awarded the crown of the Capitol; of the famous actress and singer Marianna Bulgarelli, commonly called La Romanina, and the Countess Althann, whose love and patronage were so critical to Metastasio's professional career; of the accomplished Arcadian artist and salonière Faustina[98] and 'the beautiful young princess d'Arce Orsini, composer, poetess, and general patroness of literati';[99] of the leading aristocratic salonières, women like the Countess Castiglione at Milan, the Countess Grismondi at Brescia, the Marchesa Silvia Verza at Verona, the Countess Roberti at Bassano, and, above all, of the lovely Isobella Teotocchi Albrizzi at Venice, in whose drawing rooms 'the most eminent poets, Parini, Pindemonti, Pompei, Cesarotti, were constantly to be met, together with an occasional classical sculptor or emotional singer like Canova or Pacchierotti';[100] of 'the innumerable ladies who, as soon as they have exchanged the convent for their husband's house, become refined, literary, nay learned: poetesses, composers, and presiders over intellectual society, the friends, patronesses, and counsellors of the greatest writers in Italy, yet without aspiring to the position of the Dottoressa Bassi, who lectured on Newton's *Optics* before she was twenty'.[101]

It is not just of such eminent women that Vernon Lee tells us, but also of 'the young ladies of the highest birth [who] go out on riding parties, dressed in almost masculine fashion, no one taking offence thereat, and the poets telling them that in this garb they look like Paris and Endymion';[102] of 'the ladies wearing portraits of great performers, fainting, like Beckford's Paduan lady, from musical rapture … showing their love of music in a hundred absurd fashions';[103] of the places where 'women are not left out of the literary bustle',[104] and the places where they are, such as Rome, where there was 'an absurd regulation forbidding women to perform on any stage in the Eternal City', and where women's parts in the opera were played by boys.[105] She writes of Dr Burney's visits to the music schools for girls for which Venice was famous, conjuring 'the singular sight of an orchestra entirely composed of women, who played in a masterly manner … one of the musical wonders of the eighteenth century'.[106] Elsewhere she discusses domestic life and marriage customs in relation to eighteenth-century Italian culture.[107] And she does not forget the professional performers: neither the unnamed female celebrities in anticipation of whose arrival 'the great theatre is put into order', and 'the whole town is in a tumult of excitement';[108] nor those whose names became famous, such as Maria Maddalena Morelli, who performed her extemporary poetry under the Arcadian name of Corilla Olimpica, and who was to achieve greater fame still in her fictional reincarnation as Corinne.[109]

Vernon Lee's account of the rewriting of Corilla's story reveals an astute understanding of how, in their afterlife, historical events and experiences are re-inscribed with different meanings. Having described how the *improvvisatore* was mocked and abused in Rome at the very ceremony where she received the crown of the Capitol, because by 1775 'the coronation was regarded as a farce or a profanation, the Arcadians as conceited pedants, Corilla herself as an impudent adventuress', she goes on to explain how she came to be transformed by Madame de Staël into 'a radiant sibyl, a sort of personified genius of Italy' and 'unconsciously gave rise to a masterpiece' in *Corinne*.[110] Lee's sophisticated appreciation of and interest in the process of history and how it is written, even at this early stage in her career, informs her own writing of the past and her understanding of periodisation and the histories of art. She is alert to the fact that things signify differently at different historical moments. Before and after the French Revolution, for instance, had changed the way the British viewed the French. When Dr Burney visited Paris in 1770, Lee notes, 'He had looked at this strange people without any of the fears and hatred which they were later destined to inspire. The coming revolution had not yet cast its shadow before it.'[111] And before and after Romanticism changed the way people responded to landscape. Lee observes: 'How Dr. Burney got across the Alps he does not tell us. In those days, when Alpine roads were unknown and Alpine scenery unnoticed, a journey of this sort was probably looked back upon as equally horrid and uninteresting, and unworthy, therefore, of being recorded.'[112] And he crossed the Apennines 'wholly unconscious of the delightful Radcliffian thrills of horror which Mrs. Jameson and Washington Irving were destined to render so popular; indeed the writers of the eighteenth century are so perversely cool and comfortable about the Apennine passes that you might almost imagine brigands and ghastly inn-keepers to have formed part of the travelling paraphernalia of the romanticists of our century, by whom they were introduced into Italy, together with circulating libraries and English groceries.'[113] Furthermore, she explains, the very name 'Italy' 'did not suggest what it suggests to us; it was not the field for the exercise of those faculties which are exercised there in our own day. There had been no Byron, no Sismondi, no Lady Morgan, no Ruskin; the generation of Goethe, of Madame de Staël, of Beckford, nay, even of Ann Radcliffe, had not as yet appeared.'[114] Therefore the visitor approached it in quite a different way from the modern tourist; 'did not consider Italy as a thing of the past, a remnant of antiquity, of the Middle Ages or of the Renaissance, but as a country like any other modern one; and its inhabitants neither as degenerate descendants of the Romans nor as weird children of the Renaissance'.[115]

The question of the relativity of cultural signification provides the occasion for both lighthearted and rather poignant reflection on the vagaries of reputation which again has implications for her approach to the historiography of art. Dr Burney, we are told, was not all that impressed by the boy Mozart when he encountered him,[116] while Metastasio's joking words in a mock biography, 'In the eighteenth century there lived a certain Abate Metastasio, a tolerable poet among bad ones',[117] are exposed as a cruel irony in the light of his future reputation. It also underlies Lee's frequent reflections on her own writing practice, and her frank authorial interventions, which refuse to naturalise the telling of history as anything other than a narrative which she can manipulate at will. At one point, for example, she interjects: 'According to a bad but invincible tendency of which the reader may often have to complain, we have taken the opportunity of discussing the church music of the eighteenth century in general, when there was no occasion to speak of any save the trifling performances which Dr. Burney attended; keeping our traveller waiting, standing in some dull little church listening to mediocre music.'[118] And later, having digressed once more from her reconstruction of Burney's experience of Italy to talk about eighteenth-century singers, and her own discovery of Gasparo Pacchierotti's house and garden, she recalls herself to the past of which she is meant to be writing: 'Whither have our fancies carried us? The garden at Padua, the harpsichord, the portrait – are none of them present. Pacchierotti, so far from being a mere faint recollection, is as yet a scarcely noticed reality, an obscure youth with undivined talents. Dr. Burney has never yet heard his name.'[119] Such disarming self-commentary designedly foregrounds the fact that she is not only reconstructing but constructing a period; that this is not a transparent window onto the past, but a narrative, the chronological handling of which the author is in control, and in which the very idea of what constitutes 'the past' is unstable, inevitably determined by and imbricated in similarly unstable notions of 'the present'.

Always striking is the modernity of Vernon Lee's conceptualisation of history, of her keen awareness of the fact that perceptions of the past are culturally positioned, and that history is a construction, 'only a creation of the present',[120] 'a series of … admirable theatrical views; mere delusion'.[121] Fourteen years after publishing her first book, she was to revisit eighteenth-century Italy in a 'dialogue' set in the context of a modern performance of Gluck's *Orpheus* in Rome. One of her characters is a devotee; another, a 'modern' for whom the opera 'is the work of a thoroughly bygone past, of a completely extinct art', who contends that 'produced in utter unconsciousness of what the modern soul would be, it no longer answers to the needs of us moderns'; while the third, formerly passionate about the eighteenth century, now infected by decadence, wonders: 'Are we restoring life to a thing that can live, or are we galvanising a corpse[?]'[122] The moment that Lee grasped in writing her *Studies of the Eighteenth Century in Italy* has already, it seems, passed – although we are shown the power of the voice to transport even those who most vigorously deny Gluck's appeal for a modern audience, and also the potential for his work to be re-made for the *fin de siècle*: '"Ah!" exclaimed Carlo, with suppressed enthusiasm [upon the entry of Orpheus], "that is a figure, all glittering with mystic jewel-lights, for one of your pre-Raphaelite painters, or for Gustave Moreau."'[123]

Regarding the eighteenth century

Five years later, Emilia Dilke was to publish the first volume of a vast four-part study of French art in the eighteenth century, which covers painting, sculpture, engraving, drawing, architecture, furniture and decoration. Published from 1899 to 1902, it takes an approach to the period quite different from Lee's, but is similarly distinctive and original. Like Lee, Dilke acknowledges the magnitude of the task of writing about eighteenth-century culture – 'the subject is so vast', she writes, 'that to attempt to treat it … may be likened to the child's effort to "put the sea in yonder hole"'[124] – but she eschews the selective, subjective impressionism favoured by Lee to pursue the 'scientific method' that Lee abjured. The encyclopedic comprehensiveness at which she aimed is part and parcel of such an objectivist methodology.

Not only did Dilke's academic style of presenting the eighteenth century in France differ from Lee's avowedly 'aesthetic' approach to eighteenth-century Italy, but the nature of their respective subjects was very different. While Lee interested herself principally in popular, democratic and ephemeral art forms, Dilke, despite her personal commitment to social justice and labour organisation, focused in her scholarly writing on the arts produced under the patronage of the French court, on distinctly aristocratic art forms that had an enduring appeal for the very wealthy. While Lee was fascinated by the regional, Dilke's avowed focus was on the metropolitan. And where Lee specifically determined not to discuss Italian art that was influenced by Paris and London and the pseudo-classical revival, for Dilke neo-classicism is a central theme, for she was writing of a place and time when the revivalist style 'received an extraordinary moral consecration which carried it forcibly to extreme conclusions'; when '[m]en were cut off from the richest sources of fancy by an inexorably revolutionary logic, and strict conformity to classic precedent stood for a sign of heroic character'.[125]

And yet these rather significant differences of approach may be said to have arisen out of their common concern with the social, economic and political determinants of art, with the cultural history of the eighteenth century. Like Lee, Dilke seeks to evoke the world which produced such artworks, 'to trace the action of those social laws under the pressure of which the arts take shape',[126] as well as to analyse the artefact itself, and her focus on the art of the very highly privileged may be said to have gone with the territory in the case of eighteenth-century French art. Like Lee, too, she opens the first volume of her study *French Painters of the XVIIIth Century* (1899) with a chapter on the Academy and its demise. The French Revolution had entered Lee's own story of the Arcadian Academy, but here its influence on the art establishment is, naturally enough, more prominent. Dilke relates how the French Royal Academy's fortunes were fatally associated with those of the aristocracy, '[t]heir very existence … bound up with that system of privilege and caste which the nation was rousing itself to overthrow'.[127] She describes how, as the century proceeded, the Academy made itself increasingly elitist and exclusive, securing a monopoly of exhibitions and generally 'narrowing down the common freedom of the profession which it represented, whilst enlarging the privileges which gave to itself social dignity and influence', with the result that by mid-century it had 'established that monopoly of the arts for which all along it had fought in the name of the dignity of the Crown', a monopoly which was 'now destined, by the disgust it excited in outsiders, to bring about the destruction of the body by which it was maintained'.[128] In the end, '[t]here was nothing left but to endure the strict application of the principles of liberty and equality which were destined to destroy the close fraternity that had had its origin in common sacrifices for the "bien des Arts"', and the fall of the 'Bastille de la Peinture' was the inevitable consequence.[129]

This is the context in which Dilke views the 'charming art' of the eighteenth century in France. For Dilke, it is above all an art conveying 'physical pleasure', one that celebrates the often ephemeral 'joys of the senses'.[130] Unlike the art of the previous century, the 'Grand Siècle' of which she wrote in her volume *Art in the Modern State* (1888) and which she saw as the product of a 'great centralising system', but like Renaissance art, eighteenth-century art has, for all its artificiality, according to Dilke, a kind of integrity. Truth, she argues, either in the sense of the naturalism of Dutch art or in the sense of fidelity to the 'eternal truths of life', was 'impossible to the artists of the latter half of the eighteenth century'.[131] Nevertheless, the great decorative painters *in particular*, for all their contrived artificiality, 'all reflect with an intimacy to which there is perhaps no parallel, the manners and tone of their day'.[132] '[J]ust as there never was a day in which art and life were more conventional, so there never was a time when conventions had a greater influence on character and conduct', and in the art of a great decorative painter such as Fragonard, 'far removed as it is from that of nature and of truth, we are still in a real world for the conventions of which it was made up, were an essential part of the lives of those amongst whom he lived and worked'.[133]

Dilke's own formal training as an artist equipped her to write expertly on the technical composition and material condition of the paintings which are the subject of her first volume, while her previous studies of Renaissance and seventeenth-century French art meant that she was knowledgeable about the immediate social, political and cultural world out of which the art of the eighteenth century emerged. Such an informed understanding of both the artefact and its context leads to rewarding discussion of the various schools and their most representative painters that she deals with chapter by chapter, beginning with the decorative painters, such as Boucher and Fragonard, and the painters of *fêtes galantes*, such as Watteau and Pater, and moving through the painters of familiar scenes, Chardin, Baudouin and Greuze, to portraiture and finally landscape. She writes, for example, with both a keen eye and a keen historical intelligence, about Fragonard's brilliant depictions of 'Eternal youth, perpetual pleasure, and all the wanton graces, their insincere airs masked by a voluptuous charm'; of his use of colour, particularly 'the lovely tints of beautiful flesh … wrought to the perfection of sensual charm', and those 'passages which rival the magic of Rubens, and betray the actual physical delight [he] had in painting them'; and of how 1789 brought his charmed career to a close, for, having retreated to his native Grasse, where he continued to paint in the same 'spirit of amorous gaiety as had rendered his talent delightful to the Paris of his youth', he returned to Paris 'only to find the reign of Pleasure over and the Loves and Graces fled'.[134]

Just as there was no place for Fragonard in a new order exemplified by the stern neo-classicism of David, so, in the field of architecture, in the latter decades of the century, 'Classic dwellings alone were, it was felt, worthy to shelter "l'homme libre", who now became the ideal of every painter and every sculptor who had a taste for civic virtue'.[135] But before the 'crippling zeal for "correctness"', which was for Dilke the unfortunate accompaniment of revolutionary politics, stifled all other styles, eighteenth-century France enjoyed a period of great distinction, particularly in the arts associated with the development of the modern house as a place where the wealthy could exercise their every desire for a life of luxury and ease, even if, as she wryly notes, 'the wants of men of little means were left to be satisfied by some future age'.[136] Dilke's interest in the economic framework within which artists and craftsmen worked is everywhere apparent. For example, she draws on the 'Livre-Journal' or 'day ledger' of the powerful dealer, agent and patron Lazare Duvaux, and analyses his complex role in the creation of mid-eighteenth-century *décors*.[137] Equally, the woman who had been involved with the Women's Trade Union League from its foundation in 1874, and its President from 1886 until her death, investigates the economics of production from the perspective of the artists and craftsmen engaged in making luxury items for the rich. And so she writes of the suffering and distress of the tapestry workers at the Gobelins and the Savonnerie and those engaged in the historic industries of Aubusson and Felletin, who were forced at mid-century to try to make their work look as exactly as possible like painting. 'The question of economy itself was very serious', notes Dilke, for '[t]he wages of the tapestry workers were not only always in arrears but it was impossible to establish satisfactory rates of payment, as the piece-work system continued to prevail.'[138]

Dilke is as conscious of the economics of the modern market for eighteenth-century art as she is of the contemporary economics of production. She acerbically observes: 'At the present time the chronicles of the auction room show that the arts of the eighteenth century inspire the keenest competition amongst those who look on the possession of costly furniture as one of the most expressive signs of wealth.' But whereas the eighteenth-century French financier 'was one whose tastes had been moulded not only by the pressure of tradition but by the surroundings in which he had been born', the same could not be said of the modern millionaires who are his successors.[139] To these she issues a sharp reminder that 'the values of style and construction demand some sacrifice, they can be recognized only by effort, patient attention, and cultivated habits of observation'.[140] Despite her barely concealed contempt for the shallow vulgarity of the market to which such art appeals, she devotes her volume *French Furniture and Decoration in the XVIIIth Century* to developing greater discernment of these more esoteric values of style and construction in the items of domestic luxury of which she writes.

The attention Dilke gave to the decorative arts, to the domestic culture of eighteenth-century France, as she had previously to that of Renaissance France, signifies the modernity of her historicist methodology. Although, as she put it, 'the systematic treatment of the art of the eighteenth century bristles with difficulties' because of the 'bewildering crowd of conflicting tendencies',[141] her deep conviction of the profound connectedness of the works of decoration, furniture, painting and architecture of a period made these critically neglected art forms fundamental to her analysis. Nevertheless, some reviewers of her work saw her interest in the domestic arts not as groundbreaking but as signifying her 'womanly' sensibilities.

An anonymous reviewer of her first book in the *Westminster Review*, for example, finds her 'history of the Renaissance in France … little better than a history of furniture', and concludes that 'a Renaissance whose chief results lie in the department of decorative upholstery cannot, of course, hope to vie with the splendid names and varied qualities of the Italian new birth'.[142] It was clearly appropriate for a woman to have written about 'all that skilled handicraft can do to beautify daily life and make lovely the habitations of man'.[143]

But if we reject the derogatory and dismissive implications of such contemporary views of the female intellectual and her womanly capacities, are there ways in which we might see Dilke's work as gendered? She herself was clearly interested in the gender of art. She critiques the Goncourts, for example, for giving us 'a too slight, a too feminine Fragonard', praising instead the suggestive play of his pen: 'Not a trick of coquetry in dress or manner can escape it. Lively and exact in the appreciation of every pose and movement, of the intentional coyness of the turn of a head, or the wave of a hand, it is equally cunning in the choice of a meaning breast-knot, and in all those devices of the toilet which are intended to create "a sweet disorder in the dress, kindling in cloathes a wantonnesse".'[144] Her own eye might be said to be as sharply attentive to the suggestive detail of dress as Fragonard's pen, and therefore by her account, in a nice irony, to show 'virility' (a quality which she observes in a number of the artists she discusses) rather than femininity. For example, describing the woman in Lancret's *L'Attache du Patin*, she notes how she 'contrives to show not only the blue lining of her dress, her scarlet petticoat and painfully thin white stockings, but also a white furbelow which, if in keeping with the lady's very low bodice, affords no suggestion of that comfortable warmth which the leafless trees and leaden sky of the background would seem to demand'.[145] She reads the rendition of dress in Chardin's *Toilette du Matin* with a Jamesian eye for the meaning of costume:

> No prettier lesson in coquettish dressing was ever given than the one conveyed by these two figures. Top-knots peep out scarlet from beneath the hood of the mother's black tippet, delicately blue above the fair child's forehead, the little muff in her baby hand is blue velvet and white fur, whilst by the mass book on the red stool, over which falls the red drapery which enframes the mirror on the toilet, lies another muff of green velvet and sable, cunningly chosen to give the last touch of elegance to the mother's appearance … one guesses that costumes so finished can scarcely have been donned only to go to church – mass will certainly be followed by less serious engagements.[146]

Dilke is alert to the nuanced depiction of female subjects, whether they are humble and anonymous or powerful and grand, their treatment intimate or formal, naturalistic or flattering. Of Rigaud's portrait of his mother, Marie Serre, she bids us observe the differences between this highly personal style of portraiture and the 'magnificent manner' in which he rendered 'the pompous types' of his age (he was famous for his official portraits, such as his *Louis XIV* in the Louvre), and tells of the careful provisions the artist made in his will for this portrait that meant so much to him. She is notably interested in the representation of the female body. Thus, writing of Greuze, she notes that 'there is certain to be some corner of his pictures in which the eye can detect the immature charms of one of his favourite types of girlish beauty, indiscreetly revealed with an inappropriate and picturesque elegance, verging on the theatrical'.[147] And of Latour, whose fame rests, she notes 'on his portraits of women, to whom he contrived to give a piquant and sensuous beauty which becomes a common characteristic of the most diverse types', she observes the 'mannerisms' and 'tricks of treatment' he employs to flatter his subjects and bring them 'into harmony with the fashionable type of their day': 'On everyone he confers that dimpled elevation of the corners of the mouth, a gift of which nature is chary and which cannot be acquired by art', she writes, adding, 'All seem inspired with the desire and the powers to please.'[148] Like the representations of female faces by Dilke's contemporary, Dante Gabriel Rossetti, they are 'not portraits but fantasy',[149] and signify the gender economy of the society that produced them. She probes the relationship of artist and sitter in a number of instances. Thus she describes how Fragonard, following a quarrel with the celebrated dancer 'la Guimard' whom he had painted as the Goddess of the Dance, avenged himself by disfiguring the picture, transforming her features 'into those of a menacing fury'; adding, '[s]o much bitterness has suggested, as a prelude, a little love', but also reminding us that 'the year 1770, in which Fragonard was working for "la Guimard", was the year following his marriage' and that he was then 'the man of the day'.[150] Dilke also, as Kali Israel notes, 'sardonically draws attention to images produced by self-serving men of culturally active women'.[151] We are told in *French Engravers and Draughtsmen of the XVIIIth Century*, for example, of the prodigious amateur engraver Vivant Denon that his 'chief occupation was "la gravure et les femmes"', and that '[h]e, indeed, seems to have owed much of his success and even his great position at the beginning of the nineteenth century to this means of popularity with women'.[152] Later in the volume she reproduces Flipart's engraving, after Cochon le fils, of Mademoiselle

Clairon sitting (fully clothed) as a model for a life-drawing class to a group of young male artists.

But beside such images of female objectification, Dilke shows us many examples of female agency. One of the most influential figures in the eighteenth-century art world was Madame de Pompadour, the official mistress of Louis XV, and her powerful presence in these volumes testifies to Dilke's appreciation of the multi-faceted nature of her contribution to the art of her day. Early in *French Painters* she writes at some length about the favourite's relationship with Boucher, her patronage of whom had begun with her reign. Thereafter, we are told: 'Indispensable to the favourite in her capacity of patroness of the arts, designing not only her furniture, but her fans; guiding her hand when the caprice of the moment prompted her to try her chance with the etching needle, Boucher assured for himself by this familiarity the support of Marigny and the certainty of Royal commissions of the first importance.'[153] Kali Israel sees Dilke's representation of their relationship as a key instance of the way her study 'connects male artistic inferiority, female performativity, and illegitimate and eroticized power', and suggests that, for her, 'Boucher and Pompadour together embody their inferior epoch's "artificial tone and temper"'.[154] Dilke argues that Boucher's 'defects', chief among which was '*la vulgarité élégante*' which Goncourt identified as his signature, 'contributed to his enormous success', and she paints a picture of a man whose calculated devotion to the theatrical vanities of the king's mistress paved the way to success. Yet despite her critique, she clearly respects 'the remarkable force of character, which enabled this woman to hold out so long in the difficulties of her extraordinary position', and which she finds conveyed in Boucher's portraits of her. When Dilke comments that '[t]he influence of Mme. De Pompadour … survived her death [in 1764]', she is explicitly alluding to the fact that Boucher was made first painter to the king in the following year, but she seems also to be referring to the fact that, in these portraits of her, she appears not as objectified female spectacle so much as a self-fashioned '*femme savante*', an icon of court culture signifying at once sexuality and the life of the mind. She later quotes a secondary source to the effect that the favourite's physiognomy was modelled by will rather than nature.[155]

Mme de Pompadour is repeatedly invoked in these volumes as a patron and employer responsible for exercising a powerful influence in matters of taste and directing artistic practice. Dilke judges this influence to have been 'in many respects admirably felicitous', owing to 'the rare quality of her instincts and intelligence' and the fact that '[s]he undoubtedly possessed a sincere and instinctive love of art, and sought the signs of perfection and distinction in all that was executed for her rather than the satisfaction of mere personal luxury'.[156] But the king's mistress is only the most prominent of a number of women that Dilke demonstrates to have played a significant role in the eighteenth-century art world, not the least of whom were amateur and professional artists. One whose work is reproduced in the volume on painters is Madame Vigée le Brun, whose portrait *La Princesse de Talleyrand* is described by Dilke as 'very fair and delicate in effect, and charms the eye by a harmony of pale blue, gray, and pure white' (and compares favourably with 'her well-known and flattering portraits of herself' – a more direct form of the self-fashioning that may be detected in Madame de Pompadour's portraits). Because of her husband's activities as a picture dealer, it was only at the Queen's intervention that Madame Vigée le Brun was elected to the Royal Academy,[157] but with royal support she was '*agrée et reçue*' into that august body on the same day as another female artist, Madame Guyard.

Only three pages into the first volume of her study on painters, Dilke, who had herself studied art at South Kensington, launches into a discussion of the position of female artists in the French Academy. Herself a vigorous campaigner for the rights of women to have access to life-drawing classes, she notes wryly 'the fulfilment by the administration of its often deferred promise to enable the Academy to open their Life School without charge, and the vigorous decision, taken in the same year [1706], not to receive women, in future, as "académiciennes"'.[158] Dilke goes on to explain how a few women did manage to gain admittance 'in spite of this fixed determination': Rosalba Carriera, Mademoiselle Reboul (Madame Vien), Madame Therbouche, Anne Vallayer, Mademoiselle Roslin. These two last were admitted to the Academy in the same year, but, as Dilke acerbically observes, 'these two incursions of women, rapidly following on one another, were evidently regarded as dangerous, and the Academy took occasion to record that, though they liked to encourage women by admitting a few, yet such admissions, being in some sort foreign to their constitution, ought not to be multiplied, and thenceforth it was resolved never to admit more than four'. Despite the fact that Madame Guyard, in particular, 'fought hard for the rights of women academicians, insisting … that their numbers and privileges should be increased', this notion that the admission of women was somehow 'foreign' to the Academy's constitution persisted, and was reiterated much later, in 1790, when, in the final stages before the Academy's demise, a group of officials and academicians protested that it was not fitting for 'des femmes viennent s'immiscer dans un travail qui leur est étranger'.[159]

For all their manifest differences, one of the similarities between Emilia Dilke and Vernon Lee is their preoccupation with the 'foreign'. I do not mean by this merely that they were Englishwomen who wrote about the art of other cultures. Rather, I mean to suggest all that the use of the word 'foreign' metaphorically signifies in Dilke's discussion of the French Academy's designation of women. Interestingly, both Dilke and Lee identified themselves as 'foreign'. From the beginning of her professional writing life, in Oxford, as the wife of a don (her first husband Mark Pattison), Dilke wrote as a foreigner on the margins of academia and without its sanction, unlike art historians such as Ruskin, the 'Graduate of Oxford' and later Slade Professor, and Pater, the Fellow of Brasenose. Furthermore, Dilke cultivated a distinctively foreign style in her self-presentation which was often commented on. Unhappy in her first marriage, and in poor health, she spent many months of the year away from Oxford living and working in Paris or the South of France, where she claimed to feel more at home. As she confided to a friend, in France she could 'renew the ravishing sense of being one with the earth & sky wh never comes to me till I am past Marseilles', adding 'yet I love England I love my people, though English landscape is strange and foreign to me, & here I feel at once at home'.[160] An unconventional woman, sexually as well as intellectually, whose authorial and social personae were multiple and highly performative, as Francis Pattison she seemed to find in France, both past and present, liberation from the stifling conventionalities of Oxford, while throughout her life her 'Frenchness' was a significant part of the way she fashioned her cultural identity. Vernon Lee, as an English woman who was born in France, led a nomadic existence as a child in various parts of Continental Europe ('my friends ... imagine me to have been born and brought up in a gipsy-cart'),[161] spent much of her adult life in Italy and wrote principally on Italian cultural history, felt a similar sense of exile and displacement. Her biographer notes that '[i]n England Vernon Lee never found herself completely at home' and felt that her 'sympathies were too international to be acceptable even to the least insular among her English friends'. He quotes her as writing to Kit Anstruther-Thomson: 'It's funny, though I feel so much more English than anything else (in fact only English) I cannot feel well in body or mind save on this sufficiently big and sufficiently aired and warmed continent.'[162] The consciousness of her cultural hybridity is a defining feature of Vernon Lee's writing on art, cultural history and place, and may be said to articulate with her transgressive authorial and sexual identity, and to stand in for other, unspeakable identity positions. In the case of both Vernon Lee and Emilia Dilke,

I suggest, their enactment and experience of 'foreignness', and their evident preoccupation with 'the foreign' in their writing, signify their position as female intellectuals in the business of defining culture, who speak, as foreigners, from difference, and make a virtue of their estrangement: Lee maintains 'that we all of us are the better, of whatever nationality (and most, perhaps, we rather too-too solid Anglo-Saxons) for some fusion of a foreign element'.[163] Their work on the arts of the Renaissance and eighteenth century in Italy and France participates in wider late-nineteenth-century discourses about gender and culture, providing avenues for and legitimising their exploration and articulation of the foreign, and offering them other cultural repertoires on which to draw, in the past and another country, other languages in which to speak, if in sometimes coded ways, to and about their own cultural world.

For these Englishwomen, wider discourses about gender, hybridity and difference may be said to have shaped, even enabled, their historiographical practice. Deborah Cherry has argued that, in the nineteenth century, 'History became a site for struggles over definitions of femininity.'[164] Two years before she began to write fiction, George Eliot published an article in the *Westminster Review* about the salons of women such as Madame de Sablé in seventeenth-century France because their cultural work has, she says, 'not merely an historical interest, it has an important bearing on the culture of women in the present day'.[165] Recovering through their research into and reclamation of these historical women artists and patrons a sense of the possibilities for modern women as makers and mediators of culture, Victorian women made use of past periods to authorise and further their own emancipatory projects. By including in their period surveys ephemeral and popular or domestic art forms, by rescuing the forgotten and writing the obscure into history, and by acknowledging the role of women in cultural production, female art historians took new angles on the Middle Ages, recalibrated the Renaissance from a feminine perspective, and uncovered a feminised and foreign eighteenth century, quite other to the masculinist age of reason with which the period is conventionally identified. In the next chapter we will see what they made of the arts of their own period.

CHAPTER 5

Feminine arts

In 1890, the expatriate journalist Elizabeth Robins Pennell observed, in her monthly column devoted to the affairs of women in London in the American journal *Chautauquan*: 'Women have … gone very thoroughly into journalism. You have only to go to one of the press views in a London art exhibition to find out how many are art critics, while the pictures they criticize show how many others are artists.'[1] Pennell herself, who was one of their number, produced over her long career as a professional writer many articles and reviews, often anonymously or pseudonymously, as an art critic and later a food critic for British and American periodicals, including the *Pall Mall Gazette*, the *Star*, the *Daily Chronicle*, and the *Nation*.[2] She was later to recall her industrious life as a busy professional art journalist in this period: 'Rare has been the month of May that has not found me in Paris, with my eyes and catalogue and note-book, in the *Salons*. Few have been the International Exhibitions, from Glasgow to Ghent, from Antwerp to Venice, that I have missed.' She recalls similarly 'long hours' writing' as she reviewed the London exhibitions, the results of which 'duly appeared in the long columns of many a paper, in the long articles of many a magazine'.[3] The periodical press had always been an important medium for Victorian women, not least because the convention of anonymity that prevailed until the 1860s and persisted well beyond that date enabled them to publish undercover, and most of the art criticism and histories discussed so far in this study first appeared in serial form. But in the 1880s and 1890s periodicals began to play a different and more intensified role for female art historians and critics. Journalism during the final two decades of the nineteenth century was taking an interesting cultural turn, at once a democratised medium for the popularisation of art and a vehicle for a more elevated critical discourse appropriate to the *fin-de-siècle* conception of the 'critic as artist', and women were quick to turn this to their professional advantage, strategically placing their work in a range of periodicals – from specialist art publications, literary magazines and women's journals to mainstream weekly and daily papers – in order to achieve maximum impact.[4]

Writing in genres that crossed the boundaries between journalism and literature seems to have encouraged other categorical transgressions, because it is in late nineteenth-century women's literary journalism that we most notably find the concept of art itself being redefined. If journalism is considered an art form, so too are other creative genres that have conventionally been judged to be beyond the pale. In the final decades of the century, in the pages of the periodical press, often in designated Women's Columns, female art critics write less about the Old Masters and more about the contemporary art scene – including, as Pennell points out, the work of female artists. In weeklies such as the *Illustrated London News* and the *Graphic*, and in dailies such as the *Pall Mall Gazette*, they review the Paris Salons and the current London shows, critically assessing the work of practitioners whose reputations are not yet established and secure. Furthermore they discuss not only the fine arts but also the industrial arts, the decorative arts and the domestic arts, catering not just for the elite but for the general populace. And they do so in ways that are often explicitly gendered.

As we saw in the last chapter, Emilia Dilke's very serious historical scholarship on the decorative arts as a crucial dimension of Renaissance and eighteenth-century period style met with some disparaging comments from critics, who clearly objected to what they regarded as an emasculation of the history of art into a 'history of furniture', in which 'decorative upholstery' has usurped the 'splendid names' of traditional art history.[5] Notwithstanding the importance of the decorative and applied arts for the Victorians' own period style, and the prominence of key male artists and critics, such as John Ruskin, William Morris and Charles Locke Eastlake, in promoting the ideals of fine craftsmanship, design and ornament in the home, the prevailing view was that these were inferior art forms, associated with the female domestic sphere and often produced, or at least managed and arranged, by women. One of the important ways in which second-wave feminism challenged the aesthetic values and norms of the discipline of art history was its questioning of the traditional division and ranking of 'art' and 'craft'. Anthea Callen's book *Angel in the Studio* (1979), for example, on women's contributions to the British Arts and Crafts movement upon which Ruskin and Morris were such an influence, and Rozsika Parker, in her study of embroidery, *The Subversive Stitch* (1984), drew attention to genres that have typically been disregarded by art historians as both feminine and minor domestic art forms. What is striking when we look back to women writing art history and criticism in the nineteenth century is how many who were experts in the fine arts also wrote not only about new forms of representation such as photography, the artistic status of which was fiercely debated, and the industrial and applied arts, but also about the art of the house, the arts of cooking and gardening, and, especially, the art of dress. These 'other' arts are not, of course, unconnected with one another. Victorian photographs, for example, from family portraits to self-consciously artistic tableaux, often featured elaborate forms of dress, and were framed for display, or collected in scrapbooks and albums, and used to ornament the home. And furthermore photography crossed over into the world of the fine arts, made use of by art historians and connoisseurs for purposes of attribution, for instance, and exhibited in its own right by photographic societies and galleries. But what is new and intriguing is the way in which, throughout the Victorian period and especially vigorously at the *fin*, female art historians and critics wrote about these feminine-identified genres, both frivolously and with high seriousness, as art, bringing their knowledge of both historical and contemporary fine arts to bear on their analyses of popular cultural forms, expanding the definition of what constitutes art, and bringing female producers and consumers, as well as feminine arts, into the realm of the aesthetic.

Photography

One of the earliest descriptions of the photographic aesthetic is by a woman, Elizabeth Barrett, who wrote excitedly to her friend Mary Russell Mitford on 7 December 1843:

> Do you know anything about that wonderful invention of the day, called the Daguerreotype? – that is, have you seen any portraits produced by means of it? Think of a man sitting down in the sun and leaving his facsimile in all its full completion of outline and shadow, steadfast on a plate, at the end of a minute and a half! The Mesmeric disembodiment of spirits strikes one as a degree less marvellous. And several of these wonderful portraits … like engravings – only exquisite and delicate beyond the work of the engraver – have I seen lately – longing to have such a memorial of every Being dear to me in the world. It is not merely the likeness which is precious in such cases – but the association, and the sense of nearness involved in the thing … the fact of the *very shadow of the person* lying there fixed forever! It is the very sanctification of portraits I think – and it is not at all monstrous in me to say what my brothers cry out against so vehemently … that I would rather have such a memorial of one I dearly loved, than the noblest Artist's work ever produced.[6]

The poet captures in her brief note the very essence of photography's unique indexical power – 'the *very shadow of the person*', she emphasises, 'lying there fixed forever!' – and gestures to the debates over the relationship between this new mechanical medium and the fine arts that were to be such a feature of the critical landscape in the middle decades of the century. It also captures for us the visual moment of the birth of photography, which dates from 1839 and was then in its infancy. Elizabeth Barrett is captivated by this new medium that, even then, can catch an ephemeral glimpse of a person's very shape and being (one thinks of Hopkins's coinage 'inscape'), so that their image, a matter of light and shadows, can be fixed, 'steadfast on a plate'. It is notable that, while she finds the daguerreotype to be infinitely superior to the work of even the finest engraver or portrait painter, her brothers find her preference a 'monstrous' lapse in taste.

Early photography involved a messy and technically complex process – Julia Margaret Cameron writes of having 'stained an immense quantity of table linen with nitrate of silver, indelible stains'[7] – yet it came to be associated with women, both practitioners and writers. Its suggestion, for Barrett, of mesmerism and spiritualism, and its romantic resonances, evidently appealed to her poetic sensibility, and these are the aspects of the art that were to be developed at mid-century by female photographers such as Cameron and Lady Clementina Hawarden. Hawarden took up photography in 1857, and produced some five hundred albumen prints of her daughters in their home in South Kensington over the next few years, exhibiting (and winning silver medals) with the Photographic Society of London in 1863 and 1864, and achieving critical acclaim for her experimental 'Studies', as she called them (Fig. 16).

These enigmatically beautiful images of girlhood and young womanhood constitute a sustained meditation on femininity. Untitled – their meanings open to the interpretation of the viewer – and making use of a limited repertoire of costumes and domestic props, most notably full-length mirrors, that intensifies their cumulative effect as a series of variations on a profoundly personal mother/daughter theme, they 'speak deeply to women'.[8] These are images that trigger thoughts of Roland Barthes's metaphorical suggestion that 'a sort of umbilical cord links the body of the photographed thing to my gaze'.[9] Although her striking use of light invites comparison with Turner and the Impressionists, and her choice of female subjects the Pre-Raphaelites and Whistler, her work has a distinctively feminine inflection that came to accrue to the medium of photography itself.

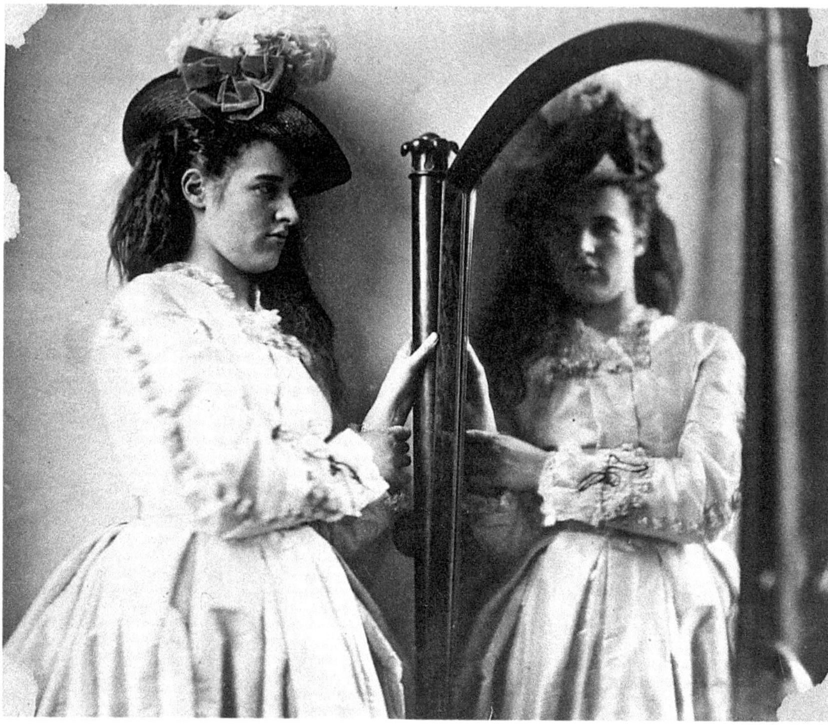

Fig. 16. Lady Clementina Hawarden, *Clementina Maude, 5 Princes Gardens* (*c.* 1863–4)

Likewise, Julia Margaret Cameron's soft-focused images of poetic subjects, modelled in picturesque dress by her family, servants and handsome local 'peasantry', as she referred to them, contributed to the feminisation of the art of photography. Although her powerful close-up portraits of male writers and artists and historical themes drew comparisons with the Old Masters – *The Times*, reviewing an exhibition of her photographs in 1873, invoked Giotto, Velázquez, Van Dyck and Reynolds – and Cameron herself cultivated such parallels (as when she gave the title 'Carlyle like a rough block of Michelangelo's sculpture' to her portrait of the historian, and described her 'La Madonna Aspertante' as 'Raphaelesque'),[10] her style and subjects, and indeed her self-representation, are for the most part decidedly feminine. Again, the mother/daughter theme is crucial to her art (Fig. 17). Her first camera was a gift in 1863 from her daughter, who subsequently died, and, as she describes in her autobiographical *Annals of My Glass House* (1874), first published in the catalogue of her 1889 London

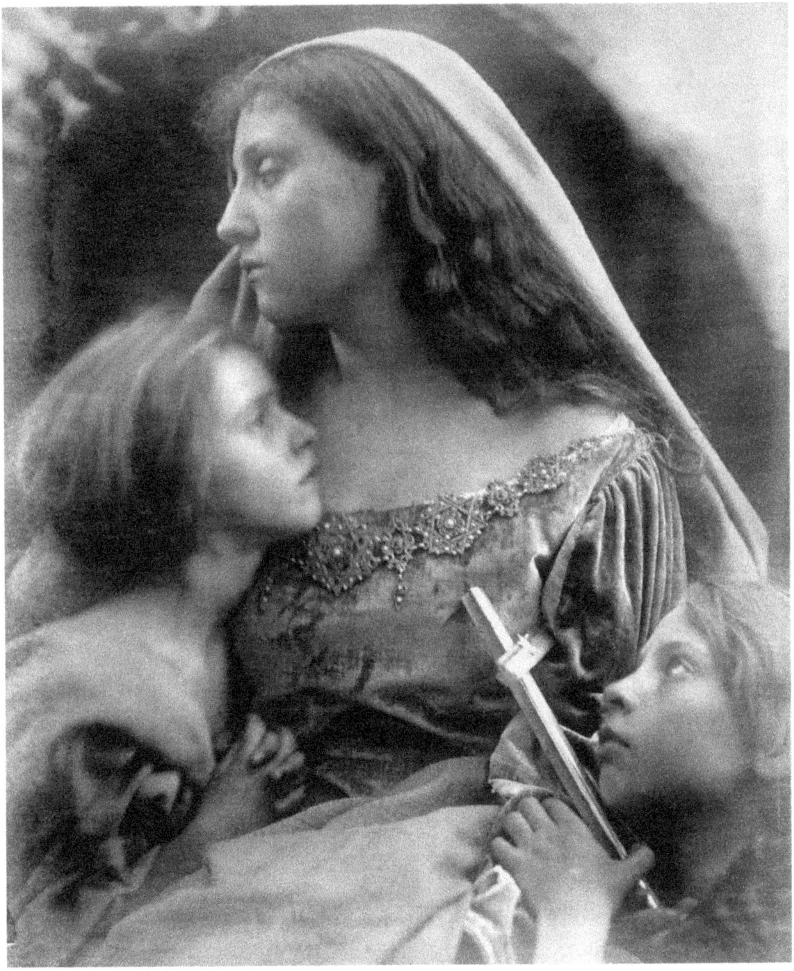

Fig. 17. Julia Margaret Cameron, *A Holy Family* (1872)

exhibition, the mechanical process of photography was always animated for her by love: 'The gift from those I loved so tenderly added more and more impulse to my deeply seated love of the beautiful and from the first moment I handled my lens with a tender ardour, and it has come to be as a living thing, with voice and memory and creative vigour.'[11]

Photography is, as Susan Sontag memorably put it, 'the inventory of mortality', and it became for Cameron a means of satisfying her 'longing' to 'arrest all beauty that came before me', as she had been unable to arrest her beloved daughter, capturing a sentiment similar to Elizabeth Barrett's own 'longing to have such a memorial of every Being dear to me in the world' and her appreciation of 'the association, and the sense of nearness' evoked by the photograph.[12]

Photography came to be regarded as a feminine art, not least because it was an art form that could be taken up in mid-life and pursued at home amidst domestic responsibilities by women such as Hawarden and Cameron, and although it obviously helped to have artistic connections, it did not require admission to a professional world from which female practitioners were excluded. Cameron declares: 'I began with no knowledge of the art. I did not know where to place my dark box, how to focus my sitter, and my first picture I effaced to my consternation by rubbing my hand over the filmy side of the glass.' Yet, with some instruction from the painter and photographer David Wilkie Wynfield, she quickly mastered the basic techniques of shallow-focus portrait photography and within a year became a member of the photographic societies of London and Scotland, submitting her first pictures for exhibition in 1865.[13] Alice Hughes, who was to become one of London's most successful society portrait photographers later in the century, had the fortune to be instructed in the art of portraiture at home by her father, the painter Edward Hughes, to whom she 'modestly ascribes most of her success' in a self-promoting interview in the *Harmsworth Magazine* in 1899.[14] However, she also studied photography at the London Polytechnic, and the photographic techniques and signature style she developed were all her own. She was evidently an astute business woman who, after engaging in amateur photography for some years, in 1891 set up a successful commercial studio in Gower Street that was eventually to employ 'an immense number of people – during the season as many as sixty at a time', although at the outset, she declares, 'I did everything myself, even to the retouching and spotting.'[15] Even in the case of Hughes, though, the art she practises is carefully feminine identified. She was famously 'A Lady Photographer Who Never Photographs Men', on the grounds that 'ladies, of course, make very much prettier pictures than do their husbands and brothers', and she established a reputation for portraits of women and mother-and-child subjects. Furthermore, she started a fashion for photographing women in large picture hats and evening dress in the manner of Reynolds and Gainsborough, and had 'decided views' about the most flattering colours and styles of dress for women having their portraits taken: 'The majority of women, whatever be their age, look well in creamy white, and there is no doubt that soft, flowing draperies add immensely to the beauty of a photograph … A simple tea-gown, open at the neck, will often produce a very much better result than an elaborate stiff dinner-dress; and this type of costume has the further advantage of being dateless – that is to say, the photograph will not grow old-fashioned.'[16]

Photography, more readily than painting, enabled some of the conventional oppositions between women's work and men's work, amateur and professional, and of course craftsmanship and art to be dissolved for women like Hughes – she, like Cameron, was keen to 'produce an artistic effect', and often chose open-air backgrounds as a way of giving her photographs 'the appearance of a painting'.[17] It was a profession that also unsettled the boundaries between home and business: she ran her first studio from the home she shared with her father. Three years before Hughes launched her business enterprise and established that this was a career that a gentlewoman could respectably pursue, Amy Levy had published her first novel, *The Romance of a Shop* (1888), which conveys how challenging it nevertheless was for middle-class women to become commercial photographers. It tells the story of four young women who, following the death of their father, decide to open a photographic studio in London, against the advice of their relatives, who fear they will lose caste. The Lorimer sisters live above their shop, and they decorate the studio itself with homely 'aesthetic' touches that at once feminise the workplace and increase its commercial appeal, so in fiction, too, the division between domestic and professional space is collapsed. The women are semantically identified with their studio and their wares – 'You will be nothing if not aesthetic,' declares one of their friends[18] – and although their business confers visual agency, they are also, as female photographers in a shop, on display, the objects of the gaze. The narrator wryly observes that 'it had got about in certain sets that all the sisters were extremely beautiful, and that Sidney Darrell was painting them in a group for next year's Academy, a *canard* certainly not to be deprecated from a business point of view'.[19] The youngest of the sisters succumbs to the attentions of a wealthy married painter and leaves the safety of the sororal studio, where women make and sell art, to become his model, unequivocally the object of the gaze. However, the other sisters resist being reduced to mere spectacle by asserting their mastery of a skilled profession. They study the technical aspects of their craft in the British Museum Reading Room, apprentice themselves to an established photographer, and demand to be taken seriously as artists. One of their first commissions is to be summoned by an aristocratic client to photograph his errant wife who has just died. Such photographs of the dead, especially beautiful women and children, were much in vogue, bearing witness to the kinds of claims made by Elizabeth Barrett of the power of photography to capture the very soul of the loved one. Gertrude's pictures of this lovely 'woman lying dead or asleep, with her hair spread out on the pillow' are declared to be her best work, and although her sister Fanny thinks it 'very strange' that the man commissioning such photographs 'should select ladies, young girls, for such a piece of work', the sex of the photographer only enhances our sense of the gender of the medium.[20]

Marriage and children are not a cue for the sisters to abandon their professional work for a conventional female existence. After her marriage, Lucy plans to carry on the business, and we are told in the epilogue that she has just 'carried off a medal for photographs of young children from an industrial exhibition', while her husband, 'no less successful in his own line', as an illustrator for periodicals such as *The Photogravure* and *The Woodcut*, 'having permanently abandoned the paint-brush for the needle … bids fair to take a high place among the black and white artists of the day'.[21] Journalism, and the new arts associated with it, is a theme in the novel. In its opening pages Gertrude Lorimer is seen playing nervously with a copy of the *British Journal of Photography* as she prepares to lay out to her sisters her plan to open a photography studio. At an early stage of the sisters' career, she refuses to be interviewed by the *Waterloo Place Gazette*, on the grounds that 'we are photographers, not mountebanks', but later 'some unauthorised person wrote a little account of the Lorimers' studio in one of the society papers, of which, if the taste was questionable, the results were not to be questioned at all', and it is acknowledged that such 'gratuitous advertisement' helps their business to thrive.[22] As the example of Alice Hughes's interview in the *Harmsworth Magazine* makes clear, feature articles in the periodical press were an opportunity for female photographers to promote both the commercial and the artistic aspects of their work, and they also provided an occasion for female journalists to write about the aesthetics as well as the profession of photography, and its suitability for women. The 'Wares of Autolycus' column in the *Pall Mall Gazette*, which appeared almost daily from May 1893 to the end of 1898, and to which Alice Meynell and other women journalists contributed articles addressed to a female readership, ran several articles on photography, including one on 'The Photographer', in a series titled 'Women's Lives', that refers to *The Romance of a Shop*:

> The business chosen by Gertrude Lorimer, that common-sensible heroine … was photography. And why not? It is a pursuit eminently fitted to woman, involving neither the nervous strain or physical fatigue of medicine, nor the noisy bustle and alert struggle of commerce. She need not

hesitate, timid and self-doubtful, even though genius be omitted from the gifts offered her by niggardly Fate. The average woman had best leave art alone; but, by force of intelligent study and thoughtful industry, she may triumph with the camera. Indeed, not only what she can do is to be pointed out, but likewise what she has done. She may turn, for an example and guide, to Mrs Cameron, who was inspired among photographers, and whose portraits explain that the mistress of the machine is not necessarily a mere automaton.[23]

This represents an interesting development on the view expressed by Elizabeth Eastlake in her pioneering article on photography published in the *Quarterly Review* in April 1857, in the year that Lady Hawarden acquired her first camera, six years before Cameron was given hers, and before either of them had demonstrated what 'the mistress of the machine' was capable of. After giving a detailed and knowledgeable history of the technical development of photography to date, Eastlake turns to consider 'the artistic part of our subject, and to those questions which sometimes puzzle the spectator, as to how far photography is really a picturesque agent, what are the causes of its successes and its failures, and what in the sense of art are its successes and failures?' – burning questions, as we have seen, in its early days.[24] She concludes:

the whole question of success and failure resolves itself into an investigation of the capacities of the machine, and well may we be satisfied with the rich gifts it bestows, without straining it into a competition with art. For everything for which Art, so-called, has hitherto been the means but not the end, photography is the allotted agent – for all that requires mere manual correctness, and mere manual slavery, without any employment of the artistic feeling, she is the proper and therefore the perfect medium.[25]

This is the work of art in the age of mechanical reproduction. Photography is the perfect medium for the nineteenth century as well: 'She is made for the present age, in which the desire for art resides in a small minority, but the craving, or rather necessity for cheap, prompt, and correct facts in the public at large. Photography is the purveyor of such knowledge to the world. She is the sworn witness of everything presented to her view.'[26] It is a democratic art form, not only because of its indiscriminate representation of everything within its sights, but also because of its reach into every corner of the population. The article opens with a wide-lens view of a world in which 'photography has become a household word and a household want', and which is

used alike by art and science, by love, business, and justice; is found in the most sumptuous saloon, and in the dingiest attic – in the solitude of

> the Highland cottage, and in the glare of the London gin-palace – in the pocket of the detective, in the cell of the convict, in the folio of the painter and architect, among the papers and patterns of the millowner and manufacturer, and on the cold brave breast on the battle-field.[27]

Produced and consumed by people in all walks of life – not least, she notes, women – photography is a pursuit that has tens of thousands of people 'practising a new pleasure, speaking a new language, and bound together by a new sympathy'; one that 'unites men of the most diverse lives, habits, and stations, so that whoever enters its ranks finds himself in a kind of republic, where it needs apparently but to be a photographer to be a brother'.[28] In Eastlake's view, photography is nothing less than a new visual language, a 'new form of communication between man and man – neither letter, message, nor picture – which now happily fills up the space between them'.[29] The cherished photographic portrait that Elizabeth Barrett responded to with such wonderment and emotion is, for Eastlake, less romantically, a 'facial map', furnishing 'accurate landmarks and measurements for loving eyes and memories to deck with beauty and animate with expression, in perfect certainty, that the ground-plan is founded upon fact',[30] yet it is similarly acknowledged to be a dynamic and revolutionary new medium of human communication, one that invites imaginative and affective confabulation. Indeed portraits, Eastlake avers, belonging as they do 'to that class of facts wanted by numbers who know and care nothing about their value as works of art', are a genre that has been improved upon by the advent of photography. Hand-touched and tinted photographic portraits offer 'a most satisfactory coalition between the artist and the machine'.[31]

Despite, or perhaps because of, its identification as a mechanical art, photography is consistently gendered as feminine in Eastlake's article, by comparison with art which is always masculine – '[t]he field of delineation, having two distinct spheres, requires two distinct labourers'. 'Her business is to give evidence of facts, as minutely and as impartially as, to our shame, only an unreasoning machine can give', but this does not constitute art. The (male) student issuing from the Academy must add to the automaton's ability to record facts '[t]he power of selection and rejection, the living application of that language which lies dead in his paintbox, the marriage of his own mind with the object before him, and the offspring, half stamped with his own features, half with those of Nature, which is born of the union – whatever appertains to the free-will of the intelligent being, as opposed to the obedience of the machine'.[32] In this explicitly sexualised account of the birth of the art work, photography is accorded a role associated with nature which must needs be married with mind. Photography is the handmaiden of 'that mystery called Art, in the elucidation of which photography can give valuable help, simply by showing what it is not'. Indeed, we are told:

> There is, in truth, nothing in that power of literal, unreasoning imitation, which she claims as her own, in which, rightly viewed, she does not relieve the artist of a burden rather than supplant him in an office. We do not even except her most pictorial feats – those splendid architectural representations – from this rule. Exquisite as they are, and fitted to teach the young, and assist the experienced in art, yet the hand of the artist is but ignobly employed in closely imitating the texture of stone, or in servilely following the intricacies of the zigzag ornament.[33]

Photography, then – like woman – is admirably equipped to be the helpmeet of art, to teach the young, and to tend to the arts of ornament, and their alignment, even in this pioneering essay by a formidable woman who was very much more than the mere helpmeet of her eminent husband, Sir Charles Eastlake – although she positions herself as such in its opening pages. Her article offers an intriguing summation of the many ways in which this 'feminine' art was at once promoted, recuperated, critiqued and positioned in relation to the fine arts in nineteenth-century art discourse.

The art of the home

'My aspirations', Julia Margaret Cameron wrote in 1864 to her friend and mentor Sir John Herschel, who coined the word 'photography' and contributed to the early development of the science, 'are to ennoble Photography and to secure for it the character and uses of High Art'.[34] While it might be said that the experimental work of Cameron and other 'mistress[es] of the machine' productively complicated the clear categorical distinction that Eastlake wishes to preserve between the fine and the industrial arts, and that their photographs were evidently understood by some of their contemporaries as constituting a new and genuinely hybrid art form, for the most part photography was viewed, if not as the recorder of fact, then as an ornamental art, whose function was to beautify the home and/or to memorialise the family. Great Aunt Julia's own photographs hung in the hallway of the Stephens's house in Gordon Square. Even the professional photographer Alice Hughes used her art as a décor item. Her interviewer for the piece in the *Harmsworth Magazine* notes that '[o]ne of the most beautiful features of Miss Hughes's fine reception-rooms is a number of beautiful Louis Quinze screens covered with exquisite specimens of her work', and lest this be mistaken for a form of advertising we are assured that many of them 'are neither for sale nor reproduction'.[35] When the Lorimer sisters move into their newly acquired studio, they spend time 'playing at photographers and decorators' in ways that elide the differences between the two: 'The objectionable Virginia cork and coloured glass of the little passage were disguised by various aesthetic devices; lanterns swung from the roof, and a framed photograph or two from Dürer and Botticelli, Watts and Burne-Jones, was mingled artfully with the specimens of their own work which adorned it as a matter of course', making of it 'a perfect bower of art and culture'.[36] While there is clearly a commercial imperative in their decorative use of the photograph, it is nevertheless represented as a marker of taste.

In a popular series of essays on the furnishing and decoration of the home, however, published a decade later in 'The Wares of Autolycus' column in the *Pall Mall Gazette* and collected and reprinted in 1897 as *The Art of the House*, the poet and journalist Rosamund Marriott Watson is critical of the fashion, particularly egregious among women, for filling the home with photographs:

> Sad, too, to think that the photograph plague, always grievous enough, should rage with by far the greater fury in homes whose presiding fairy happens to be of the less – decoratively – scrupulous sex. Photos, photos everywhere, would seem to be the watchword of the modern housewife – on the walls, the overmantel; on the countless 'occasional' tables that bring the artless visitor to the borders of profanity, on the grand piano, on the protean but undying chiffonier. Only the chairs as yet remain uninvaded by that smirking or languishing company. And the sole spark of promise is that they have the saving excuse of perishability. But this will not bring us back the dainty miniature, the tender silhouette, the pleasant portraiture of days when likenesses were fit and few, and the card physiognomy of every casual acquaintance was not held in decorative esteem and shrined in a frame but a little less foolish than itself.[37]

Women are here deemed to be responsible for what Marriott Watson figures as the spread of a contagious disease and, as in the case of their manifold other excesses and lapses in taste, she makes it her business to put them right.

Her work, like other columns, books and manuals on the domestic arts published in the period, is founded on a paradox: that women, who are ostensibly naturally fitted out to be homemakers, are frequently not so equipped, and need be taught how to realise and fulfil their essential nature. 'The judicious use of wallpaper, the right selection and disposal of furniture, is taken for granted as being thrown in with the rest of the feminine arts', she observes, and yet there is reason to entertain misgivings about a housewife's 'heaven-born ability for grouping flowers to the best advantage' and for arranging her own drawing room.[38] In her introductory essay 'Some Principles of Decoration', she draws attention to such ironic anomalies as professional interior designers being hired 'to make the place look homely',[39] yet of course the purpose of her own intervention is to lend a professional eye to the aesthetics of the home, and to help women artfully achieve what so evidently does not come naturally to them as the designated homemakers. The domestic arts must be mastered as 'accomplishments', each of which 'is a separate science in itself … founded on principles as well-defined as those that govern the composition of a sonnet, a picture, or a fugue'.[40] A well-respected poet, Marriott Watson could claim to have expert credentials in the first at least of these forms, and so writes with some authority that '[t]he arrangement of furniture is just as difficult and dangerous an art as landscape gardening or sonnet-making … The art of innuendo, the study of implication, are no less subtle where the juxtaposition of inanimate matter is concerned than when words are the components to be juggled with.'[41] This is, indeed, the *art* of the house, and Marriott Watson is, she implies, an educated and cultured woman who is well equipped to advise on the aesthetics of the home.

Talia Schaffer has written with great insight about the shifting cultural meanings of domestic handicrafts and the gendering of home decoration in the nineteenth century which provide a context for the works of Marriott Watson and other women writing on the domestic arts throughout the period. She points to the contradictory and symbiotically evolving relationship between ornamental arts produced by women and the mainstream industrial arts, mapping a trajectory from mid-century, when handcrafted goods emulated industrialism and 'ornamental manufacture' occupied a prominent place at the Great Exhibition, through the 1870s, when handicraft, with its connotations of women's decorous industriousness in their separate sphere of the home, went out of vogue, and new conceptions of craftsmanship were ushered in by William Morris and Walter Crane. In a nuanced discussion of the complex appropriations and reappropriations of interior design aesthetics as men such as Charles Locke Eastlake (nephew of Sir Charles Eastlake), with his *Hints on Household Taste: in Furniture, Upholstery and Other Details* (1868), entered what had traditionally been regarded as a female realm, she explores what happened when male art specialists turned their attention to interior design. Their intervention transformed what had once been an ineluctably amateur and feminine form of domestic creativity into a professional, and decidedly more masculine, field, one which valorised the display of antiques and fine collectibles rather than valueless female craftwork, and which required in the decorator a knowledge of art and architectural history and skills of connoisseurship.[42]

Women writing about the decorative arts were always required to negotiate these competing gendered discourses, and Schaffer has shown how for some women, such as Elizabeth Gaskell, George Eliot and Margaret Oliphant, it was fiction that formally enabled the development of a more subtle language about female handicraft, much as we have seen that novels provided a fictional space in which women could write about the fine arts. What we find in the case of women like Marriott Watson who wrote about the domestic arts professionally is that their work frequently contains a ritual denunciation of female handicraft and women's unsophisticated aesthetic taste in order to establish their own critical credentials, at the same time that it plays upon the idea that the female author can bring a privileged knowledge of domestic culture to bear on questions of interior design, thereby adding a different kind of authority to the professional field. Marriott Watson herself, whose interior design ideology is, as Schaffer notes, like that of other contributors to the 'Wares of Autolycus' column, 'deeply marked by the tensions of writing a "feminine" column in the decidedly nonfeminine venue of the *Pall Mall Gazette*',[43] engages in such manoeuvres in *The Art of the House*. She clears the way for her own domestic aesthetic by vigorously denouncing both the aesthete and the amateur female decorator before going on to write about interiors 'in a discourse that was continuous with the complex, allusive, imagistic, and psychologically dense language of her own poetry'.[44] Lamenting 'the widespread superstition that the sense of sight needs no education', she also regrets the lack of attention given by most women to 'the inner development of the houses in which they are to live and move and have their being', a phrase suggestive of the profound connection between the identity and inner being of a woman and her home. 'Indeed', she writes, 'it were difficult to over-estimate the intimacy of the relations between ourselves and what, for want of a better word, may be called our setting.'[45] The home is an extension of its owner's very subjectivity, and it must be adapted to reflect and express her interiority.

This perception of the close identification of the mistress with her house permeates Marriott Watson's language, which is at once alive with metaphor and alert to the materiality of things. As Schaffer points out, Marriott Watson writes the house as a corpulent Victorian matron, stuffed with furnishings that are the objective correlative of women's grotesquely misshapen bodies: the inelegant Victorian sofa, with its 'hippopotamus-like form, the dreary buttoned-down upholsteries – now in leather, now in rep, now, worst of all, in ruby or emerald velvet, or in satin; the dropsical turned legs, the foolish undulations of the back as it dwindled unbeautifully less – a little more than midway between head and foot'; the regulation pianoforte, '[t]he incorrigible "grand", with its gross proportions, its amorphous unwieldiness of bulk, its bloated legs, grotesquely indented with inadequate little ankles, like the fat lady in a country fair … It is only fit to mate with the toad-like ottoman of yesterday.'[46] Her lexicon here and throughout the most virulently critical passages of the book is replete with language that invokes contemporary debates around heredity and degeneration. Inanimate furnishings are anthropomorphised, and endowed with an imaginative life of their own: 'your walls are sure to bear mute witness against you from your rising up to your down-lying. "Sleepless with cold, commemorative eyes", the peacock frieze in unblessed union with the realistic flowery wallpaper stares mute reproach at you so long as it, and you, may endure.'[47] Worse still, modern Morris and Jacobean wallcoverings are represented as sexually predatory, violating the woman in her home: 'The figures force themselves upon you, they are always with you, in decided patterning, importunate anecdote, insistent, and demonstrative. They press uninvited into the world you live in, for world of their own they have none.'[48] Published in the same period as Charlotte Perkins Gilman's short story 'The Yellow Wallpaper' (1892) and Freud's early articles on hysteria, there is more than a suggestion of *fin-de-siècle* female neuroses in Marriott Watson's art of the house. She despairs, for example, of women's mania, once they have 'tasted blood' and 'the craving [has grown] with indulgence', for 'run[ning] amuck' with a paint-brush, and painting over fine furniture: 'but there's no help for it, unless perchance the hand-painting habit comes to be recognized at last as one of the dire diseases of the day, and a Home be instituted for the restraint and special treatment of its victims and the general good of the community at large'.[49]

Poorly decorated and designed homes are evidently not the peaceful haven from the world they are meant to be but sites of violent abuse and nervous irritation: 'new fenders and old fireplaces swear at each other', and the saddleback chair's 'stuffy, clinging surface sets the nerves on edge'.[50] Yet with due attention, a woman's domain can be full of imaginative possibility, nowhere more so than in the bedroom, where she can practise her feminine arts most creatively:

> The fit plenishing of a sleeping chamber demands at least as intelligent consideration, as nice a sense of selection, as the composition of any other kind of nocturne, be it in words, in music, or in paint … A well-arranged bedroom, where comfort and good taste combine to live in unity together, is like the shadow of a great rock in a weary land, a place wherein to doff your will (and your worries to boot), as raiment laid away, and give yourself over to the unconsciousness or the divine irresponsibility of dreams. It is, or should be, an enchanted castle, whence every night you may set forth, bound, now for the deep seas of forgetfulness, now for the vague, fantastic outlands that lie over the Mountains of the Moon, down the Valley of the Shadow. As you drift away, it is but meet and natural to demand that your last drowsy glances should fall on fair harmonies of form and colour, that your parting impressions shall be touched to pleasantness and peace.

The scene is set for the woman to doff her will along with her clothing, and give herself over to fantasy – ideally in an ancient bedchamber, decorated with oak furniture, designed 'to mate with the [oak-panelled] walls'.[51]

Like other writers on the art of the house, Marriott Watson comments throughout her work on the appropriateness or otherwise of different historical period styles for the modern home, and is alert to the ways in which domestic ornaments, clocks not least, express their times: 'The evolution of the timepiece shows so much in common with the human development brought forth by the hours it registers – the development of life and thought – that you might almost take its history for the history of civilization itself: the spirit of the age speaking, or keeping silence, in its clocks'. By contrast with '[t]he comparative quietude of the past, the slower movement of life as it was lived long since; the deeper dependence on natural elements that belonged to more primitive periods than our own', which were reflected in its timepieces – the sun-dial, the water-clock, the hour-glass – modern clocks represent the very nature of modern time: 'the fret and fever of modern existence, the hurly-burly and turmoil of to-day are very adequately typified in our loud-voiced timekeepers, ticking away for dear life, as it were; vociferous of haste, of hours packed with teeming circumstance. Their tongues are sharp with hurried admonition, imperative with shrewd reminders.'[52] Modern clocks here morph into modern sharp-tongued, shrewish women. Marriott Watson will quite often recommend to her readers that they include in their decorative scheme an item that invokes some time past when the pace of life was different: a variety of small elegantly ornamented eighteenth-century clock, available in modern reproduction; a porcelain tea set, with scenes after Watteau, depicting 'ladies with hoops and powdered hair, receiving gallants with full-skirted coats and high-heeled shoes, in stately gardens'; a fifteenth-century Italian cassone decorated with gilded, painted or carved scenes, that makes an 'appeal to sense and imagination alike', and stirs the fancy 'to all manner of strange realizations that simulate memory, and are partly pleasure and part regret'; an old Persian rug, 'born of an ancient civilization, another race and time, and placed much as a master of painting places his composition on the canvas'.[53] Regretful that 'the grand manner in decoration is no more with us', she turns to the past and, like the female art historians who recast and feminised the Renaissance and the eighteenth century, she mobilises historical design in ways that are distinctively gendered. Furthermore, she identifies herself not with the monstrous modern female decorator or with those other contemporary 'monstrosities', the aesthetes, but with an earlier tradition of domestic artist and with the kind of 'housewifely sentiment' exemplified by Mrs Tulliver in *The Mill on the Floss* 'weeping over her linen-chest and her best china'.[54]

The Victorians were notable for their interest in the past, paradoxically as a consequence of their acute consciousness of their own modernity. There was a new awareness of the historical moment of the present (Richard D. Altick reminds us that '[s]ignificantly, the Victorian period was the first in English history to be christened while it was still in progress'),[55] but also of its contingency, of its place in the linear history by which the past becomes the future, and this is an issue that preoccupied writers on the domestic arts equally with mainstream art historians as they struggled to locate themselves in a history of interior design. Marriott Watson muses on a future time when 'survivals of the better-equipped past' – all these clocks, cassone chests, rugs, antique beds, delicately painted porcelain tea sets, hand-embroidered linens that are such helpful props for the mistress of the house in her own day – 'shall have ultimately crumbled and gone', and 'a new and regenerate school of furniture' will emerge, 'something with vitality, that will reflect the feeling of the time in which it was brought forth'.[56] Looking to her own times, despite Victorian Britain's claims to leadership in modern design, she is sceptical about what passes for domestic arts in the modern home having enduring value, predicting that 'after the lapse even of a poor fifty years or so, but little will be left of our gimcrack modern chattels, our "art suites", our hand-painted impedimenta'. Interestingly, she attributes much of the blame for the woeful impoverishment of modern interior design to the Great Exhibition of 1851, the supposed apogee of modernity:

> [T]he great orgie of '51 has left almost indelible traces, traces that the process of time and change can alone obliterate, and that at a snail's pace. Ill weeds thrive apace, and the trail of the Great Exhibition, that very monster which gave birth to a longer-lived monstrosity, the Crystal Palace, is, decoratively speaking, over us all. It is forever being disclosed afresh under some new form, and we who perforce cannot wait to see the future, must cling to the skirts of the past, rejoicing that so much of the *vieux truc mais toujours bon* is left to us.[57]

The extended metaphor of the snail's slimy trail and the persistent trope of degeneration renders the Great Exhibition as an insidious venereal disease from which 'we' must seek refuge in a feminised past until such time as there is a justifiable renewal of confidence in contemporary design.

If Marriott Watson's identification of the Great Exhibition as a key cause of the bankruptcy of the modern domestic aesthetic, exemplified by 'our gimcrack modern chattels, our "art suites", our hand-painted impedimenta', seems surprising, it is worth turning to Schaffer's discussion of the intriguing paradox that '1851 can be read as the climax of the domestic handicraft movement, when handicrafts were publically showcased as prime examples of Great Britain's manufacturing prowess'.[58] But whereas at mid-century '"industry" aligned handicraft with mechanical manufacture', and both signified contemporaneity, 'within twenty years, William Morris and his fellow reformers would redefine craft and machine work as inherently oppositional, making it hard even to remember how allied they seemed at the Great Exhibition'.[59] As perceptions of handicraft's relation to modernity shifted, so did its association with the pre-industrial past, with the consequence that '[a]fter the 1850s, making domestic handicraft became an aggressively historicizing act'.[60]

Importantly, though, even in the 1850s, women writing about the arts, not least in relation to the Great Exhibition, had themselves drawn connections between modern and medieval craftwork, pointing out that the very idea of craftsmanship in Europe goes back to the Middle Ages, making the arts of the earlier period a suitable educational model for the present. Hannah Lawrance, for example, who reviewed both the Great Exhibition (1851) and the Manchester Art Treasures Exhibition (1857), celebrates the contribution to the arts made by medieval monastic orders which produced not only beautifully illuminated manuscripts but also fine craftsmanship by 'mosaic workers, painters of glass, carvers of wood and stone, and workers in metal', and she finds in the diversity of this work, and its connection of the beautiful and the functional, an inspiration for the nineteenth century.[61] She points to the beneficial effects of the arts, fine and applied, for the nation as a whole, citing the Plantagenets, under whose rule 'domestic architecture advanced … not only for the nobles, but the citizens', urban 'dwelling-houses' featured 'richly-decorated ceilings … carvings and paintings on the walls, and … hangings', and ordinary people would worship in a church that was 'a very gallery of art, and well fitted to awaken artistic feeling', from its 'gorgeous altar plate' to its 'delicately enamelled' chalice, or from its 'jewelled pyx' to 'the altar books blazing with vermillion, and azure, and gold'.[62] Furthermore, as Benjamin Dabby argues, she finds in medieval art a direct connection between the progress of art and the 'commencement of England's commercial greatness'.[63] While 'art was cultivated, art manufactures improved also', she avers. Under the Plantagenets, 'the whole people became lovers of art' and art's 'great patrons': 'a willing people, undertook those noble works throughout the land, which the united wealth of monarch, prelates, and nobles, had without their help been inadequate to complete'.[64]

Lawrance was disappointed by the failure of the Great Exhibition, in its conception, organisation and content, to convey either the virtues of medieval British art or its modern relevance, and she found its Gothic displays 'piecemeal', chaotically organised and unhistorical. However, she was to find much more effective use made of Plantagenet culture six years later at the Manchester Art Treasures Exhibition, which was, importantly, she pointed out, a community-led initiative that was genuinely supported by the people of Lancashire for the public good, and was laudably 'intent upon connecting the beautiful with the useful'. In her review of the exhibition she invokes an earlier industrial exhibition held in Oldham in 1854, which had likewise taken the opportunity to demonstrate the connections between Britain's medieval art and contemporary applied arts and industrial innovations, praising it for its 'suggestive and educating influence'. Informed by 'sympathy with the past', the Art Treasures Exhibition included a large collection of medieval British artefacts of which, she wrote approvingly, 'sculpture … decorative furniture, – works in gold and other precious metals, – armour, – implements of chase, – musical instruments, – glass … china, delft, – tapestry, – antiquities, costume, may be given as leading examples'.[65]

The art of dress

When she herself wrote of 'fine arts', Lawrance explained, she used the phrase 'in its widest extent',[66] and it is undoubtedly the case that the Great

Exhibition, with its emphasis on the compatibility of art and industry, tended to broaden the signification of both terms, introducing categories such as 'ornamental industry' and 'imitative arts', and encouraging debate, as did the invention of photography, about the boundaries between the fine arts and other kinds of aesthetic expression.[67] William Whewell wrote of the 1851 Exhibition, housed within the vast single glass structure of the Crystal Palace, that it seemed to dissolve the laws of space and time: 'By annihilating the space which separates different nations, we produce a spectacle in which is also annihilated the time which separates one stage of a nation's progress from another.'[68] The great 'crystal shop' or 'glass bazaar', as *Punch* dubbed the Exhibition, unsettled the boundaries not only between nations, between past and present, between the fine and the applied arts, and between art and commodity, but also between viewer and spectacle.[69] The crowds of visitors were themselves behind glass, on display. *Chambers' Edinburgh Journal* exclaims at 'the gorgeous assemblage of objects of art – snow-white statues, brilliantly-coloured tapestries, golden vases, sparkling fountains, inscribed crimson flags, the sign-boards of nations – and last, not least, the streaming, the loitering, the sitting and standing crowds of well-dressed people from all quarters of the globe – all are felt to be beyond the reach of words'.[70] Many writers did, notwithstanding, endeavour to write about the overwhelming spectacle presented by this cornucopia of gorgeous art objects, including the well-dressed exhibition-goers, and women in particular analysed the art of dress displayed by their contemporaries as the modern counterpart of the various historical and multicultural costumes on display.

Perhaps the most notable of these commentators on women's dress at the Great Exhibition was the art historian Mary Merrifield, whose highly regarded books *The Art of Fresco Painting* (1846), *Original Treatises on the Arts of Painting* (1849) and *Practical Directions for Portrait Painting in Watercolours* (1851) had established her reputation as a formidable scholar with particular expertise in the painterly techniques of the Old Masters, especially as colourists. In 1854 she collected and reprinted in a single volume entitled *Dress as a Fine Art* a number of articles she had written for Sharpe's *London Magazine* and the *Art Journal*, some in direct response to the contemporary fashion on display at the Great Exhibition.[71] An essay 'On the Harmony of Colours in its application to Ladies' Dress' originally written for the *Art Journal*, for example, begins:

> One of the most important advantages of the Great Exhibition has been the comparison which it enabled us to make between our progress as a nation, and that of our continental neighbours, in those various useful and

> elegant arts which contribute so much to the comfort and enjoyment of life. In many branches of industry the English need not fear competition with any nation; in others we must admit our inferiority. Since the opening of the Exhibition, the public journals have abounded in censures on the arrangement of colours in the British department, which was said to be far inferior to that of the foreign contributors. It has also been asserted that the dress of the English ladies is, generally speaking, chargeable with the same defect. Our own impressions, and subsequent observation, induce us to think the charge is not without foundation. Colours, the most heterogeneous, are often assembled on the same person; and on the same figure may sometimes be seen all the hues of the peacock, without their harmony.[72]

Merrifield goes on to enumerate all the ways in which Englishwomen make mistakes in their dress, and fail to make an 'agreeable … impression on the spectator' by paying regard to the 'optical effect' of their colour selection. They choose the colour of their outfits with no regard to their complexion, for example, or their stature: 'How frequently … do we see the dimensions of a tall and *embonpoint* figure magnified to almost Brobdignagian proportions by a white dress, or a small woman reduced to Lilliputian size by a black dress!'[73] She notes that 'we English have always been more remarkable for our partiality to gay or glaring colours, than for our skill in adapting them to the person, or arranging them so as to be in harmony with each other', and invokes the history of British costume as proof that 'this remark applies to our ancestors as well as to ourselves'.[74] This is because, she observes, '[t]o many persons the law of the harmony of colours is a sealed book',[75] and so drawing on her vast fund of knowledge about the use of colour historically in the arts, as well as her understanding of modern scientific colour theory, she goes on to explain the principles of the harmony and contrast of colours, and then to apply them to dress.

Her focus here is on Caucasian women, she explains, on the grounds that 'our lords and masters have something better to do than to study the effects of colours on their complexions', and that an 'infinite variety of complexion … characterizes the white nations', whereas by contrast '[t]here is so little variation in the complexions of the individuals of the other races, and, moreover, so little probability that these pages should ever fall into the hands of the coloured races'.[76] She does, however, praise West Indians for their choice to wear brilliant colours, which the laws of colour and tone support, as evidence of their good taste, and comments that '[t]he partiality of the orientals for brilliant colours, and gold brocades and gauzes, such as we have seen in the Great Exhibition, and which are the produce of India and China, are in accordance with the same laws, and are in fact the most becoming colours these people could have selected', evidence likewise of 'the good taste displayed by the orientals as a class'.[77] Englishwomen, alas, pay insufficient attention to the laws of colour either in the sense of dressing to suit their complexions or with regard to 'harmony of arrangement', as she demonstrates by noting the colours on the dresses of the first six ladies she encounters at the Great Exhibition. 'The very thought' of some of the colour combinations she meets with 'sets one's teeth on edge', she reports, and she finds herself admiring most of all the sober dress of a Quaker woman, for the 'semi-neutral colours which they so generally adopt, are very becoming to the complexion', as portrait painters both past and present know so well.[78]

Merrifield turns to work by painters such as Parmigianino, Titian, Reynolds and Riedel for examples of becoming modes of wearing the hair, to Van Dyck for large sleeves, and to Lely, Kneller, Reynolds and Gainsborough for their distinctive use of costume. For an understanding of colour, she points out that 'there are in this country by Raphael, Titian, Paolo Veronese, and other great masters, paintings which reveal [the principles of harmony of colour] to an intelligent observer, and to which access is readily obtained by all who are willing to study them', and she herself illustrates her points 'by examples from pictures by the old masters; beginning with those in the National Gallery', including Andrea del Sarto, Sebastian del Piombo, and Van Dyck, and then moving to Continental galleries – a Titian in Brescia, a Veronese in Venice, some Bernardino Luinis in Milan.[79] Interestingly, in her *Practical Directions for Portrait Painting in Water-Colours* (1851) she writes about costume in art from another perspective, recommending to the amateur portraitist that they consult the paintings of the Old Masters in order to dress their subject in a way that will be aesthetically pleasing and will make the best of their attributes. 'With the present knowledge of art that pervades the wealthy classes', she notes, 'the painter will not frequently have to encounter strong contrasts of glaring colours, but as he will have to treat coloured draperies, it may not be amiss to refer to some of the pictures of Sir Joshua Reynolds and Vandyck, in order to show their arrangements of colours'.[80] And she recommends to the portraitist, as she does to women with regard to their dress, that they follow Van Dyck, Rubens, Rembrandt, Velázquez, Marillo, Correggio and other masters in placing white next to the skin of women and children.

An important aspect of Merrifield's approach to her subject, then, is her illustration of the scientific theories she elucidates with examples from historical and contemporary painters, and again this has the effect of eliding the differences between the art of dress and the fine arts, and reinforcing the claim made by the title of her 1854 collection that dress is, indeed, a fine art. Their identification is made explicit at the beginning of the book, when she distinguishes between art and artifice in the matter of costume: 'No deception is to be practised, no artifice employed, beyond that which is exercised by the painter, who arranges his subjects in the most pleasing forms, and who selects colours which harmonise with each other; and by the manufacturer, who studies pleasing combinations of lines and colours.'[81] Thereafter she constantly refers to artists to support her points: to the ripe female figures of Rubens; the uncovered bosoms of Van Dyck portraits; the flattering practice of placing white drapery between a woman's skin and her richly coloured bodice in portraits by Eastlake, Lehmann and Uwins; the figure-hugging laced-up bodice worn by the subject of *Titian's Mistress*; Etty's nudes, whose waistlines have been distorted by the wearing of tight-laced stays. Merrifield enters the debate about the issue of tight-lacing, and strategically makes use of it to address the fact that women are denied access to life classes, and therefore have no 'general knowledge of form, and of the principles of beauty as applied to the human frame'. She points out that '[t]he study of form on scientific principles, has hitherto been limited entirely to men; and if some women have attained this knowledge, it has been by their own unassisted efforts – that is to say, without the advantages which men derive from lectures and academical studies'. Through the medium of writing about dress, Merrifield takes the opportunity to comment that '[i]n this, as in other acquirements, the pursuit of knowledge, as regards women, is always attended with difficulties', and to urge, as other women did, that female students be allowed to attend life classes:

> While fully concurring in the propriety of having separate schools for male and female students, we do think that a knowledge of form may be communicated to all persons, and that a young woman will not make the worse wife, or mother, for understanding the economy of the human frame, and for having acquired the powers of appreciating its beauties. We fear that there are still some persons whose minds are so contracted as to think that, not only studies of this nature, but even the contemplation of undraped statuary, are contrary to the delicacy and purity of the female mind; but we are satisfied that the thinking part of the community will approve the course we recommend.[82]

A proper art education is advocated for women, but meanwhile she suggests to her female readers that the best way to acquire such knowledge of the human form as at least will enable them to appreciate the art of dress is through the contemplation of good pictures and sculpture, in the form of casts and engravings if they don't have access to original art works. Indeed, '[o]ne of these casts [of a female figure] ... should be found on the *toilette* of every young lady, who is desirous of obtaining a knowledge of the proportions and beauties of the figure', in order that she may understand the importance of symmetry, harmony and proportion, and see for herself that disproportionately small waists make her figure 'not only deformed, but positively ugly', so that 'tight-lacing will die a natural death'.[83]

Merrifield was not the only serious art historian to write about dress as a fine art, and nor was she the first to take the opportunity of an article on dress to address her readers on the subject of female education. Elizabeth Rigby (later Eastlake) published an anonymous review of three books on costume under the title 'The Art of Dress' in the *Quarterly Review* (1847), a piece that was reprinted in 1852 with a companion article on music as *Music and the Art of Dress*. Posing as a male writer, Rigby declares in her opening paragraph: 'For centuries we agreed that education was a dangerous thing for [woman] – only because we felt how much better use she would make of it than ourselves: and Milton taught his daughters to pronounce Greek and Latin, so that they might read the classics aloud for his pleasure, but forbade their understanding the meaning of a word for their own – for which he deserved to be blind.' By contrast, she observes, her anonymity conferring an additional degree of irony, '[n]ow, we not only make them welcome to help themselves to any of the fruits of science, or flowers of literature, as plentifully as they please, but are too happy, as all Editors and Publishers will testify, when we can prevail upon them to help us as well'. Rigby's review covers male as well as female dress, and she points out, in another defence of women, that 'whilst our poets, moralists, and clergy have been satirizing and denouncing the extravagancies and absurdities of female apparel, we have been flaunting and strutting away, under cover of our own fire, far more extravagant and absurd than they'; indeed, she adds, 'we cannot point to one single excess or caprice which has appeared on the beautiful person of woman, that has not had its counterpart, as bad or worse, upon thc ugly body of man'.[84]

With these preliminaries out of the way, Rigby embarks on the subject of her piece, the art of dress, stressing its crucial importance, particularly for women, for whom it becomes 'a sort of symbolical language – a kind of personal glossary – a species of body phrenology, the study of which it would be madness to neglect'; 'to a proficient in the science, every woman walks about with a placard on which her leading qualities are advertised'.[85] Like Merrifield, she turns to painters to illustrate her own views on women's dress, for '[t]he portrait-painter ... is after all the only real authority for the true spirit of a costume'.[86] Older women, for example, and likewise 'those ladies who, though not precisely in the yellow leaf, are somewhat on the turn', should model their style of dress on Holbein's portraits, for it 'is of all others the best adapted to secure an honourable retreat for waning charms', though he does also draw costumes that would grace a young woman as well: 'Holbein's pencil is as graceful [in his drawings of the head-dresses of Catherine Howard, Lady Audley and the Lady of Richmond] as if it had been guided by Eastlake', she notes, with a flattering and flirtatious compliment, under cover of anonymity, to the man she would marry a couple of years later.[87] Van Dyck preferred to paint younger women, she observes, or at least women wearing a style of dress more suited to youth – not always appropriately, and sometimes 'desperately out of season', with 'cheeks doubly painted, first by herself, and then by Vandyke'.[88] Sir Joshua Reynolds's painted 'excessively beautiful' costumes: 'We go through a gallery of his portraits with feelings of intense satisfaction, that there should have been a race of women who could dress so decorously, so intellectually, and withal so becomingly.' It is conceded that their costumes would not be very practical for modern women to adopt – they are not made for 'extraordinary movement' – but regretted that '[f]rom that time to this we consider there has not been a costume fit for a woman to wear'.[89]

Eastlake's historical survey ends with an attack on 'the unbecoming absurdities which fill the fashion books and encumber our walls'.[90] Naturally enough, this view of the aesthetic deficiencies of contemporary dress was not shared by the Victorian fashion industry, nor by the magazines that prided themselves on their fashion plates. Some women's magazines, indeed, were decidedly aspirational. The Editor of the *Ladies' Treasury*, for example, declared in 1860 that its fashion images, comparably with its architectural, landscape and portrait engravings, were 'executed, as we need scarcely remind our readers, in the highest style of art'.[91] Their primary business was to advise their female readers on the latest styles, and they invoke such cultural standards in order to appeal to a certain market. However, as the century wore on, and dress reform came to play a central role in the culture of Aestheticism, the lines between women's fashion pages and advice manuals on the one hand and, on the other, writing about the aesthetics of dress that was genuinely informed by a knowledge of histories and theories of art, became less easy to draw. Mary Elizabeth Haweis, author of books such as *The Art of Beauty* (1878) and *The Art of Dress* (1879), is a case in point. Talia Schaffer has noted a tension in her interesting attempt to bring Ruskinian theories of art to bear on dress, by insisting upon the importance of principles such as artistic truth, proportion, integrity and usefulness, between the high cultural critical influences she invokes and the journalistic fashion magazine style her writing espouses, a tension encapsulated by the fact that her first articles on fashion were published in both the *Art Magazine* and the *Queen*.[92] This does indeed make for an 'uneasy union', one that is not always wholly consistent or successful. Yet it is a fascinating instance of an experimental hybridised form of criticism that pushes at the boundaries of art writing, brings it to new readerships, and gives a feminine inflection to the mainstream cultural aesthetic propounded by men such as Ruskin, Morris and Charles Locke Eastlake.

In the final two decades of the century, writers such as Haweis and George Fleming (Constance Fletcher) continued to encourage women to learn how to dress by looking at paintings, as Merrifield and Rigby had recommended at mid-century. As Schaffer notes, 'Haweis told her readers to draw their sleeves and caps from Renaissance paintings', while 'Fleming asked her readers to imagine themselves as figures in a painting and dress themselves according to the rules of composition'.[93] Furthermore, in the pages of the more intellectual journals, attention is also given to the counter-influence of fashion upon art. 'The Wares of Autolycus', for example, comments wryly on the omnipresence of the crinoline in mid-nineteenth-century art: 'The illustrator of that time not only waited, as it were, upon the crinoline, enlarged his space to give it room, swept other things out of its way, and studied the repetitions of its decorations; he also introduced it where it had really no right to be. Never, in modern times, was a fashion treated with so grave a homage of anachronism, and so confessed to be a rule and law of the very being of woman, having not only present effect, but retrospective force as well.'[94] The jury is out on '[w]hether painters lead the fashions of the time, or guide them, or follow them', but the subtle reciprocities of art and dress are a subject of debate. For a contributor to the column writing in the following year 'there is undoubtedly a unanimity' between fashion and art, for example in the matter of colour:

> Time was when violets and purples in all their variety were rejected as rigidly inside as outside the studio … But as open-air painting became a commonplace of the schools, the violet tones came quietly back and the golden ebbed away … Woman, with usual intrepidity, ran up the violet ensign. She summarized what the painters were doing with their halfmeasures and hesitation for she simply trimmed herself with the strongest dyes that the chemical dye-vat could give her. Art was making two bites of a

> cherry. Not so fashion. With a purple velvet lily and a magenta rose you know precisely where you are. Meanwhile the painters were shedding a more and more diffused violet ray over their out-of-door work, their flesh, their whites, and their shadows; and they were not only painting in a violet manner, they were also painting violet things.

This writer's conclusion is that '[w]oman has made art dance to foolish tunes from time to time'.[95]

Modernity

In an article for the *Chautauquan* of 1892, Elizabeth Robins Pennell observes acerbically of an exhibition 'Les Arts de la Femme' that she attended in Paris, 'A walk around the galleries convinces the unbiased visitor that, throughout the ages, dress has been the one all-important thought of woman. But little that is shown does not relate immediately to costume.'[96] The aesthetics of dress is certainly a constant theme in 'The Wares' column at this time, as it was in Fenwick Miller's 'Ladies' Column' in the *Illustrated London News*, especially in the reportage of society events at the fashionable Grosvenor Gallery or the studios of celebrity painters. 'In Mrs Jopling's studio there were several dresses of such silk', enthuses Fenwick Miller, responding to the beautifully costumed female artists, themselves works of art on display, at one of her shows. 'Miss Alice Havers, the artist, had a costume of black silk broché in rounds with a short mantle of brown plush … Mrs Jopling herself had a charming costume of golden-brown plush.'[97] Wherever women are gathered at a public cultural event, the art of fashion is invoked alongside the other arts. One article, devoted to the 'parrot-coloured raiment' and brilliant lighting effects created by the choreographer and costume designer Miss Loie Fuller, celebrates her invention of 'a new science of clothes, not at all after Carlyle', and notes her colourful influence on women's fashion more broadly; another explores 'the philosophy of dress', and concludes that 'the prime consideration … in the art of dressing would appear to this rash enthusiast to be a proper community between the body and its raiment'.[98] Katharine Tynan is reported, in a speech at a dinner for female writers, to have 'made amends' for her 'tremendous opinions as to the superiority of Miss C. Rossetti to any male contemporary in poetry … by a most impulsive compliment to the show of beauty and of frocks'.[99] The femininity of the audience is emphasised here and in reviews of other arts events; indeed, the overwhelming impression in these pages is of women of all classes gathering for cultural occasions, whether gorgeously attired society ladies at the RA and Grosvenor shows, the '[n]umbers of smart women puzzl[ing] their pretty heads over Mr. Linley Sambourne's political cartoons at the Fine Art Society's Galleries on Saturday afternoon', or women of a lower class frequenting private views in the hope they will be served with free tea.[100]

But amidst such scenes of female sociability, mingling among the fashionable art set, the 'smart women puzzl[ing] their pretty heads' and the ladies in search of free tea at the exhibitions and galleries of late-nineteenth-century London and Paris, were the serious female art critics, eager to see the latest shows, their pencils sharpened to produce copy for the press, and ready to give an opinion on the new, or newly curated, art on display. Women such as Alice Meynell, Elizabeth Robins Pennell and a host of other sister journalists and critics were key figures in the formation of artistic taste at the *fin*.[101] They wrote about exhibitions of 'feminine' arts, to be sure – a show at the Royal School of Arts Needlework; an exhibition of cookery at the Portman Rooms; French pottery and Tiffany lamps at the Tiffany Studio; pottery and porcelain at the Paris Exposition[102] – but they also wrote about the industrial arts and about the fine arts, reviewing shows of new and recent work and reporting on the contemporary gallery and studio scene. If some focused on the art of the home, others took as their subject the art of the street. A review by Pennell of the first English exhibition of poster art, held at the Royal Aquarium in 1894, 'Posters in London', examines the new urban art form that has swept London, Paris, Germany and New York, and is the 'latest fad' among collectors, bringing to her analysis of 'modern methods of street decoration' her formidable knowledge of the fine arts as well as of 'the artistic treatment of the *affiche*'.[103]

They were eclectic in approach, receptive to all manner of artistic genres, and avowedly international, alert to what was happening in Continental Europe, the United States and beyond, with regard to both individual artists and artistic movements. Cecilia Waern, for example, wrote knowledgably about domestic, industrial and monumental public art. Author of a monograph on the art of the American painter and artist in glass John LaFarge, published in 1896, she had reviewed his work for the *Atlantic Monthly* the previous year, when he was invited to hold a one-man show at the Salon of the Champ de Mars. Remarking on the need for 'sympathy with and observation of things outside the narrow domain of critical formulas applied in art galleries', Waern locates LaFarge's glass work in relation to historical traditions of stained glass art, and writes sensitively about the Japanese paintings and the sketches and watercolours he produced during a year-long sojourn in the South Seas.[104] She also wrote on the newly completed decorative panels painted for the Boston Library by influential French artist Pierre Puvis de Chavannes, drawing on her knowledge of European fresco and mural painting to comment on the value and effect for the viewer of seeing such work in the location for which it was produced, rather than in a museum or gallery.[105]

Waern was similarly in touch with art closer to home, and wrote thoughtfully about the contemporary European art scene. Like a number of other female art critics of the time, such as Alice Meynell and Elizabeth Robins Pennell, she was interested in Impressionism, a term, she averred in an article of 1892 in the *Atlantic Monthly*, 'at present more discussed than understood'.[106] 'Some Notes on French Impressionism' proposes that what matters is 'the painter's manner of seeing things', because 'artists are the eyes or seers of the period in which they live, and our own vision is, consciously or unconsciously, influenced by theirs'.[107] Waern's understanding of how ways of seeing, though naturalised, are in fact culturally framed, even constructed and determined, strikes a very modern note. It is not, therefore, in her view, productive to try to resist modern movements in art; rather, we should seek to understand them. Indeed, '[t]he less we instinctively like their vision and presentment of life, the more it behooves us to examine impartially the principles that have guided them. We might otherwise run the risk of rejecting in theory that which is forcing itself upon us in practice.'[108] Waern is alert to these artists' understanding of 'the laws of optical effect'.[109] Among the various different styles of Impressionist art, she identifies one feature that is common to all: 'They aim at being the reproduction of one impression on the artist's eye, and through his eye on his mind; not of a set of collateral impressions fused into one.'[110] What all Impressionist artists have in common, for all their palpable differences, then, is 'the visual unity of their picture'. She goes on to explain how it is that their art 'is more likely to give you a broad, open-air impression, and to produce the illusion of looking at a real scene, than would a landscape painted by an artist who had allowed his eye to travel painfully from object to object', because '[i]t is well known that the eye cannot rest on two things simultaneously'.[111] It is their insistence on focus, on representing 'the unity of impression', reinforced by 'the influence of Japanese art and of instantaneous photography' – other art forms of the moment – that has produced among the Impressionists 'results that are characteristically modern', she argues, and that 'represent an almost immeasurable widening of the resources of Western art'.[112]

Critics such as Waern are thus attuned to the ways in which the radically new perspectives of art such as this are expressive of modernity.[113] She writes of one of Manet's small paintings of a horse race, 'I know of but few pictures that so appeal to the intensely modern feeling of collective sympathy.'[114] Impressionism does not make of painting 'merely another form of colored photography'; rather, it

> aims to reproduce, as nearly as possible, the same kind of physical impression on the spectator's eye that was produced on the eye of the artist by the object seen in nature; to make one immediate impression on our retina; to let it come in at once, as it were, through the front door, and, calmly or brightly, announce its presence. It is for us to say if it does so, and if there is enough, in the painter's vision, of the mystical essence called pictorial truth, or rather the truths that are apprehensible by the age in which we live.[115]

It is 'the age in which we live' that is captured by Impressionist art – its forms, its movements, its colours, its light, and its science. Waern writes about the modern optical theories and technical creeds that underpin the work of the pointillists and other luministes, for example. But she also captures the moment of Impressionism in a more personal and human way when she describes how her interest in Vincent Van Gogh, who in 1892 had recently committed suicide and whose work was only beginning to gain a reputation, took her to Gauguin's studio and Le Père Tanguy's art supplies shop in Montmartre. There she was able to view piles of canvases by Impressionist and Post-Impressionist painters and to talk at length to the modest figure who had done so much to support and promote their work. She gives no indication that she is aware of Van Gogh's portraits of Julien Tanguy, yet she herself clearly responds to her encounter with the man around whom a mythology was already forming ('No one knows what or where he eats; he sleeps in a closet among his oils and varnishes') in the intimacy of his shop, which exudes a powerful sense of the materiality of the art works and of the material conditions in which they were produced and circulated.[116] It is a glimpse into a picturesque corner of Montmartre that conjures the real confraternity of painters and dealers who make up a historically specific artistic community, an eyewitness account that adds texture, immediacy and authority to her formal analysis of Impressionism as an art-historical movement.

Vignettes such as this, like the many images and exhibition reviews and gallery pamphlets of the period, suggest how embedded women were in the contemporary art scene, how engaged they were with the newest work, and how nuanced their interpretations of it often were. Waern was one of a number of female critics who were receptive to Impressionism before it was widely appreciated in Britain. Alice Meynell, for example, wrote enthusiastically about Degas as early as 1882 as part of a series of articles on Impressionist art for the *Magazine of Art*, a decade before the exhibition of *L'Absinthe* in London's Grafton Gallery provoked such an outcry in the press, and she went on to become a supporter of the French-influenced Newlyn School.[117] In the same year George Fleming (Constance Fletcher) wrote the pamphlet for an exhibition of the Italian landscape painter and revolutionary Giovanni (Nino) Costa at the Fine Art Society, in which she is evidently familiar with Impressionist art, from which she distinguishes Costa's work.[118] A decade later, and contemporary with Waern, Elizabeth Robins Pennell is arguing that painters such as Degas, Manet, Whistler and, above all, Claude Monet, 'have revolutionized the art of painting in our day', and by the time she reviews the Impressionist exhibition at the Grafton Gallery in 1905, when 'even the British public … has got used to seeing their work, and is therefore no longer scandalized, much as it may still disapprove', Impressionism has become, in a retrospective view, 'one of the most interesting and defiant phases in the art of the last century'.[119]

As this summative assessment of nineteenth-century art might suggest, one of the reasons why women were inclined to regard Impressionism sympathetically was because of its defiance of the art establishment, and its exclusion from the Academy. It was their anti-academic stance that drew women like Pennell to certain groups and movements within British art too. In an article she wrote titled 'Art in the Victorian Era' for the *Nation* in 1897, on the occasion of Queen Victoria's Diamond Jubilee and its associated exhibitions, it is the Pre-Raphaelites she praises for their part in 'the revolt against Victorian vulgarity', against, that is, 'the vulgarizing of art, with full Academical authority, that was the most discouraging feature of the time, as we look back to it':

> For theirs was a revolt as truly as the Romantic movement, some twenty years earlier, had been in France. Ruskin, the prophet, Madox Brown, the master, and Rossetti, Millais and Holman Hunt, the brave crusaders, threw down the gauntlet no less boldly, no less uncompromisingly, than the young men of the *Cénacle*, when they rallied around the red waistcoat of Gautier on that famous night at the Théâtre-Français.[120]

Because of 'the rebellion, the reaction' of Pre-Raphaelitism, and the impetus it gave for renovation across the arts (including house decoration, which was 'almost revolutionized, thanks to the Pre-Raphaelite firm of Morris, Marshall, Falkner & Co'), Pennell concludes that '[a]ltogether the second period of the Victorian era was as promising as the first had been discouraging'.[121] But the potential she sees for a regeneration of British art is, decidedly, no thanks to the art establishment. According to Pennell, 'The Academy – the official representative of art – raises no higher standard in 1897 than it did in 1837. At the National Gallery today, as years ago when it was first exhibited at Burlington House, Mr. Frith's "Derby Day" is the picture that holds the crowd.' 'On the whole', she avers, 'conditions are healthier than when the Eggs and the Landseers and the Eastlakes were accepted as masters.' But the Academy cannot take credit for this:

> For this improvement, to be sure, you need not look to the Academy, forced to open its doors to distinguished foreigners like Mr. Sargent and Mr. Abbey, forced to recognize sculptors of the eminence of Mr. Gilbert and Mr. Ford. The Academy has never yet, until it could not help itself, extended its approbation or sympathy to the genuine movements, the vigorous pronouncements of the younger men. To its shame be it said, it has remained at a standstill, while the art of England has progressed.[122]

It was not only younger men who were excluded from the Royal Academy, of course. Although two female painters, Angelica Kauffmann and Mary Moser, were among its founding members in 1768, since that time no women had been made Academicians, and it would not be until 1922 that the first female painter, Annie Swynnerton, would be elected as an Associate. Furthermore, women had been denied access to the Royal Academy Schools until the 1860s, when a handful of women were permitted to enrol as students, although they were not granted access to life-drawing classes until 1893, despite the interventions of women such as Meynell, Emilia Dilke, Fenwick Miller and Pennell.[123] Its exclusion of women was undoubtedly one reason for the hostility expressed by many female critics towards the Royal Academy in this period. For example, an article on Mary Moser's painting published in 'The Wares of Autolycus' in 1895 takes the opportunity to comment on the broader topic of women as artists, their place in the profession, and their exclusion in the nineteenth century from the Academy. Moser's artistic achievement is judged in light of the tastes of her day:

> when Mary Moser began to paint from nature she was breaking with a tradition that must have added sensibly to the distress of nations. What she did was done as her companions and contemporaries did it, and held that it should be done; it was not done to astonish Georgian Kings and Queens and Deans with the resources of feminine ingenuity. It took its place in her time. Sir Joshua Reynolds praised it. It was tried by the common rule. To us today, as it is to be seen in the Diploma Gallery at Burlington House, it does not seem conspicuously good, but Mary Moser may still prefer to please her age than to please ours.

The article concludes with some remarks on the gender politics of the art world, then and now, and a direct swipe at the modern-day Royal Academy:

> If she was flattered, if her sex made her success somewhat more salient than it might have been if achieved by a man, and so helped her to her membership too easily, the Royal Academy cannot be too warmly congratulated on the thoroughness of its repentance. Nothing that a woman will paint can make her an Academician in this century. It is not a question of merit, inasmuch as the bar is candidly confessed beforehand. So set up, that bar is, it may be worth noting, entirely illegal.[124]

In a 'Wares of Autolycus' column published in the previous year, Alice Meynell had similarly questioned the legality of the Academy's position on women, drawing obliquely on her sister the painter Elizabeth Butler's experience of exclusion:

> when one woman was very near getting the honours … the question was whether the Royal Academy should or should not be 'altered' to allow for her election. It is, however, to make the present custom of exclusion legal that the laws would have to be altered … the Royal Academy might put itself into order by a law incapacitating for membership all painters who are women, or all painters having blue eyes, or all painters, say, born in Kent. One non-artistic and non-technical exclusion will be as reasonable as another.[125]

Florence Fenwick Miller was to reiterate, as part of a sustained public campaign against women's exclusion, Meynell's point that George III's conferral of a Royal Charter upon a founding membership that included two female painters meant that it was not illegal for women to be elected to the Royal Academy. Throughout the 1890s and into the twentieth century she argued vigorously that women such as Elizabeth Butler, and also Henrietta Rae, Clara Montalba, Louise Jopling, Lucy Kemp-Welch, Marianne Stokes and Helen Allingham, were artists of a calibre to be elected Academicians. In 1910, she was still asking: 'When will there be a woman artist RA I wonder?'[126]

As if to compensate for this systematic exclusion from the Academy, female critics writing throughout the Victorian period made it their business to ensure that women were not also excluded from the art-historical canon by celebrating the achievements of both historical and contemporary women in the arts. As we saw in the last chapter, Anna Jameson had contemplated writing a study of female artists, and in the event devoted a section of *Visits and Sketches at Home and Abroad* (1834) to a discussion of women painters.[127] Reviewing *Modern Painters* in the 1850s, Hannah

Lawrance criticised Ruskin for his failure to acknowledge the role of both sexes, and all classes, in the production of beautiful and useful art, arguing that since the Middle Ages, 'from the noble even to the peasant', artistic progress had involved a collaboration between the sexes.[128] In an article of 1870, on 'The Education and Employment of Women', she claimed that women in her own times, like their ancestors, held 'precisely the same position as men' in 'the two highest departments of intellectual exertion – literature and the arts'.[129]

By this time Elizabeth F. Ellet had published an entire volume on the history of women's art. However, *Women Artists in All Ages and Countries* (1859) makes no attempt, by its author's own admission, 'to give elaborate critiques or a connected history of art'; rather, 'The aim has been simply to show what woman has done, with the general conditions favourable or unfavourable to her efforts, and to give some impressions of the character of each distinguished artist as may be derived from a faithful record of her personal experiences.'[130] For the reviewer of the book in the *Athenaeum*, this renders her study of little value: 'Her notices are scarcely at all critical; they run through the centuries, between long piles of local and ephemeral reputations, with now and then a bright name upon the roll, and the female artists in the category are presented, with rare exceptions, upon one level of frigid and formal excellence.'[131] Though 'floating down the current which has set in from the intellect-of-women point of view', Ellet is no feminist. While acknowledging that modern women have greater freedom and improved education and professional opportunities than ever before that 'have encouraged the advancement of women as artists beyond any point reached in preceding ages', she dissociates herself from contemporary supporters of 'the so-called "emancipation" which would urge [woman] into a course against nature, and contrary to the gentleness and modesty of her sex'. She writes about a sample of nineteenth-century women artists: about David's female pupils, for example, among them Constance Marie Charpentier and Angélique Mongez; about Regnault's students, including Madame Anzon and Sophie Guillemard; and cites women such as Constance Mayer, Madame Elie and Philiberte Ledoux, who painted in the manner of Greuze.[132] However, they are lucky if they get a sentence each of bland description, and it was not until Ellen C. Clayton published *English Female Artists* in 1876 that a more comprehensive account of the history of women's art in England appeared.

Clayton bluntly observes: 'Our native painters … have left but faintly impressed footprints on the sands of time. They do not glitter in the splendor of renown, like their sisters of the pen or of the buskin.'[133] Presumably because of the paucity of women artists in England, Clayton devotes some space in her history of *English Female Artists* to women who are 'unfortunately not Englishwomen', such as Susannah Homebolt, Lavinia Teerlinck and Artemisia Gentileschi,[134] but she writes about a good range of English artists active in the nineteenth century, and her book remains useful as a reference book, even though it does not discuss the art itself in any depth. Clayton does attempt to address the question of why England has historically produced so few women artists. She accounts for their absence before the reign of Henry VIII by the fact that '[i]n those rough, rude ages, females could not work beyond the boundaries of their homes, or the walls of their convent'. Furthermore, '[t]he more needy class were not sufficiently educated to be capable of any description of art workmanship'.[135] She was to be somewhat more caustic about the ideological forces that militate against women's ambitions in a volume on *Female Warriors* published three years later:

> Whisper it not in Gath that a woman should dare ever to transgress the lines laid down by Popular Prejudice. A woman is a subordinate accident in creation, quite an afterthought, a supplementary notion, a postscript … Man (though he is permitted to include in his superb all-comprehensive identity, woman) is big, strong, noble, intellectual: a Being. Woman is small, weak, seldom noble, and ought not to be conscious of the significance of the word Intellectual … If it be proved by hard facts that woman is not a poor, weak creature, then she must be reprimanded as being masculine. To brand a woman as being masculine, is supposed to be quite sufficient to drive her cowering back to her 'broidery-frame and her lute.[136]

By the end of the century, women critics were attempting more serious analysis of the work of female practitioners in terms of their negotiation of gender issues. Helen Zimmern, for example, wrote an article in 1900, 'The Work of Miss Bessie Potter', for the *Magazine of Art* in which she describes the Chicago-based sculptor as 'mainly a woman's sculptor', noting: 'She finds her subjects in American modern women, those nervous, highly-strung, excitable products of a virile people which is made up of all races and all climes.' Zimmern characterises sculpture as a 'masculine' art, but attributes Potter's particular skill to her female identity. Discussing her sculpture entitled 'Young Mother', for example, Zimmern describes how '[t]he young sculptor has caught to perfection the tone and atmosphere which is most attractive, and herein she turns to advantage her sex, with its fine sensibilities. Yet rarely under her hands does a figure lose in strength or force, as is almost universally the case with women sculptors who are apt to fall short in this masculine art.'[137] Meynell wrote in a similar vein, often anonymously, about her sister Elizabeth Butler's work in another masculine-identified genre, that of battle painting, though she also celebrated the 'feminine' art practice of Laura Alma-Tadema, bringing her own authority as a female critic to her assessment of the artist's womanly themes and style.[138] Likewise Fenwick Miller praised the 'masculine' realism of celebrity *animalière* Rosa Bonheur, whose painting *The Horse Fair* had caused a sensation when it was exhibited in London in 1855, equally with the fashionable femininity of both the art and the person of Louise Jopling.[139] A reviewer of the Women's Building, part of the 1893 Chicago World's Fair, praised the mural decoration of the vestibule, dedicated to the representation of women's work, for showing that 'women may be masters of art, and can treat strong subjects successfully, as well as men', singling out Annie Swynnerton's depiction of Florence Nightingale in the Crimea for showing 'how strong women's art can be in colour, design, and sentiment'.[140]

If it was still rare for individual women artists to have entire articles devoted to their work, by the 1890s they were standardly included in reviews of group exhibitions, although even so in mixed shows the main focus is often on the male artists. Were there not space constraints, Waern says in 'Some Notes on French Impressionism', she 'should delight to linger … on Miss Mary Cassatt's truly womanly studies of mothers and children, or felicitous, free translations of the exquisite synthetic art of the Japanese'.[141] Pennell did not generally make a point of giving special attention to female artists, but even she writes about paintings exhibited by Mrs Stanhope Forbes and Mrs Alma-Tadema in the spring shows at the Royal Academy and the New Gallery in 1892, and she ends her review of the 1905 Impressionist show at the Grafton Gallery with an only slightly qualified endorsement of the work of Berthe Morisot:

> As for Madame Morisot, as now seen, she calls for little reserve in one's tribute to her. She places a model before the mirror at a not very interesting moment of the toilet, or a sitter doing nothing at all in a garden, and her color is so delicate, her values so right, that one sees only the tender harmony of grays or pale golds. And if her little marines point without mistake to their origin in Manet, they are the work of an intelligent pupil. Few other women who have ventured to practice an art from which their sex seems to disqualify them, can approach her.[142]

Pennell does not here venture an explanation for why it is that women are disqualified by their sex from becoming eminent artists, but elsewhere she suggests that many women seem merely to 'play with an art or profession to which men devote their lives. They dabble a little in paint, and then hope to compete with men who have studied for years.' She relates how a female student at the Royal Academy Schools won a prize for design, and was commissioned to decorate the dining hall at Girton, but gave up 'because of the labor it would entail'.[143] Pennell returns to the puzzling question of '[w]hy the woman artist has been rare' in a summative article entitled 'Art and Women', written unusually under her own name, and her last for the *Nation,* published in 1918.[144] The question is puzzling because, in her view, 'the hindrances to her path certainly have been less' than for, say, female physicians and lawyers. Women 'were not banished in the past from the studio and the workshop, where, no doubt, a training would have been theirs had their genius imperatively called for it'. The problem seems to be that such genius is conspicuously lacking in womankind: 'from the Louvre to the Uffizi, from the Prado to the Rijks, you may look in vain for a woman to rival Velásquez as portrait painter, or Tintoretto as decorator, or Michelangelo as sculptor, or Rembrandt as etcher – or rather, you may look in vain for almost any woman at all'. Nor were women interdicted from practising art: 'Indeed, when the ladylike virtues were most at a premium, art was never included among the unladylike vices. To dabble in paint was a polite accomplishment for the ladies', and presumably, she argues, other women would have had the chance, like Mary Moser and Angelica Kauffmann, to adopt art as a profession, had they had a modicum of talent. Yet with the exception of Madame Vigée Le Brun no comparable artists presented themselves until Rosa Bonheur and then Berthe Morisot and Mary Cassatt came along. Bonheur she describes as 'a woman of unusually masculine physique and temperament', with 'something of … virility … in her work'; Morisot, as a good student of Impressionism, who produced work that was 'a re-echo of the right thing intelligently understood', but without originality; Cassatt, as 'the disciple, not the prophet' of Impressionism, but 'an artist in all she does, and a fine craftsman', who, Pennell notes approvingly, 'works as a man works'.

Cassatt was born in 1844, and was active in the later nineteenth century. Surveying the changes that have taken place in her lifetime, Pennell is struck by what a revolution there has been for female artists over that period:

> When she began to work, women artists were few. Now they are numbered by the hundreds, by the thousands. The schools everywhere are as open to them as to men. They can brave the Latin Quarter without danger to their reputation. American scholarships send them to Paris … Societies of women artists are many; so are their exhibitions. The Salons of Paris, the Academy, the International, and other galleries of London welcome the work of women on their walls.

However, even with all this, and the obvious barriers removed, 'the world still waits for the woman genius'. In sum: 'In the past hardly any women adopted art as a profession. During the last fifty years or so, they have rushed into art in crowds. And art is as unchanged by their rush as it was by their indifference.' Pennell confesses to be baffled by the fact that women have accomplished so little in art, and ends her article on the bleak note: 'the reason, when it is understood, may explain our true limitations as women better than any theory hitherto offered by the student of sex'.[145]

If the experience of female artists had changed as radically as Pennell suggests in the last half of the nineteenth century, so had that of women entering the professions of art history and critical journalism over the same period. No longer was it a matter of a few intrepid women like Anna Jameson and Elizabeth Eastlake raising their voices to question Ruskin's hegemonic catechism (Pennell had pronounced in 1892 'Ruskin's teachings are already obsolete, save in the provinces'); rather, women took their place alongside men – if not equally, no longer separately – in a critical community that had become vastly expanded and democratised by the transformative power of the mass media. Pennell's article 'Art and Women' appeared in 1918, and already the nineteenth-century world she retrospectively surveyed must have felt very distant. The Great War, then in its final months, had brought about decisive changes in the gender order. Around 8.4 million women gained the vote in 1918, and female candidates could for the first time seek election. However, for Virginia Woolf, the really decisive shift that separated her own generation from that of her Victorian parents, the moment when, as she momentously put it, 'human character changed', had taken place nearly a decade earlier, 'on or about December 1910'.[146] And the cultural watershed to which she refers had nothing to do with general elections or female suffrage: it was an art exhibition – specifically, the first Post-Impressionist show, organised by her friend the artist and art critic Roger Fry – an exhibition whose significance in modern cultural history has been in part determined by the critical essay a female writer wove around it in 1923. It would be another fifty years before second-wave feminism would review the history and historiography of art from a perspective newly sharpened by the Women's Movement, but the wide range of art literature discussed in this study demonstrates that Victorian art historians and critics were giving serious attention to the place of women in, and their absences from, that history, and to the question posed by Linda Nochlin in 1971, 'Why Have There Been No Great Women Artists?', long before they were the subject of modern critical debate.[147]

Conclusion

The decision to limit the subject of this book to women was a conscious one. I chose to write about female art historians and critics, rather than about nineteenth-century art writing as a whole. By segregating the work of women, it may be argued that I have unfairly denied them a place in the mainstream, almost as egregiously as those cultural historians who have ignored them altogether. The most enlightened of the Victorian women who are my subject would likely deplore my decision on the grounds that women whose work is good need no special pleading. Harriet Grote, Elizabeth Eastlake and Jenny Lind founded the Society of Female Artists in 1855 because women painters were not taken seriously and had difficulty in finding professional training and exhibiting their work publicly. But art historians such as Hannah Lawrance had misgivings. She praised the Society's founders for their initiative, but maintained that it was always better for women to exhibit alongside men; establishing an association 'exclusively for themselves', she said, was to risk marginalisation.[1] And other women critics and artists shared her view. Alice Meynell and her sister Elizabeth Butler appreciated the value of female networks, but neither favoured all-women exhibitions.[2] Florence Fenwick Miller, like Meynell, would review only mixed shows, because segregated exhibitions of lady artists were often of such low quality that they harmed the reputation of women artists as a whole: 'We all know that the feeble, commonplace, timid work that is on the whole what is shown there does not represent in fact the attainment of women in art, yet we cannot clear our judgment of the illusion and the third rate shows give an impression that women's work is inevitably third rate.'[3] Like George Eliot in her review essay 'Silly Novels by Lady Novelists' (1856), Miller argued that women were their own worst enemies: tolerating and condoning poor-quality work by women practitioners tainted the reputation of their whole sex. 'There is no sex in art', she declared.[4] Pennell was blunter still in her rejection of the aims of the Society for Women Artists, as it was called by the end of the century: 'If women are painters, well and good. But let them take their chances accordingly, and not with clamorous reminders that they are women after all, and therefore to be treated with the tenderness and chivalry due to their sex.' She concludes, rather brutally: 'If they cannot paint, they should not exhibit.'[5]

By the same token, I might ask if the female critics whose work I have curated in this all-women book should have been allowed to take their chances in a mixed collection. A number of them, after all, have had one-woman retrospectives in the form of dedicated monographs that testify to their currency and growing reputations in the twenty-first century. Anna Jameson, Emilia Dilke, Elizabeth Eastlake, Alice Meynell and Vernon Lee are now acknowledged as major contributors to the Victorian art world, and others such as Michael Field are acclaimed for an oeuvre that includes their writing about art. So does my decision to hive these women off into a group defined by their sex legitimise claims that their work was not as good or as important as that of their male peers? That they were not truly integrated in the professional field? Does it re-inscribe a Victorian gender binary about which enlightened Victorian women were themselves sceptical?

My reasons for treating female art critics as a discrete category are threefold. First, it is clear that these women themselves valued their female professional networks and genealogies, and consciously fashioned gendered identities as professional writers, and I have wished to capture this in my own analysis. Second, focusing on female critics has enabled me to identify patterns within women's writing about art that may be invisible when looking at either the full range of art literature or at the work of a single author. The systemic institutional and personal constraints imposed upon women, for example, and their strategies for overcoming or circumventing them become clearer when they are considered as a professional group. And finally, the fact that women have been omitted from most accounts of the nineteenth-century art world means they now need to be highlighted in terms of their gender if they are to take their rightful place in future histories. In the associated field of Victorian art, Jan Marsh and Pamela Gerrish Nunn curated a pioneering exhibition of Pre-Raphaelite women artists in 1998. Their aim was to correct the impression left by the 1984 Pre-Raphaelite blockbuster at the Tate Gallery that there were none. A consequence of the 1998 exhibition and of other feminist interventions is that the Tate's 2012 Pre-Raphaelite show stresses the importance of female practitioners.[6] It is my belief that the sisterhood of Victorian critics benefits from a similarly separatist approach, not because they cannot stand up alongside their male peers, but because they have been for too long invisible. They need to be newly understood by a new generation.

The project of feminism, in art history as well as in other fields, is only in part a recuperative one, involving the recovery of neglected women. More importantly, it challenges us to think about representation, and about the social and political functions of culture. In this respect, it seems crucial to reflect on what women had to say about art in a period when art criticism had an unprecedentedly important role in public discourse and the formation of cultural values. When Oscar Wilde's character Gilbert announces in 'The Critic as Artist' in 1890 that '[i]t is to criticism that the future belongs', and imagines an 'educational system' which would 'try and develop in the mind a more subtle quality of apprehension and discernment', he is summing up the Victorian belief that it is imperative to engage critically with the arts.[7] This is a critical ethos that women helped to create. Wilde envisages the development of a whole academic discipline, and it is only fair that the formative role of women in its foundation should be acknowledged and understood, rather than ridiculed or diminished.

I have argued against the perception of some twentieth-century feminist art historians that their Victorian predecessors were, at a formative moment for the academic discipline and the profession, complicit in the creation of an almost exclusively masculine canon. It is my contention that in formal art histories as well as in other genres of Victorian writing (the novel, translations, guidebooks, poetry, journalism) there are many examples of feminist interventions in debates about art. At a historical moment when neither the profession nor the discipline were fully defined, women took the chance to be undisciplined. They exploited the ambiguous terrain of the middlebrow and they seized the opportunity to have a role in the establishment of the highest academic and professional standards. To banish these women from the critical canon would be as significant an omission as to leave out female practitioners from the canon of art itself.

As I hope this study will have made clear, I have no wish to suggest that there were categorical differences between the way men and women looked at or wrote about art in the nineteenth century. I have instead sought to explore the historical conditions in which women experienced and represented art, the differences between women, and how such factors shaped, and were shaped by, both gender and genre. As Joan Scott has argued, it is incumbent upon historians of women to attend to the 'changing, and often radically different, historical contexts within which women as subjects came into being', to recognise that 'collective identities are invented as part of some effort of political mobilisation', to think about 'how identity was established, how women with vastly different agendas identified with one another across time and social positions', and to try to explain '[w]hat were the mechanisms of such collective and retrospective identification'.[8]

Looking at art, I suggest, and writing about art – about the experience of looking at pictures, about visual aesthetics and about art's histories – is highly gendered, often in very complex ways. My subjects include a number of women whose identities were consciously self-fashioned. Some dressed in mannish clothes and wore their hair cropped, some assumed a male name, some a male voice – not unusual in the nineteenth century. But I have endeavoured nevertheless to explore, with some historical and textual specificity, the mechanisms by which they identified collectively and retrospectively as and with women. I have attempted to think about the extent to which, for all their differences in class, sexuality, education and intellect, they looked like (they saw, and were seen, as) women.

I am interested in the connections between the stories these women told about themselves, and their engagement with art and the material and cultural circumstances in which they wrote. I am specifically concerned with how their writing about art was culturally mediated. Women had to negotiate significant social, intellectual and institutional barriers to become professional writers, and it seems to me important to assess their work in light of the discursive constraints upon what they were able to say. I have concentrated on how women critics approached and mediated the work of canonical or near-canonical painters, but I have also considered their writing about contemporary art practice and new art forms, as well as their development of new, and often gendered, critical categories. The women I have considered may not, as Deborah Cherry and others observe, have been all that interested in writing about women artists (although, as we have seen, some were); but their writing, their historiography, and their ways of seeing and of theorising vision are often extraordinarily imaginative and adventurous in ways that, as I have tried to suggest, may be linked to their gender. They thus gave both women and men new models for looking at and writing about art that have provided a foundation for modern ways of seeing and understanding art and its histories.

In 'Inapprehensiveness', one of the last poems he wrote before his death in 1889, Robert Browning has his male and female characters invoke John Ruskin and Vernon Lee as a way of commenting ironically on sexual difference, and on how things look to men and to women.[9] The poem begins with the male speaker and his female companion standing 'simply friend-like side by side / Viewing a twilight country' in an apparently shared gaze. But the woman '[breaks] silence', asserting her desire to control the field of vision, wishing she had her perspective glass. Such optical devices are, as Jonathan Crary reminds us, 'sites of both knowledge and power that operate directly on the body of the individual',[10] and the perspective glass here signifies the woman's wish to define and control her position vis-à-vis not only the view but also her companion. Meanwhile the 'unnoticed' man by her side, desperate for her 'regard', 'needing but a look', wills her to break her 'inapprehensive stare', silently imploring her, 'let your eyes meet mine'. But the woman continues actively to look, taking pleasure in her gaze, insisting upon her role as observer. She utterly confounds the specular status her companion wishes to confer upon her, by refusing to be the willing object of his fantasising and coercive gaze. The view reminds her of something she has read – 'not', she thinks, 'by Ruskin' – in response to which the disgruntled male speaker caustically offers at the end of the poem the suggestion that the name she is searching for is perhaps Vernon Lee (its placement as the poem's final words gives it particular weight). The invocation of Ruskin and Vernon Lee allows us to locate the poem within the larger frame of the sexual politics of spectatorship, and underlines the different, indeed competing, viewing positions of masculinity and femininity within the modern ocular field.

Fifteen years later, in a 'Postscript on Ruskin' that may also suggest a postscript to my book, Vernon Lee wrote a warmly celebratory commemorative article on Ruskin's work and his legacy to the modern world. In it, she commends his 'many-sided genius'. She acknowledges her own indebtedness to him, not least for the ways he taught her, and a whole generation, how to look at art, and to understand that 'art was sprung from daily life and fit for daily life's consumption'.[11] It is a piece that also flags up their differences, though – differences that are, interestingly, cast as generational rather than sexual. Ruskin was, in her view, hampered rather than enabled by his faith: 'alas, the universe of Ruskin is (despite its singing streams and rejoicing mountains) inert, mechanical; a dead weight lugged about by a personal (and on the whole inefficient) creator, and requiring to be poked and scolded by Ruskin himself'.[12] His particular religious cosmology was 'foisted on him by the past', and is not, Lee predicts, what will survive for future generations; nor will his dogmatic taxonomy of art. 'Ruskin's deliberate intention was to place Turner above Claude, Gothic above Renaissance, the Middle Ages above modern times, hand labor above machinery, Protestantism above Catholicism, and Biblical interpretation above scientific'; but, she argues, 'this programme matters little and soon will matter not [at] all'. Rather, it is the broad tenor of his writings, through which '[h]e has shown us art, history, nature, enlarged, transformed and glorified through the loving energy of his spirit', that will endure.[13]

Lee writes as Ruskin's disciple, but also as his peer. Her express purpose is to sum up his achievement and his intellectual legacy, to encourage after-comers to read his work. She draws a sharp distinction between Ruskin's contemporaries, who tolerated 'the system of symbolical metaphysics and dogmatic morals' in which he set his aesthetic intuitions 'with so tedious an ingenuity', and 'our modern habits of thought', which have no patience for 'this artificial framework'.[14] She points out that '"modern" meant for Ruskin, not our latter-day habits of mind … but the mental habits … of the second and third quarters of the nineteenth century; of that period of chaotic materialism, of hand to mouth ruthless egoism, against which not only Carlyle came to protest, but Karl Marx also'.[15] Lee addresses herself in particular to her younger readers because, she says, she is convinced that, 'far-spreading as was his influence on his immediate contemporaries, and large as is the debt (though often second-hand and unacknowledged) due to him by the following generation, the very best of Ruskin's efficacy can be expected in the future'.[16]

What is striking as we read her words over a century later is, first, that she was right in her assessment of what it was that future generations would value in Ruskin's work; and, second, that the woman who wrote with such authority and insight about his legacy for future generations would herself sink into undeserved obscurity for much of the twentieth century. A portrait of Vernon Lee by her childhood friend John Singer Sargent (Fig. 18) represents her as a voracious observer. Her spectacles mark out the circumference of her gaze and frame her wide-awake eyes, seeming to signify not myopia but, paradoxically, her capacity to see. Many visitors to Tate Britain, who could readily identify the subject of Charles Fairfax Murray's 1875 portrait of John Ruskin, won't recognise this woman with the penetrating eyes (so unlike Sargent's more familiar society portraits of beautiful, fashionably dressed women). The caption tells the modern viewer that Vernon Lee, who bequeathed the portrait to the

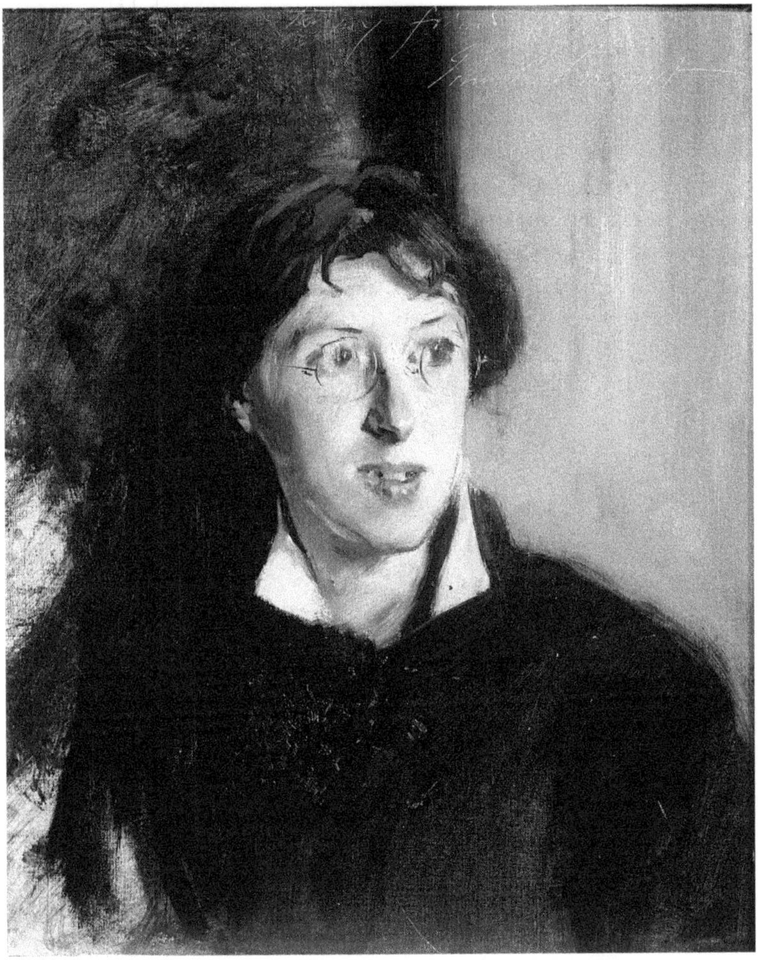

Fig. 18. John Singer Sargent, *Vernon Lee* (1881)

Tate Gallery at her death in 1935, 'was the pseudonym of the writer Violet Paget (1856–1935), best known for her books on Italian Renaissance art'. In this study I have tried to restore those books, and the hundreds of books, articles, poems, novels, guidebooks and catalogues by other women who wrote about art in the nineteenth century, to our picture of the Victorian art scene. In her own attempt to 'try to bring [modern readers] back to a study of Ruskin', Vernon Lee distinguished between what was essential in his work and what was ephemerally of its time. I have followed the same approach in regard to Lee herself and to my other female subjects. I hope the book I have written will demonstrate that Victorian women wrote compellingly about their engagement with visual culture. I hope it will show that they made significant and enduring contributions to the historiography of art; and that Ruskin and Pater, marvellous though they were, were not the only voices making themselves heard in the nineteenth-century art world. Indeed, I suggest they can only be understood now in the context of a broader public discourse on art that is acknowledged to have included women.

Notes

Introduction

1 Bernard Berenson Archive. MS Letters between the Berensons and Katharine Bradley and Edith Cooper. Villa I Tatti, Florence (Venice, 11 October 1893).

2 Quoted in Alison Brown, 'Vernon Lee and the Renaissance: From Burckhardt to Berenson', *Victorian and Edwardian Responses to the Italian Renaissance*, ed. John Easton Law and Lene Østermark-Johansen. Aldershot, Hants.: Ashgate, 2005, p. 197.

3 Harold I. Shapiro, *Ruskin in Italy: Letters to his Parents 1845*. Oxford: Clarendon, 1972, pp. 215–16.

4 See A. M. Holcomb, 'Anna Jameson: The First Professional English Art Historian', *Art History* 6 (1983): 171–87 (178).

5 See Rachel Teukolsky's excellent book, *The Literate Eye: Victorian Art Writing and Modernist Aesthetics*. Oxford and New York: Oxford University Press, 2009, pp. 3ff.; and John Paul M. Kanwit, *Victorian Art Criticism and the Woman Writer*. Columbus: Ohio State University Press, 2013, pp. 2–3, 11–30.

6 Notable exceptions are Claire Richter Sherman with Adele M. Holcomb, ed., *Women as Interpreters of the Visual Arts, 1820–1979*. Westport, Conn., and London: Greenwood, 1981; Pamela Gerrish Nunn, 'Critically Speaking', *Women in the Victorian Art World*, ed. Clarissa Campbell Orr. Manchester University Press, 1995, pp. 107–24; Meaghan Clarke, *Critical Voices: Women and Art Criticism in Britain 1880–1905*. Aldershot, Hants.: Ashgate, 2005; and Kanwit, *Victorian Art Criticism and the Woman Writer*, 2013. There is a growing body of work on the art-historical writing of individual women such as Vernon Lee. See, for example, recent articles in *Victorian Studies*: Stefano Evangelista, 'Vernon Lee in the Vatican: The Uneasy Alliance of Aestheticism and Archaeology', 52, 1 (Autumn 2009): 31–41; Jonah Siegel, 'The Material of Form: Vernon Lee at the Vatican and Out of It', 55, 2 (Winter 2013): 189–201; Athena Vrettos, '"In the clothes of dead people": Vernon Lee and Ancestral Memory', 55, 2 (Winter 2013): 202–11.

7 Deborah Cherry, *Painting Women: Victorian Women Artists*. London: Routledge, 1993, p. 116.

8 Martin Jay, 'Scopic Regimes of Modernity', in *Vision and Visuality*, ed. Hal Foster. Seattle: Bay Press/Dia Art Foundation, 1988, pp. 3–23 (p. 3).

9 Jonathan Crary, *Techniques of the Observer: On Vision and Modernity in the Nineteenth Century*. Cambridge, Mass., and London: MIT Press, 1990. W. J. T. Mitchell takes issue with Crary's lack of interest in 'the empirical history of spectatorship, in the study of visuality as a cultural practice of everyday life, or in the observer/spectator's body as marked by gender, class, or ethnicity', and in particular with his statement that 'no example … can be located empirically'. See W. J. T. Mitchell, *Picture Theory: Essays on Verbal and Visual Representation*. Chicago and London: University of Chicago Press, 1995, pp. 19–21.
10 Elspeth Probyn, *Sexing the Self: Gendered Positions in Cultural Studies*. London: Routledge, 1993, p. 40.
11 See, for example, Germaine Greer, *The Obstacle Race: The Fortunes of Women Painters and their Work*. London: Weidenfeld & Nicolson, 1979, p. 1; Cherry, *Painting Women*, p. 72.
12 Alice Meynell, 'A Woman in Grey', in *Prose and Poetry: Centenary Volume*, ed. Frederick Page *et al.*, with a bibliographical and critical introduction by V. Sackville-West. London: Cape, 1947, pp. 208–12 (pp. 208–9).
13 Laura Mulvey, 'Visual Pleasure and Narrative Cinema', *Screen* 16, 3 (Autumn 1975): 6–18.
14 Meynell, *Prose and Poetry*, p. 7.
15 See *The Works of John S. Sargent, R.A. With an Introductory Note by Mrs Meynell*. London: William Heinemann; New York: Charles Scribner's Sons, 1903.
16 Meynell, *Prose and Poetry*, p. 17.
17 Ibid., pp. 222–6.
18 Alice Meynell, *The Spirit of Place and Other Essays*. London and New York: John Lane, The Bodley Head, 1899, pp. 77–80 (pp. 78–9).
19 Meynell, *The Spirit of Place*, pp. 92–100 (pp. 93, 92). This aspect of her work recalls Vernon Lee's description of the Tuscan landscape, which is similarly shaped by the eyes of the beholder: 'Ever changing as you move, hills rising or sinking as you mount or descend, furling or unfurling as you go to the right or to the left, valleys and ravines opening or closing up, the whole country altering, so to speak, its attitude and gesture as quickly almost, and with quite as perfect consecutiveness, as does a great cathedral when you walk round it' (*Laurus Nobilis: Chapters on Art and Life*. London: John Jane, The Bodley Head, 1909, pp. 161–202).
20 Meynell, *The Spirit of Place*, pp. 86–91 (p. 90).
21 See 'Shadows', in Meynell, *The Spirit of Place*, pp. 101–6; 'Cloud', in *Essays by Alice Meynell*. London: Burns & Oates, 1914, pp. 184–7; 'Newlyn', *Art Journal* (1889): 97–102, 137–42.
22 'Walls', in Meynell, *Prose and Poetry*, pp. 276–9 (p. 278); 'Solitude', in Meynell, *The Spirit of Place*, pp. 16–22 (p. 19).
23 Aliquis, 'Art Critics of Today', *Art Journal* (July 1892): 193.
24 Clarke, *Critical Voices*, p. 9.
25 Quoted in Talia Schaffer, *The Forgotten Female Aesthetes: Literary Culture in Late Victorian England*. Charlottesville and London: University Press of Virginia, 2000, p. 167.

26 Quoted in June Badeni, *The Slender Tree: A Life of Alice Meynell*. Padstow, Cornwall: Tabb House, 1981, p. 70.
27 Quoted in Viola Meynell, *Alice Meynell: A Memoir*. London: Jonathan Cape, 1929, p. 161.
28 'An American Talks about Art', *Magazine of Art* 1 (May 1878): 202–5 (205).
29 Vernon Lee, *Limbo, and Other Essays*. London: Grant Richards, 1897, p. 59.
30 'The Point of Honour', in *Essays by Alice Meynell*, pp. 165–8 (pp. 165, 166).
31 Michel Foucault, *The Order of Things: An Archaeology of the Human Sciences*. London: Tavistock Publications, 1970, pp. 3–16.
32 *The Works of John S. Sargent, R.A.*, pp. 6–7, 10.
33 Alice Meynell, 'A Question of Propriety', *Tablet* (6 June 1885): 882–3. See Meaghan Clarke's discussion of the controversy in *Critical Voices*, pp. 63–7, and in 'Translating Nudus: Modernity and the British Academy's New Clothes', in *Critical Exchange: Art Criticism of the Eighteenth and Nineteenth Centuries in Russia and Western Europe*, ed. Carol Adlam and Juliet Simpson. Bern: Peter Lang, 2009, pp. 167–89.
34 'The Colour of Life', in Meynell, *Prose and Poetry*, pp. 219–22 (p. 220). See Schaffer, *The Forgotten Female Aesthetes*, pp. 176–9.
35 Meynell, *Prose and Poetry*, pp. 219, 222.
36 An argument that is also made by Pamela Gerrish Nunn in 'Critically Speaking', p. 109. John Paul M. Kanwit, too, argues for a more inclusive view of Victorian art criticism, and explores the engagement of novelists with contemporary ideas about art, in *Victorian Art Criticism and the Woman Writer.*
37 Anna Jameson, 'Andrea Mantegna', *Penny Magazine* 12 (1843): 436. Reprinted in *Memoirs of Early Italian Painters and of the Progress of Painting in Italy*. 2nd edn, London: John Murray, 1868, pp. 108–27 (p. 121).
38 See Teukolsky, *The Literate Eye*, p. 10.
39 Charlotte Brontë, *Jane Eyre*, ed. Richard J. Dunn. New York and London: W. W. Norton & Company, [1848] 1971, p. 5. See Antonia Losano, *The Woman Painter in Victorian Literature*. Columbus: Ohio State University Press, 2008.
40 Elizabeth Robins Pennell, 'Les Arts de la Femme', *Chautauquan* 16 (1892): 212–14 (212).

1 The profession of art history

1 Griselda Pollock, *Differencing the Canon: Feminist Desire and the Writing of Art's Histories*. London and New York: Routledge, 1999, pp. 11–12.
2 Nathaniel Hawthorne, *Our Old Home, and English Notebooks*, 2 vols., 4th edn (Boston: Houghton Mifflin Company, 1912), vol. II, p. 521.
3 On Sophia Peabody Hawthorne, see Julie E. Hall, '"Coming to Europe", Coming to Authorship: Sophia Hawthorne and her Notes in England and Italy', *Legacy: A Journal of American Women Writers* 19, 2 (June 2002): 137–51; and chapter 4 of Annamaria Formidella Elsden, *Roman Fever: Domesticity and Nationalism in C19th American Women's Writing* (Columbus: Ohio State University Press, 2004), pp. 71–94.

4 Nathaniel Hawthorne, *The Marble Faun*, ed. Susan Manning. Oxford University Press, 2002, p. 46.
5 Ibid., p. 50.
6 Adele Holcomb, 'Anna Jameson: The First Professional English Art Historian', *Art History* 6 (1983): 171–87.
7 Aliquis, 'Art Critics of To-Day', *Art Journal* (July 1892): 193–7 (193).
8 Germaine Greer, *The Obstacle Race: The Fortunes of Women Painters and their Work*. London: Weidenfeld & Nicolson, 1979, p. 1.
9 Deborah Cherry, *Painting Women: Victorian Women Artists*. London and New York: Routledge, 1993, p. 72.
10 N. N. Feltes, *Modes of Production of Victorian Novels*. University of Chicago Press, 1989, p. 42. For further discussion of the question of professionalism in the nineteenth century, see H. Perkin, *The Rise of Professional Society: England since 1880*. London: Routledge, 1990. On women and the profession of writing in the period, see Linda H. Peterson, *Becoming a Woman of Letters: Myths of Authorship and Facts of the Victorian Market*. Princeton University Press, 2009; Judith Johnston and Hilary Fraser, 'The Professionalization of Women's Writing: Extending the Canon', in *Women and Literature in Britain 1800–1900*, ed. Joanne Shattock. Cambridge University Press, 2001, pp. 231–50; Mary Jean Corbett, *Representing Femininity. Middle-Class Subjectivity in Victorian and Edwardian Women's Autobiographies*. Oxford University Press, 1992; Deirdre David, *Intellectual Women and Victorian Patriarchy: Harriet Martineau, Elizabeth Barrett Browning, George Eliot*. London: Macmillan, 1987; Dorothy Mermin, *Godiva's Ride: Women of Letters in England, 1830–1880*. Bloomington: Indiana University Press, 1993; Thais E. Morgan, ed., *Victorian Sages and Cultural Discourse: Renegotiating Gender and Power*. New Brunswick: Rutgers University Press, 1990; Julia Swindells, *Victorian Writing and Working Women: The Other Side of Silence*. Cambridge: Polity, 1985.
11 Laurie Kane Lew, 'Cultural Anxiety in Anna Jameson's Art Criticism', *Studies in English Literature* 36 (1996): 829–56 (838–9).
12 For a nuanced discussion of how women located themselves within the emerging profession of authorship in the nineteenth century see Linda H. Peterson, *Becoming a Woman of Letters: Myths of Authorship and Facts of the Victorian Market*. Princeton University Press, 2009.
13 Lew, 'Cultural Anxiety In Anna Jameson's Art Criticism', p. 831.
14 Ibid., pp. 842, 846.
15 G. F. Waagen, *Peter Paul Rubens, his Life and Genius*, trans. R. R. Noel, ed. Anna Jameson. London, 1840, pp. vi, vii.
16 Harold I. Shapiro, *Ruskin in Italy: Letters to his Parents 1845*, Oxford: Clarendon, 1972, pp. 215–16.
17 *The Works of John Ruskin*, ed. E. T. Cook and Alexander Wedderburn. 39 vols. London: George Allen, 1903–12, vol. 35, p. 373.
18 See, for example, A. M. Holcomb, 'Anna Jameson: The First Professional English Art Historian', *Art History* 6 (1983): 171–87; David A. Ludley, 'Anna Jameson and D. G. Rossetti: His Use of Her Histories', *Woman's Art Journal*

12 (1992): 29–33; Judith Johnston, *Anna Jameson: Victorian, Feminist, Woman of Letters*. Aldershot, Hants.: Scolar, 1997, especially chapter 6.

19 Lew, 'Cultural Anxiety In Anna Jameson's Art Criticism', p. 840.

20 Holcomb, 'Anna Jameson: The First Professional English Art Historian', pp. 177, 180–1. Holcomb cites a paper by Carol Gibson-Wood, 'Some Observations on Anna Jameson's *Memoirs of the Early Italian Painters*', delivered at the Universities Art Association of Canada Conference in Calgary, 18 February 1982, which looks at Jameson's German sources.

21 Holcomb, 'Anna Jameson: The First Professional English Art Historian', p. 178.

22 See Adele M. Ernstrom, 'Elizabeth Eastlake's *History of Our Lord as exemplified in works of art*: Theology, Art and Aesthetic Reaction', *Art History* 35, 4 (September 2012): 750–77; and John Paul M. Kanwit, *Victorian Art Criticism and the Woman Writer*. Columbus: Ohio State University Press, 2013, chapter 3, pp. 53–75, on the part played by women such as Eastlake in the development of art criticism as a professional discipline in Britain.

23 *Journals and Correspondence of Lady Eastlake*, ed. Charles Eastlake Smith. 2 vols., London: John Murray, 1895, vol. 1, p. 248. On Lady Eastlake, see also Susanna Avery-Quash and Julie Sheldon, *Art for the Nation: The Eastlakes and the Victorian Art World*. London: The National Gallery Company, 2011.

24 J. D. Passavant. *Tour of a German Artist in England with Notices of Private Galleries, and Remarks on the State of Art*, trans. [Elizabeth Rigby]. 2 vols., London: Saunders and Otley, 1836, vol. 1, p. v.

25 Gustav Friedrich Waagen, *Treasures of Art in Great Britain: Being an Account of the Chief Collections of Paintings, Drawings, Sculptures, Illuminated Mss., &c., &c*, trans. Elizabeth Rigby Eastlake. 4 vols., London: J. Murray, 1854 and 1857.

26 Elizabeth Eastlake, *Five Great Painters*. 2 vols., London: Longmans, Green and Co., 1883, vol. 1, p. 18.

27 Ibid., p. 216.

28 Anonymous review of Elizabeth Ellet, *Women Artists in All Ages and Countries*, *Athenaeum* (24 December 1859): 849, quoted in Pamela Gerrish Nunn, 'Critically Speaking', *Women in the Victorian Art World*, ed. Clarissa Campbell Orr. Manchester and New York: Manchester University Press, 1995, pp. 107–24 (p. 117).

29 Anonymous review of Ellen. C. Clayton, *English Female Artists*, *Art Journal* (1 August 1876): 256.

30 *Journals and Correspondence of Lady Eastlake*, vol. 2, p. 276.

31 Ibid.

32 Elizabeth Eastlake, 'Giovanni Morelli: The Patriot and Critic', *Quarterly Review* 173 (July 1891): 235–52 (235, 236, 238).

33 Ibid., pp. 235, 241.

34 Ibid., p. 248. See Elizabeth Eastlake, 'Photography', *Quarterly Review* 101 (April 1857): 442–68.

35 Eastlake, 'Giovanni Morelli', p. 251.

36 *Journals and Correspondence of Lady Eastlake*, vol. 2, pp. 91, 137.
37 *Mary Berenson: A Self-Portrait from her Letters and Diaries*, ed. Barbara Strachey and Jayne Samuels. London: Victor Gollancz, 1983, p. 47 (letter from Mary Costelloe to Hannah Whitall Smith, 12 September 1891).
38 Mary Whitall Costelloe, 'The New and the Old Art Criticism', *Nineteenth Century* (May 1894): 828–37 (832, 834–5).
39 Berenson Archive, Elizabeth Eastlake to Mrs Costelloe, 2? February, 1893.
40 [Mary] Merrifield, *The Art of Fresco Painting as Practised by the Old Italian and Spanish Masters, with a Preliminary Inquiry Into the Nature of the Colours Used in Fresco Painting*, ed. A. C. Sewter. London: Alec Tiranti, 1952, p. ix.
41 Ibid., 'Preface'.
42 Julia Cartwright, *Beatrice d'Este, Duchess of Milan 1475–1497: A Study of the Renaissance*. London: J. M. Dent and Sons; New York: E. P. Dutton and Co., 1926, p. v.
43 Julia Cartwright, *Isabella d'Este, Marchioness of Mantua 1474–1539: A Study of the Renaissance*. 2 vols., London: John Murray, 1903, vol. 1, p. ix.
44 See Angela Emanuel, ed., *A Bright Remembrance: The Diaries of Julia Cartwright, 1851–1924*. London: Weidenfeld & Nicolson, 1989, p. 266. Interestingly, other female art historians, such as Anna Jameson and Vernon Lee, also had to contend with the criticism that their ideas were not their own.
45 Berenson Archive, Maud Cruttwell to Mary Berenson, Paris, 1900.
46 Emilia Dilke, *French Painters of the Eighteenth Century*. London: George Bell & Sons, 1899, pp. 115–16. NB Baptised Emilia Francis Strong, she married Mark Pattison in 1861, and published her early work under the name Francis Pattison. After his death and her marriage to Sir Charles Dilke, she published as Emilia Dilke.
47 Ibid., p. vi.
48 Kali Israel, *Names and Stories: Emilia Dilke and Victorian Culture*. New York and Oxford: Oxford University Press, 1999, pp. 255–6.
49 Colin Eisler, 'Lady Dilke (1840–1904): The Six lives of an Art Historian', in Claire Richter Sherman and Adele M. Holcomb, eds., *Women as Interpreters of the Visual Arts, 1820–1979*. Westport, Conn.: Greenwood, 1981, pp. 147–80.
50 [Emilia Pattison], unsigned review, *Westminster Review* n.s. 43 (1873): 639–41.
51 George Eliot, *Middlemarch*. Harmondsworth: Penguin, 2012, chapter 22, pp. 240, 241.
52 See Barbara Caine's account of the problematical relationship between mother and daughter in 'Mothering Feminism/Mothering Feminists: Ray Strachey and *The Cause*', *Women's History Review* 8, 2 (1999): 295–310.
53 Claire Richter Sherman with Adele M. Holcomb, eds., *Women as Interpreters of the Visual Arts, 1820–1979*. Westport, Conn., and London: Greenwood, 1981, p. 40.
54 Mrs Callcott, *Essays Towards the History of Painting*. London: Edward Moxon, 1836, pp. 5–6.
55 'Handbook to the Public Galleries of Art', *Gentleman's Magazine* n.s. 18 (1842): 227, quoted in Johnston, *Anna Jameson,* p. 154.

56 'Handbook to the Public Galleries of Art', *British and Foreign Review* 14 (1843): 55.
57 Lew, 'Cultural Anxiety in Anna Jameson's Art Criticism', pp. 832, 838, 834.
58 Ibid., p. 831.
59 Mary Merrifield, Review of Jameson, *Legends of the Madonna*, *Edinburgh Review* 97 (January 1853): 230–9 (231).
60 Ibid., p. 231.
61 Ibid., p. 233.
62 *Medieval and Renaissance Treatises on the Arts of Painting*. Mineola, N.Y.: Dover Publications, 1999 (1966), pp. v, vii, x. xi.
63 See Caroline Palmer, 'Colour, Chemistry and Corsets: Mary Philadelphia Merrifield's *Dress as a Fine Art*', *Costume* 47, 1 (January 2013): 3–27.
64 Elizabeth Eastlake, 'Photography', *Quarterly Review* (April 1857): 442–68 (465).
65 Vernon Lee, *Euphorion: being Studies of the Antique and the Mediaeval in the Renaissance*. 2 vols., London: T. Fisher Unwin, 1884, vol. 1, p. 21.
66 Homi K. Bhabha, *The Location of Culture*. London and New York: Routledge, 1994, p. 1.
67 *The Autobiography of Margaret Oliphant*, ed. Elisabeth Jay. Oxford and New York: Oxford University Press, 1990, p. 155.
68 Berenson Archive, Bernard Berenson to Michael [Katherine Bradley], Florence, 11 December 1893.
69 Quoted in Vineta Colby, *Vernon Lee: A Literary Biography*. Charlottesville and London: University of Virginia Press, 2003, pp. 161–2.
70 Berenson Archive, Michael to Mary, 133, Villa Rosa, Saturday, 1895. For amusing accounts of this visit, see Ms. letter 135, and *Works and Days: From the Journal of Michael Field*, ed. T. and D. C. Sturge Moore. London: John Murray, 1933, pp. 264–5.
71 Miranda Seymour, *Ottoline Morrell: Life on the Grand Scale*. London: Hodder & Stoughton, 1992, p. 38.
72 Berenson Archive, Maud Cruttwell to Mary Berenson, Paris, 17 December 1900.
73 Berenson Archive, Maud Cruttwell to Mary Berenson, Paris, n.d., 1900.
74 Berenson Archive, Maud Cruttwell to Mary Berenson, Paris, 17 December 1900.
75 Berenson Archive, Maud Cruttwell to Mary Berenson, Paris, n.d., 1900.
76 Ibid.
77 Ibid.
78 Berenson Archive, Elizabeth Eastlake to Mrs Costelloe, 2 February 1893.
79 Berenson Archive, Elizabeth Eastlake to Mrs Costelloe, 22 September 1892.
80 Berenson Archive, Elizabeth Eastlake to Mrs Costelloe, 2 February 1893.
81 Ernest Samuels, *Bernard Berenson: The Making of a Connoisseur*. Cambridge, Mass.: Harvard University Press, 1979, pp. 120–1.
82 Berenson Archive, Elizabeth Eastlake to Mrs Costelloe, 2 February 1893, 22 September 1892.

83 Berenson Archive, Elizabeth Eastlake to Mrs Costelloe, 2 February 1893.
84 Berenson Archive, Elizabeth Eastlake to Mr Berenson, 19 June 1893.
85 Ibid.

2 The art of fiction

1 Berenson Archive, Maud Cruttwell to Mary Berenson, Paris, n.d., 1900.
2 Maud Cruttwell, *Fire and Frost*. London: John Lane, The Bodley Head, 1913, p. 3.
3 Ibid., pp. 5, 19ff.
4 Ibid., p. 12.
5 Ibid., p. 58.
6 Ibid., p. 301.
7 Ibid., p. 6.
8 Unlike his wife, who is 'short, and rather fat' – poor Mary Berenson struggled with her weight, and was taunted by Bernard for being fat.
9 Cruttwell, *Fire and Frost*, pp. 23–4.
10 Ibid., pp. 96–7.
11 Vernon Lee, *Limbo, and Other Essays*. London: Grant Richards, 1897, pp. 28–9.
12 Cruttwell, *Fire and Frost*, p. 97.
13 Edmund Gosse, Introduction to Gemma Ferrugia, *Woman's Folly*, trans. Helen Zimmern. London: Heinemann 1895, p. vi. And see, for example, Mary Merrifield, 'The Need of Sanitary Knowledge to Women', *Dublin University Magazine* 76 (September, 1870): 843–8, and articles published in the *Art Journal* and *Sharpe's London Magazine* collected as *Dress as a Fine Art*. London: Arthur Hall, Virtue, & Co., 1854; Louisa Twining, *Workhouses and Women's Work*. London: Longman, Brown, Green, Longmans, & Roberts, 1858; Emilia Dilke, 'Benefit Societies and Trades Unions for Women', *Fortnightly Review* n.s. 45 (June 1889): 852–6, and 'Woman Suffrage in England', *North American Review* 164 (February 1897): 151–9; Elizabeth Pennell, *Life of Mary Wollstonecraft.*: Boston: Roberts Bros., 1884 and 'A Century of Women's Rights', *Fortnightly Review* 54 (o.s.), 48 (n.s.) (September 1890): 408–17.
14 See Pamela Gerrish Nunn's argument in 'Critically Speaking', in Orr, *Women in the Victorian Art World*, pp. 107–24.
15 See Antonia Losano, *The Woman Painter in Victorian Literature*. Columbus: Ohio State University Press, 2008.
16 See discussions of this painting in Deborah Cherry, *Beyond the Frame: Feminism and Visual Culture, Britain 1850–1900*. London and New York: Routledge, 2000, pp. 28–30, 35–7; and Marsha Meskimmon, *Women Making Art: History, Subjectivity, Aesthetics*. London and New York: Routledge, 2003, pp. 75–80.
17 Anne Brontë, *The Tenant of Wildfell Hall*, ed. Stevie Davies. London: Penguin, 1996, p. 47.
18 Margaret Oliphant, *The Three Brothers*. New York: D. Appleton and Co., 1870, p. 89.

19 Dinah Mulock Craik, *Olive and The Half-Caste*, ed. Cora Kaplan. Oxford University Press, 1996, pp. 119, 304.
20 'The Sisters in Art', *Illustrated Exhibitor and Magazine of Art* 2 (1852): 214–16, 238–40, 262–3, 286–8, 317–19, 334–6, 347–8, 362–4.
21 Virginia Woolf, *To the Lighthouse*, ed. Stella McNichol and Hermione Lee. London: Penguin, 1992, p. 94.
22 Ella Hepworth Dixon, *The Story of a Modern Woman*. London: Methuen, 1894, pp. 54, 42.
23 Anne Thackeray Ritchie, *Miss Angel And Fulham Lawn*. London: Smith, Elder, & Co., 1908, p. 92.
24 For interesting discussions of Dicksee's painting, see S. P. Casteras, '"The Necessity of a Name": Portrayals and Betrayals of Victorian Women Artists', in *Gender and Discourse in Victorian Art and Literature*, ed. A. H. Harrison and B. Taylor. DeKalb: Northern Illinois University Press, 1992, pp. 207–32; and Cherry, *Beyond the Frame*, pp. 178–80.
25 See Heather Tilley, 'Blindness and Writing, 1800–72'. Unpublished PhD thesis, University of London, 2009.
26 Charlotte Brontë, *Villette*, ed. Mark Lilly and Tony Tanner. London: Penguin, 1979, p. 275.
27 Frances Trollope, *Domestic Manners of the Americans*, ed. Donald Smalley. New York, 1949, pp. 268–9.
28 George Eliot, *Middlemarch*. Harmondsworth: Penguin, 2012, chapter 19, pp. 204, 205.
29 Ibid., p. 209.
30 Deborah Cherry and Griselda Pollock, 'Woman as Sign in Pre-Raphaelite Literature: A Study of the Representation of Elizabeth Siddall', *Art History* 7, 2 (June 1984): 206–27 (223).
31 Mary Elizabeth Braddon, *Lady Audley's Secret*, ed. Jenny Bourne Taylor. London: Penguin, 1998, p. 72.
32 Vernon Lee, *Miss Brown*. 3 vols., Edinburgh: William Blackwood and Sons, 1884, vol. 1, pp. 25, 126, 309.

3 Girl guides: travel, translation, ekphrasis

1 Claire Richter Sherman with Adele M. Holcomb, eds., *Women as Interpreters of the Visual Arts*. Westport, Conn., and London: Greenwood Press, 1981, p. 24.
2 See Sara Mills, *Discourses of Difference*. London: Routledge, 1991, pp. 41–2.
3 See Lesa Scholl, *Translation, Authorship and the Victorian Professional Woman: Charlotte Brontë, Harriet Martineau and George Eliot*. Aldershot, Hants.: Ashgate, 2011; and Judith Johnston, *Victorian Women and the Economies of Travel, Translation and Culture, 1830–1870*. Aldershot, Hants.: Ashgate, 2012.
4 Vernon Lee, *Euphorion: being Studies of the Antique and the Medieval in the Renaissance*. 2 vols., London: T. Fisher Unwin, 1884, vol. 1, p. 16.
5 Judith Johnston, *Anna Jameson: Victorian, Feminist, Woman of Letters*. Aldershot, Hants.: Scolar, 1997, p. 101.

6 Ibid.
7 'Diary of an Ennuyée', *Westminster Review*, 6 (1826): 325–41 (339). Quoted in Johnston, *Anna Jameson*, p. 101.
8 Mariana Starke, *Information and Directions for Travellers on the Continent*. 7th edn, London: John Murray, 1829, Advertisement.
9 Starke, *Information and Directions for Travellers on the Continent* (1829), Advertisement.
10 Mariana Starke, *Information and Directions for Travellers on the Continent*. 5th edn, London: John Murray, 1824, p. v.
11 Starke, *Information and Directions for Travellers on the Continent* (1829), Advertisement.
12 Starke, *Information and Directions for Travellers on the Continent* (1824), Advertisement.
13 Ibid., p. viii.
14 Robyn Cooper, '"The Crowning Glory of Pisa": Nineteenth-Century Reactions to the Campo Santo', *Italian Studies* 37 (1982): 72–100.
15 Starke, *Information and Directions for Travellers on the Continent* (1829), p. 94.
16 Ibid., p. 96.
17 See Peter de Bolla, *The Education of the Eye: Painting, Landscape, and Architecture in Eighteenth-Century Britain*. Stanford University Press, 2003, especially chapter 5, for a discussion of the 'sentimental look', which he traces back to the 1760s.
18 Elizabeth Rigby, 'Lady Travellers', *Quarterly Review* 76 (June 1845): 98–136 (98).
19 Ibid. p. 99.
20 Ibid.
21 Ibid., p. 103.
22 Rigby briefly refers to *Letters from the Baltic*, without acknowledging that it is her own work, in her review.
23 Elizabeth Rigby, *Letters from the Shores of the Baltic*. 2nd edn, London: John Murray, 1842, pp. 28–9; Elizabeth Eastlake, 'Life and Works of Thorvaldsen', *Edinburgh Review* 142 (July 1875): 1–29.
24 Michel Foucault, 'Of Other Spaces', *Diacritics* (Spring 1986): 22–7 (25).
25 Rigby, *Letters from the Shores of the Baltic*, pp. 65–7.
26 Anna Jameson, *Memoirs of Early Italian Painters and of the Progress of Painting in Italy*. 2nd edn, London: John Murray, 1868, p. xix; Kate Thompson, *A Handbook to the Public Picture Galleries of Europe*. London: Macmillan, 1877, pp. vi–viii.
27 Jameson, *Memoirs of Early Italian Painters*, p. ix; Thompson, *Handbook to the Public Picture Galleries of Europe*, pp. v–vii.
28 Maud Cruttwell, *A Guide to the Paintings in the Florentine Galleries the Uffizi, the Pitti, the Accademia: A Critical Catalogue with Quotations from Vasari*. London: J. M. Dent & Company; New York: E. P. Dutton & Co., 1907, p. v.
29 Ibid., pp. v–vi.
30 Ibid., p. vi.

31 Ibid., p. vii.
32 Sherry Simon, *Gender in Translation: Cultural Identity and the Politics of Transmission*. London and New York: Routledge, 1996, p. 5.
33 Johnston, *Anna Jameson*, p. 128. See pp. 127–35, 141–53 for full discussion.
34 Jameson, *Memoirs of Early Italian Painters*, pp. xi, xii, xvii, xix.
35 See Diana Maltz, 'Engaging "Delicate Brains": From Working-Class Enculturation to Upper-Class Lesbian Liberation in Vernon Lee and Kit Anstruther-Thomson's Psychological Aesthetics', in *Women and British Aestheticism*, ed. Talia Schaffer and Kathy Alexis Psomiades. Charlottesville: University Press of Virginia, 1999, pp. 211–29.
36 André Lefevere, 'Translation: Its Genealogy in the West', in *Translation, History and Culture*, ed. Susan Bassnett and André Lefevere. London: Pinter, 1990, p. 15
37 Richard Stein, *The Ritual of Interpretation: The Fine Arts as Literature in Ruskin, Rossetti and Pater*. Cambridge, Mass.: Harvard University Press, 1975.
38 Walter Benjamin, 'The Task of the Translator', in *Illuminations*, ed. Hannah Arendt, trans. Harry Zohn. London: Pimlico, 1999, pp. 70–82 (p. 79).
39 Sarat Maharaj, 'Perfidious Fidelity: The Untranslatability of the Other', in *Global Visions: Towards a New Internationalism in the Visual Arts*, ed. Jean Fisher. London: Kala Press in association with the Institute of International Visual Arts, 1994, pp. 28–35 (p. 28).
40 Simon, *Gender in Translation*, pp. 134–5.
41 Benjamin, 'The Task of the Translator', p. 76.
42 Simon, *Gender in Translation*, p. 1.
43 See James A. W. Heffernan *Museum of Words: The Poetics of Ekphrasis from Homer to Ashbery*. University of Chicago Press, 1993, pp. 8–10, and his article 'Speaking for Pictures', *Word and Image* 15, 1 (January–March 1999): 19–34.
44 'Poetical Catalogue of Pictures in Lit. Gaz.', *The Poetical Works of Letitia Elizabeth Landon (L.E.L.)*, ed. William B. Scott. London: George Routledge & Sons, n.d., p. 256.
45 Ibid., p. 300.
46 Deborah Cherry and Griselda Pollock, 'Woman as Sign in Pre-Raphaelite Literature: A Study of the representation of Elizabeth Siddall', *Art History* 7, 2 (June 1984): 206–27, (p. 208). Revised by Pollock and republished in Pollock, *Vision and Difference : Femininity, Feminism and the Histories of Art*. London: Routledge, 1988, pp. 91–114. See also 'A Photo-essay: Signs of Femininity', pp. 115–19.
47 Maud Cruttwell, *A Guide to the Paintings in the Churches and Minor Museums of Florence*. London: J. M. Dent & Company, 1908, p. 166.
48 Emily Pfeiffer, *Sonnets*. London: Field and Tuer, The Leadenhall Press; New York: Scribner and Welford, 1886, p. 24. The volume includes other ekphrastic poems on paintings by Edward Burne-Jones and G. F. Watts. See pp. 77–86.
49 Ibid., p. 25.
50 Ibid., p. 11.
51 *The Journals of George Eliot*, ed. Margaret Harris and Judith Johnston. Cambridge University Press, 1998, pp. 356–7.

52 George Eliot, *Romola*, ed. Andrew Brown. Oxford: Clarendon Press, 1993, pp. 155, 162.
53 Ibid., p. 395.
54 *Essays of George Eliot*, ed. Thomas Pinney. London: Routledge and Kegan Paul, 1968, pp. 446–7.
55 Benjamin, 'The Task of the Translator', pp. 77, 82.
56 Berenson Archive. MS Letters between the Berensons and Katharine Bradley and Edith Cooper. Villa I Tatti. Ms. 201.
57 Berenson Archive Ms. 181.
58 Michael Field, *Works and Days MS*. British Library, Add. MS. 46779–80 MS. 46780 f.124.
59 Ana I. Parejo Vadillo, '*Sight and Song*: Transparent Translations and a Manifesto for the Observer', *Victorian Poetry* 38, 1 (2000): 15–34 (17).
60 Michael Field, *Sight and Song*. London: Elkin Mathews and John Lane, 1892, p. v. Subsequent references will be cited parenthetically in the main text by page number.
61 *Works and Days: From the Journal of Michael Field*, ed. T. and D. C. Sturge Moore. London: John Murray, 1933, p. 3 (from a letter to Robert Browning, 29 May 1884). NB I quote where possible from this published edition of extracts from the journal for ease of reference.
62 Heffernan, *Museum of Words*, p. 8.
63 Martha Vicinus, 'The Adolescent Boy: *Fin-de-Siècle* Femme Fatale?' in *Victorian Sexual Dissidence*, ed. Richard Dellamora. University of Chicago Press, 1999, pp. 83–106 (pp. 83–4).
64 Angela Leighton, *Victorian Women Poets: Writing Against the Heart*. Brighton: Harvester, 1992, pp. 213–14; Michael Field, BL Add. MS. 46779 f.104v; Berenson Archive.
65 Michael Field, *Underneath the Bough: A Book of Verses*. London: George Bell & Sons, 1893, p. 79.
66 Norman Bryson, *Vision and Painting: The Logic of the Gaze*. New Haven: Yale University Press, 1983, p. 122.
67 Field, *Works and Days*, p. 48.
68 Field, BL Add. MS. 46779, f.117.
69 Vicinus, 'The Adolescent Boy', p. 93.
70 Field, *Works and Days*, pp. 56–7.
71 *The Complete Prose Works of Matthew Arnold*, ed. R. H. Super. Ann Arbor: University of Michigan Press, 1960–70, vol. 3, p. 258.
72 See *The Works of John Ruskin*, ed. E. T. Cook and Alexander Wedderburn. London: George Allen, 1903–12, vol. 3, for his extended discussion of the importance of 'truth'; and vol. 15, p. 17, for his view that '[t]he whole technical power of painting depends on our recovery of what may be called the *innocence of the eye*'.
73 Bryson, *Vision and Painting*, pp. 91–2.
74 Field, *Works and Days*, p. 48.
75 Ibid.
76 Kathy Alexis Psomiades, '"Still Burning from this Strangling Embrace": Vernon Lee on Desire and Aesthetics'. *Victorian Sexual Dissidence*, ed. Richard Dellamora. University of Chicago Press, 1999, pp. 21–41 (p. 37).

77 British Library, Ms. 46780ff, cited in Vadillo, '*Sight and Song*: Transparent Translations and a Manifesto for the Observer', p. 17.
78 Bernard Berenson, *The Florentine Painters of the Renaissance*. New York, 1896, p. 84.
79 Berenson Archive, Ms. 178.
80 Berenson Archive, Ms. 212.
81 Berenson Archive, Ms. 178.
82 Ibid.
83 Berenson Archive, Ms. 242.
84 Berenson Archive, Ms. 162.
85 British Museum, Ms. 46779, 63a.
86 Ibid., 64.
87 Ibid., 90a.
88 Ibid., 90.
89 Ibid., 89a, 89.
90 Ibid., 90.
91 George Eliot, *Middlemarch*. Harmondsworth: Penguin, 2012, chapter 63, p. 702. I am grateful to Vicky Mills for drawing my attention to this and the following analogy.
92 Field, *Works and Days*, pp. 54–5.
93 Ibid., p. 57.
94 British Museum, Ms. 46779, 116a.
95 Ibid., 117a.
96 Ibid.
97 Anna Jameson, Legends of the Madonna as represented in the fine arts: forming the third series of Sacred and Legendary Art. 3rd edn, London: Longman, Brown, Green & Longman's 1864, p. xiii
98 *The George Eliot Letters*, ed. Gordon S. Haight. 9 vols., New Haven: Yale University Press, 1954–78, vol. 2, pp. 471–2.
99 See Carolyn Burdett, 'Introduction: Psychology/Aesthetics in the Nineteenth Century', and '"The subjective inside us can turn into the objective outside": Vernon Lee's Psychological Aesthetics', *Psychology/Aesthetics in the Nineteenth Century, 19: Interdisciplinary Studies in the Long Nineteenth Century* 12 (2011) http://19.bbk.ac.uk/index.php/19/issue/view/80.
100 Vernon Lee and Clementina Anstruther-Thomson, *Beauty and Ugliness and Other Studies in Psychological Aesthetics*. London: John Lane, Bodley Head, 1912, pp. 25–6. See Burdett, '"The subjective inside us can turn into the objective outside"', and Lynda Nead, *The Haunted Gallery: Painting, Photography, and Film c. 1900*. New Haven, Conn.: Yale University Press, 2007, pp. 39–40, 56–8.
101 Lee and Anstruther-Thomson, *Beauty and Ugliness*, p. 17.
102 See Elizabeth Grosz's article 'Sexual Difference and the Problem of Essentialism' (in *The Essential Difference: Another Look at Essentialism*, ed. Naomi Schor and Elizabeth Weed. Bloomington: Indiana University Press, 1988, pp. 82–97), where she discusses the ideological 'cognates' of

essentialism – biologism, naturalism and universalism. In Lee's aesthetic, organicism displaces biologism (which might admit sexual difference).

103 Diana Maltz, 'Engaging "Delicate Brains"', p. 221.

104 Dame Ethel Smyth, *What Happened Next*. London: Longmans Green, 1940, p. 160.

105 W. B. Yeats, 'Sight and Song', in *W. B. Yeats: Uncollected Prose*, ed. John P. Frayne. 2 vols., London: Macmillan, 1970, vol. 1, pp. 225–6.

106 Martin Jay, 'Scopic Regimes of Modernity', in *Vision and Visuality*, ed. Hal Foster. Seattle: Bay Press/Dia Art Foundation, 1988, pp. 3–23 (p. 4).

4 Women's periods

1 Joan Kelly, *Women, History and Theory: The Essays of Joan Kelly*. Chicago and London: The University of Chicago Press, 1984, p. 19.

2 Judith Lowder Newton, 'History as Usual? Feminism and the "New Historicism"', in *The New Historicism*, ed. H. Aram Veeser. New York and London: Routledge, 1989, pp. 152–67 (p. 155).

3 Natalie Zemon Davis, '"Women's History" in Transition: The European Case', *Feminist Studies* 3, 3/4 (Spring/Summer 1976): 83–103.

4 Newton, 'History as Usual?' p. 155.

5 E. F. S. Pattison, 'Art and Morality', *Westminster Review* n.s. 35 (January 1869): 148–84 (156, 163).

6 Ibid., p. 178.

7 See 'The Use of Looking at Pictures', *Westminster Review* n.s. 44 (October 1873): 415–23 (421).

8 E. F. S. Pattison, 'John Ruskin, *Lectures on Art* and *Catalogue of Examples* (Oxford, 1870)', *Academy* 1 (10 September 1870): 305–6 (305).

9 Quoted in Emilia F. S. Dilke, *The Book of the Spiritual Life*, including a Memoir of the author by Sir Charles Dilke. London: John Murray, 1905, p. 5.

10 Vernon Lee, *Euphorion: being Studies of the Antique and the Mediaeval in the Renaissance*. 2 vols., London, 1884, vol. 1, pp. 213–14.

11 Ibid., vol. 2, p. 15.

12 Ibid., p. 17.

13 Vernon Lee, *Belcaro: Being Essays on Sundry Aesthetical Questions*. London: T. Fisher Unwin, 1887, p. 205.

14 Ibid.

15 Vernon Lee and C. Anstruther-Thomson, *Beauty and Ugliness, and Other Studies in Psychological Aesthetics*. London: John Lane, The Bodley Head, 1912, p. 31.

16 See Hilary Fraser, 'Women and the Ends of Art History: Vision and Corporeality in Nineteenth-Century Critical Discourse', *Victorian Studies* 42, 1 (Autumn, 1998/99): 77–100.

17 E. F. S. Pattison, 'Walter Pater: *Studies in the History of the Renaissance* (London, 1873)', *Westminster Review* n.s. 43 (April 1873): 639–41.

18 Pattison, 'The Use of Looking at Pictures', p. 419.

19 See Kali A. K. Israel, 'Style, Strategy, and Self-Creation in the Life of Emilia Dilke', in *Constructions of the Self*, ed. George Levine. New Brunswick: Rutgers University Press, 1992, pp. 213–45; Kali Israel, 'The Resources of Style: Francis Pattison in Oxford', *Radical History Review* 72 (1998): 122–62; and *Names and Stories*. Oxford University Press, 2000.
20 Israel, 'Style, Strategy, and Self-Creation in the Life of Emilia Dilke', p. 232.
21 Ibid.
22 E. F. S. Pattison, 'Germain Pilon', *Portfolio* 2 (1871): 72–5 (75).
23 E. F. S. Pattison, *The Renaissance of Art in France*. 2 vols., London: C. Kegan Paul & Co., 1879, vol. 1, pp. 12, 13, 24–6.
24 Israel, 'Style, Strategy, and Self-Creation in the Life of Emilia Dilke', p. 231.
25 Ibid., p. 237.
26 See Israel, *Names and Stories*, pp. 5–6.
27 Ibid., p. 173.
28 See Jan Marsh, '"The Old Tuscan Rapture": the Response to Italy and its Art in the Work of Marie Spartali Stillman', in Alison Chapman and Jane Stabler, eds., *Unfolding the South: Nineteenth-Century British Women Writers and Artists in Italy*. Manchester University Press, 2003, pp. 159–82.
29 Deborah Cherry, *Painting Women: Victorian Women Artists*. London and New York: Routledge, 1993, p. 198.
30 Ibid., p. 199.
31 In Rozsika Parker and Griselda Pollock, *Old Mistresses: Women, Art and Ideology*. London: Routledge and Kegan Paul, 1981. There is a growing body of work on Renaissance women artists and their place in the canon by modern scholars. See, for example, Babette Bohn, 'The Antique Heroines of Elisabetta Sirani', *Renaissance Studies* 16 (2002): 52–79; Mary D. Garrard, *Artemisia Gentileschi: The Image of the Female Hero in Italian Baroque Art*. Princeton University Press, 1989; Mary D. Garrard, *Artemisia Gentileschi around 1622: The Shaping and Reshaping of an Artistic Identity*. Berkeley and London: University of California Press, 2001; Fredrika Jacobs, *Defining the Renaissance Virtuosa: Woman Artists and the Language of Art History and Criticism*. Cambridge University Press, 1997; Caroline Murphy, 'Lavinia Fontana and le Dame della Città: Understanding Female Artistic Patronage in Late Sixteenth-Century Bologna', *Renaissance Studies* 10 (1996): 190–208; Caroline Murphy, 'Lavinia Fontana and Female Life Cycle Experience in Late Sixteenth-Century Bologna', in Geraldine A. Johnson and Sara F. Matthews Grieco, eds., *Picturing Women in Renaissance and Baroque Italy*. Cambridge University Press, 1997; Caroline Murphy, *Lavinia Fontana: A Painter and her Patrons in Sixteenth-Century Bologna*. New Haven and London: Yale University Press, 2003; Bernardina Sani, *Rosalba Carriera: Catalogue Raisonné*. Venice: Umberto Allemandi & Co. 2007. An exhibition of the works of Artemisia Gentileschi was held at the Musée Maillot in Paris in 2012.
32 Adele M. Holcomb, 'Anna Jameson: The First Professional English Art Historian', *Art History* 6, 2 (June 1983): 171–87.
33 Ibid., 184.

34 Adele M. Holcomb, 'Anna Jameson (1794–1860): Sacred Art and Social Vision', in *Women as Interpreters of the Visual Arts, 1820–1979*, ed. Claire Richter Sherman, with Adele M. Holcomb. Westport, Conn., and London: Greenwood Press, 1981, p. 113.
35 *Letters of Anna Jameson to Ottilie von Goethe*, ed. G. H. Needler. London, New York, Toronto: Oxford University Press, 1939, p. 124 (21 April 1840).
36 Anna Jameson, *Visits and Sketches at Home and Abroad*. 2 vols., 2nd edn, London: Saunders and Otley, 1835, vol. 2, pp. 175–6. See *At Home in Renaissance Italy*, ed. Marta Ajmar-Wollheim and Flora Dennis. London, V&A Publications, 2006, p. 219.
37 Jameson, *Visits and Sketches*, p. 177.
38 Ibid., p. 173.
39 Ibid., p. 175.
40 Ibid., pp. 171–3, 179.
41 Ibid., p. 177.
42 Ibid., pp. 177–8.
43 Ibid., p. 178.
44 Ibid., p. 177.
45 Robert Browning, *The Poems, Volume II*, ed. John Pettigrew, supplemented and completed by Thomas J. Collins. Harmondsworth, Middlesex: Penguin, 1981, pp. 899–908, ll. 14, 29.
46 Jameson, *Visits and Sketches*, vol. 2, pp. 178–9. Compare Florence Fenwick Miller's declaration in 1898: 'There is no sex in art' ('Ladies' Page', *Illustrated London News* (26 February 1898): 310), discussed in the Conclusion.
47 *The Poems of Tennyson*, ed. Christopher Ricks (Longman's Annotated English poets). London: Longmans, Green & Co, 1969; revised edn in 3 vols., 1987. 'The Princess', VII, l. 285.
48 Virginia Woolf, *A Room of One's Own, Three Guineas*, ed. Morag Shiach. Oxford University Press, 1992, p. 101.
49 Vernon Lee, *Euphorion: being Studies of the Antique and the Medieval in the Renaissance*. 2 vols., London: T. Fisher Unwin, 1884, vol. 1, p. 99.
50 Ibid., pp. 139, 141.
51 Ibid., p. 160.
52 Emilia Dilke, *Art in the Modern State*. London: Chapman and Hall, 1888, p. 28.
53 Lee, *Euphorion*, vol. 1, p. 46.
54 Julia Cartwright, *Beatrice d'Este, Duchess of Milan 1475–1497: A Study of the Renaissance*. London: J. M. Dent and Sons; New York: E. P. Dutton and Co., 1926, pp. v–vi.
55 Ibid., p. v.
56 Ibid., p. vi.
57 Ibid.
58 Julia Cartwright, *Christina of Denmark, Duchess of Milan and Lorraine 1522–1590*. London: John Murray, 1913, p. v.
59 Cartwright, *Beatrice d'Este*, p. vi.
60 Ibid., pp. vii–viii.

61 Julia Cartwright, *Isabella d'Este, Marchioness of Mantua 1474–1539: A Study of the Renaissance*. 2 vols., London: John Murray, 1903, vol. 1, pp. viii–x.
62 Ibid., vol. 2, p. 391.
63 Cartwright, *Beatrice d'Este*, pp. v–vi, vi–viii.
64 Cartwright, *Isabella d'Este*, vol. 1, pp. viii–ix.
65 Deborah Cherry, *Beyond the Frame: Feminism and Visual Culture, Britain 1850–1900*. London and New York: Routledge, 2000, p. 169. Romano's portrait was also an influence on Edward Burne-Jones's *Sidonia Von Bork* (1860). See Edward Clifford, *Broadlands as It Was*, London: privately printed, 1890, p. 55.
66 Lee, *Euphorion*, vol. 1, p. 16.
67 Ibid., pp. 10–11.
68 Ibid., p. 16.
69 Quoted in Peter Gunn, *Vernon Lee: Violet Paget, 1856–1935*. London: Oxford University Press, 1964, p. 9.
70 Lee, *Euphorion*,, vol. 1, p. 21.
71 Ibid., vol. 1, p. 18–22.
72 Vernon Lee, *Studies of the Eighteenth Century in Italy*. London: W. Satchell and Co., 1880, p. 293–4.
73 Ibid., p. 294.
74 Ibid., p. 295.
75 Vernon Lee, *Juvenilia: Being a Second Series of Essays on Sundry Aesthetical Questions*, 2 vols., London: T. Fisher Unwin, 1887, vol. 1, p. 136.
76 Lee, *Studies of the Eighteenth Century in Italy*, p. 2.
77 Ibid., p. 1.
78 Ibid., pp. 8, 10.
79 Ibid., p. 64.
80 Ibid., p. 121.
81 Ibid., p. 4.
82 Ibid., p. 10.
83 Ibid., p. 67.
84 Ibid., p. 122.
85 Ibid., p. 19.
86 Ibid., p. 215.
87 Ibid., p. 56–7.
88 Ibid., p. 160.
89 Ibid., p. 30–1.
90 Ibid., p. 112–13.
91 Ibid., p. 120.
92 Ibid., p. 157.
93 Vernon Lee, *Althea: A Second Book of Dialogues on Aspirations and Duties*. London: Osgood, McIlvaine & Co., 1894, p. x.
94 Lee, *Studies of the Eighteenth Century in Italy*, p. 268.
95 Tom Gunning, 'The Cinema of Attractions: Early Film, its Spectator, and the Avant-Garde', in Thomas Elsaesser, ed., *Early Cinema: Space, Frame, Narrative*. London: BFI, 1990, pp. 56–62 (p. 57).

96 Lee, *Studies of the Eighteenth Century in Italy*, p. 95.
97 Ibid., p. 120.
98 Ibid., pp. 18–20.
99 Ibid., p. 47.
100 Ibid., pp. 54–5.
101 Ibid., p. 33.
102 Ibid., p. 35.
103 Ibid., p. 94.
104 Ibid., p. 33.
105 Ibid., p. 124.
106 Ibid., p. 101.
107 Ibid., p. 34.
108 Ibid., p. 35.
109 Ibid., pp. 56–8.
110 Ibid., pp. 58–9.
111 Ibid., p. 70.
112 Ibid., p. 79.
113 Ibid., p. 114.
114 Ibid., pp. 79–80.
115 Ibid., p. 81.
116 Ibid., p. 116.
117 Ibid., p. 143.
118 Ibid., p. 85.
119 Ibid., p. 122.
120 Vernon Lee, *The Spirit of Rome: Leaves from a Diary*. London: John Lane, The Bodley Head, 1906, p. 142.
121 Ibid., pp. 115–16.
122 Lee, *Althea*, pp. 60, 62.
123 Ibid., p. 64.
124 Emilia Dilke, *French Painters of the XVIIIth Century*. London: George Bell and Sons, 1899, p. vi.
125 Ibid., p. 34.
126 Emilia Dilke, *French Engravers and Draughtsmen of the XVIIIth Century*. London: George Bell and Sons, 1902, p. v.
127 Dilke, *Painters*, p. 7.
128 Ibid., p. 12.
129 Ibid., p. 21.
130 Ibid., p. 1.
131 Ibid., p. 73.
132 Ibid., p. 70.
133 Ibid., p. 73.
134 Ibid., pp. 70, 71.
135 Emilia Dilke, *French Architects and Sculptors of the XVIIIth Century*. London: George Bell and Sons, 1900, p. 5.
136 Ibid., pp. 5, 7–8.

137 Emilia Dilke, *French Furniture and Decoration in the XVIIIth Century.* London: George Bell and Sons, 1901, p. 163.
138 Ibid., pp. 110, 115.
139 Ibid., p. 203.
140 Ibid., p. vi.
141 Ibid., p. 1.
142 *Westminster Review* 55 (April 1879): pp. 595–6.
143 Ibid. See Elizabeth Mansfield, 'Victorian Identity and the Historical Imaginary: Emilia Dilke's *The Renaissance of Art in France*', *Clio: A Journal of Literature, History and the Philosophy of History* 26, 2 (Winter 1997): 167–88 (186–7, 170); and Eisler, 'Lady Dilke', 170.
144 Dilke, *Painters*, p. 71.
145 Ibid., p. 106.
146 Ibid., p. 122.
147 Ibid., p. 132.
148 Ibid., p. 163.
149 Griselda Pollock, *Vision and Difference: Femininity, Feminism and the Histories of Art*. London: Routledge, 1988, p. 122.
150 Dilke, *Painters*, p. 65.
151 Israel, *Names and Stories*, p. 65.
152 Dilke, *Painters*, p. 3.
153 Ibid., p. 54.
154 Israel, *Names and Stories*, pp. 187–8.
155 Dilke, *Painters*, p. 158.
156 Dilke, *Furniture*, p. 73.
157 Dilke, *Painters*, p. 157.
158 Ibid., p. 3.
159 Ibid., p. 17 ('it is not fitting that women should dabble in work they know nothing about').
160 See Israel, *Names and Stories*, p. 181.
161 Vernon Lee, *The Sentimental Traveller: Notes on Places*. London: John Lane, The Bodley Head, 1908, p. 3.
162 See Gunn, *Vernon Lee*, pp. 167–8.
163 Ibid., p. 28.
164 Cherry, *Painting Women*, p. 192.
165 George Eliot, 'Woman in France: Madame de Sablé', *Westminster Review* (October 1854). Reprinted in *George Eliot: Selected Essays, Poems and Other Writings*, ed. A. S. Byatt and Nicholas Warren. London: Penguin, 1990, pp. 8–37 (p. 36).

5 Feminine arts

1 *Chautauquan* 12 (1890): 772.
2 She also wrote travelogues, memoirs, and biographies of Mary Wollstonecraft, her uncle the folklorist Charles Godfrey Leland, her friend James Abbott McNeill Whistler and her husband Joseph Pennell.

3 Elizabeth Robins Pennell, *Nights: Rome, Venice in the Aesthetic Eighties; London, Paris in the Fighting Nineties*. Philadelphia and London: J. B. Lippincott, 1916, pp. 19–20.

4 See Meaghan Clarke, *Critical Voices: Women and Art Criticism in Britain 1880–1905*. Aldershot, Hants.: Ashgate, 2005; Meaghan Clarke, 'New Woman on Grub Street: Art in the City', in *Gissing and the City: Cultural Crisis and the Making of Books in Late-Victorian England*, ed. John Spiers. Palgrave Macmillan, 2005, pp. 31–40; Linda H. Peterson, *Becoming a Woman of Letters: Myths of Authorship, Facts of the Market*. Princeton University Press, 2009, chapter 6, especially pp. 178–80.

5 *Westminster Review* 55 (April 1879): 595–6; and Julie Codell, 'When Art Historians Use Periodicals: Methodology and Meaning', *Victorian Periodicals Review* 34, 3 (Fall 2001): 284–9.

6 *Illuminations: Women Writing on Photography from the 1850s to the Present*, ed. Liz Heron and Val Williams. Durham, N.C.: Duke University Press, 1996, p. 2.

7 Extract from Julia Margaret Cameron, *Annals of My Glass House* (1874), reprinted in *Illuminations*, ed. Heron and Williams, pp. 8–13 (p. 10).

8 Linda M. Shires, *Perspectives: Modes of Viewing and Knowing in Nineteenth-Century England*. Columbus: Ohio State University Press, 2009, p. 73.

9 Roland Barthes, *Camera Lucida: Reflections of Photography*. trans. Richard Howard. New York: Hill, 1981, p. 81.

10 Cameron, *Annals of My Glass House*, in *Illuminations*, ed. Heron and Williams, p. 10.

11 Ibid., p. 8.

12 Ibid., pp. 9, 2. See Susan Sontag, *On Photography*. New York: Anchor, 1977, 1990, p. 70.

13 Cameron, *Annals of My Glass House*, p. 9.

14 'A Lady Photographer Who Never Photographs Men; A Talk with Miss Alice Hughes', reprinted in *Illuminations*, ed. Heron and Williams, pp. 3–7 (p. 3).

15 Ibid., p. 6.

16 Ibid., pp. 4–5.

17 Ibid., p. 4.

18 Amy Levy, *The Romance of a Shop*. Cambridge: Black Apollo Press, 2012, p. 38.

19 Ibid., p. 103.

20 Ibid., pp. 50, 47.

21 Ibid., p. 172. See Elizabeth F. Evans, '"We Are Photographers, Not Mountebanks!": Spectacle, Commercial Space, and the New Public Woman', in *Amy Levy: Critical Essays*, ed. Naomi Hetherington and Nadia Valman. Athens: Ohio University Press, 2010, pp. 25–46.

22 Levy, *The Romance of a Shop*, pp. 53, 103.

23 'The Photographer', 'The Wares of Autolycus', *Pall Mall Gazette* (8 July 1895). See also the 'Wares' column on photography of 31 August 1893.

24 Elizabeth Eastlake, 'Photography', *Quarterly Review* 101 (April 1857): 442–68 (459).

25 Ibid., p. 465.
26 Ibid., p. 465.
27 Ibid., p. 443.
28 Ibid., p. 443.
29 Ibid., p. 465.
30 Ibid., p. 465.
31 Ibid., p. 467.
32 Ibid., p. 466.
33 Ibid., pp. 466–7.
34 Colin Ford, *Julia Margaret Cameron: A Critical Biography*. J. Paul Getty Trust Publications, 2003, p. 83.
35 Hughes, in *Illuminations*, p. 6.
36 Levy, *The Romance of a Shop*, pp. 41, 40.
37 Rosamund Marriott Watson, *The Art of the House*. London: George Bell and Sons, 1897, p. 150.
38 Ibid., p. 2.
39 Ibid., p. 1.
40 Ibid., p. 2.
41 Ibid., pp. 79–80.
42 See Talia Schaffer, *The Forgotten Female Aesthetes: Literary Culture in Late-Victorian England*. Charlottesville and London: University Press of Virginia, 2000, especially chapter 3; and *Novel Craft: Victorian Domestic Handicraft and Nineteenth-Century Fiction*. New York: Oxford University Press, 2011.
43 Schaffer, *The Forgotten Female Aesthetes*, p. 87.
44 Ibid., p. 87.
45 Watson, *The Art of the House*, pp. 1, 152–3.
46 Ibid., pp. 73, 158. See Schaffer, *The Forgotten Female Aesthetes*, pp. 99–101.
47 Watson, *The Art of the House*, p. 7.
48 Ibid., p. 17.
49 Ibid., pp. 151–2.
50 Ibid., pp. 40, 67.
51 Ibid., pp. 164–5.
52 Ibid., p. 89.
53 Ibid., pp. 115, 175, 96.
54 Ibid., p. 153.
55 Richard D. Altick, *The Presence of the Present: Topics of the Day in the Victorian Novel*. Columbus: Ohio State University Press, 1991, p. 8.
56 Watson, The Art of the House, p. 171.
57 Ibid.
58 Schaffer, *Novel Craft*, p. 36. See her discussion of 'The Great Exhibition and Imitative Arts'.
59 Ibid., p. 37.
60 Ibid., p. 44.
61 Hannah Lawrance, 'Legends of the Monastic Orders', *British Quarterly Review* 12 (1850): 477–500 (479).

62 Hannah Lawrance, 'The Manchester Exhibition', *British Quarterly Review* 24 (1856): 462–92 (476, 478). Quoted in Benjamin Dabby, 'Female Critics and Public Moralism in Britain from Anna Jameson to Virginia Woolf'. Unpublished PhD thesis, University of Cambridge, 2013, p. 147. I am indebted to Benjamin Dabby for sharing his research on Hannah Lawrance.
63 Lawrance, 'Manchester Exhibition', pp. 480–1. This, and the following extracts, are quoted and discussed in Dabby, pp. 147-51.
64 Ibid., pp. 479, 481.
65 Ibid., p. 466.
66 Ibid.
67 See Schaffer, *Novel Craft*, pp. 36–41.
68 William Whewell, *The General Bearing of the Great Exhibition on the Progress of Art and Science*, Inaugural Lecture (25 November 1851), p. 6. This and the next two quotations are taken from Isobel Armstrong, *Victorian Glassworlds: Glass Culture and the Imagination 1830–1880*. Oxford University Press, 2008, p. 147.
69 *Punch* 18 (January–June 1850): 90.
70 *Chambers' Edinburgh Journal* (31 May 1851): 336–40 (337).
71 See Caroline Palmer, 'Colour, Chemistry and Corsets: Mary Philadelphia Merrifield's *Dress as a Fine Art*', *Costume* 47, 1 (January 2013): 3–27.
72 Mary Merrifield, *Dress as a Fine Art*. London: Arthur Hall, Virtue, & Co., 1854, p. 127.
73 Ibid., p. 128.
74 Ibid., p. 129.
75 Ibid., p. 132.
76 Ibid., p. 141.
77 Ibid., p. 157.
78 Ibid., pp. 158–60.
79 Ibid., pp. 166–8.
80 Mary Merrifield, *Practical Directions for Portrait Painting in Water-Colours*. London: Winsor and Newton, 1851, p. 25.
81 Merrifield, *Dress as a Fine Art*, p. 2.
82 Ibid., pp. 22–3.
83 Ibid., pp. 24, 22.
84 Elizabeth Rigby, 'The Art of Dress', *Quarterly Review* 79 (1847): 372–99 (373).
85 Ibid., pp. 375–6.
86 Ibid., p. 390.
87 Ibid., pp. 392, 390, 391–2.
88 Ibid., p. 393.
89 Ibid., pp. 395, 398–9.
90 Ibid., p. 399.
91 Eliza Warren Francis, 'Editorial', *Ladies' Treasury* 4 (1860).
92 Schaffer, *The Forgotten Female Aesthetes*, pp. 108–10.
93 Ibid., p. 103.
94 'The Wares of Autolycus', *Pall Mall Gazette* (3 November 1894): 5.
95 'The Wares of Autolycus', *Pall Mall Gazette* (3 May 1895).
96 Elizabeth Robins Pennell, *Chautauquan* 16 (1892): 214.

97 Florence Fenwick Miller, 'Ladies' Page', *Illustrated London News* (9 April 1887): 407. Cited in Clarke, *Critical Voices*, p. 94.
98 'The Wares of Autolycus', *Pall Mall Gazette* (2 August 1893; 1 May 1895).
99 'The Wares of Autolycus', *Pall Mall Gazette* (2 June 1893): 5.
100 'The Wares of Autolycus', *Pall Mall Gazette* (7 June 1893): 5; (14 June 1893).
101 As Meaghan Clarke demonstrates in her excellent study of the subject, *Critical Voices: Women and Art Criticism in Britain 1880–1905*. Aldershot, Hants.: Ashgate, 2005.
102 'The Wares of Autolycus', *Pall Mall Gazette* (22 November 1894 and 28 October 1893); Anna B. Leonard, 'Exhibition of French Pottery at the Tiffany Studios', *Keramic Studio* 1 (1899): 82–3; Mira Edson, 'A Tiffany Lamp', *Keramic Studio* 1 (1899): 226; Anna B. Leonard, 'Pottery and Porcelain at the Paris Exposition', *Keramic Studio* 2 (1900): 73–5.
103 Elizabeth Robins Pennell writing as 'N.N.' in *The Nation* (15 November 1894). Reprinted in *Brushes with History: Writing on Art from* The Nation, *1865–2001*, ed. Peter G. Meyer. New York: Thunder's Mouth Press/Nation Books, 2001, pp. 56–60.
104 Cecilia Waern, 'Some notes on the Art of John La Farge', *Atlantic Monthly* 75 (May 1895): 690–3 (690).
105 Cecilia Waern, 'Puvis de Chavannes in Boston', *Atlantic Monthly* 79 (February 1897): 251–7.
106 Cecilia Waern, 'Some Notes on French Impressionism', *Atlantic Monthly* (April 1892): 535–41 (535).
107 Ibid., p. 536.
108 Ibid.
109 Ibid., p. 537.
110 Ibid., p. 536.
111 Ibid.
112 Ibid., pp. 536–7.
113 In a review essay of 1899 titled 'Some Prospects of Modern Art', the novelist and biographer Una Ashworth Taylor stresses that the reality the modern French subject painter endeavours to depict 'must be a reality characteristic of its own and no other period. Life must be reproduced only under those salient forms which stamp it as modern; it must be portrayed in its most perceptible points of divergency from the life of all other epochs.' *Edinburgh Review* (July 1899): 48–69 (59).
114 Waern, 'Some Notes on French Impressionism', p. 537.
115 Ibid.
116 Ibid., p. 541.
117 Alice Meynell, 'Pictures from the Hill Collection', *Magazine of Art* (1882): 80–1. See Clarke, *Critical Voices*, pp. 70–6.
118 *Notes by George Fleming on a Collection of Pictures by Professor G. Costa: Exhibited at the Fine Art Society*. London: The Fine Art Society, 1882.
119 N.N., 'The Salon in the Champ de Mars', *Nation* (25 June 1891); N.N., 'The Impressionists in London', *Nation* (9 February 1905). Reprinted in Meyer, ed., *Brushes with History*, pp. 51–2, 80.

120 N.N., 'Art in the Victorian Era', *Nation* (1 July 1897), reprinted in Meyer, ed., *Brushes with History*, pp. 69–74. Though Pennell had noted in an article on Millais a couple of years earlier that this narrative of rebellion had in fact served the PRB rather well: 'The Pre-Raphaelites were rebels – rebels against Academic convention and tradition ... but whatever neglect or insult was offered to the work of the Pre-Raphaelites was always sure in the end to prove the kindest of advertisements. Better, after all, to have one's painting called an atrocity, or abomination, or any other hard name, than to have absolutely nothing said about it' (N.N., 'Millais', *Nation* (27 August 1896): 156–7).

121 N.N., 'Art in the Victorian Era'. Una Ashworth Taylor, in 1900, looking back at 'the principal features of the movement, whose nativity involved so complete a change in the ideals of art', remarks: 'The ideals themselves – ideals of the wider scope of art, of its possible application to the common surroundings of daily life; ideals of the right of all men, so far as it lies in them, to participate in the enjoyment of the outward fairness art may impart to the general environment – are diffused not only among artists, but likewise among artisans and handicraftsmen, and have found practical embodiment in a widely spread system of education in those "lesser arts" which for centuries had fallen into abeyance, or become the prey of the mechanical copyist' ('Morris and Rossetti', *Edinburgh Review* (April 1900): 356–79 (356).

122 N.N., 'Art in the Victorian Era'.

123 See Clarke's discussion of the life drawing controversy, *Critical Voices*, pp. 65–7.

124 'Wares of Autolycus', *Pall Mall Gazette* (10 May 1895).

125 Alice Meynell, 'Wares of Autolycus', *Pall Mall Gazette* (12 January 1894): 5.

126 See Florence Fenwick Miller, 'Ladies' Page', *Illustrated London News* (5 June 1897): 790; (12 March 1898): 380; (14 February 1903): 244; (29 January 1910): 174. All cited in Clarke, *Critical Voices*, p. 93. Clarke differentiates Fenwick Miller's exclusive focus on the Royal Academy from Meynell's and Pennell's broader acknowledgement of modern developments in art practice, pointing out that 'Fenwick Miller's continued espousal of RA membership as the pinnacle of achievement for women artists' amounted to 'a conservative affirmation of the traditional art world' which they did not share (Clarke, *Critical Voices*, p. 94).

127 Anna Jameson, *Visits and Sketches at Home and Abroad*. 2 vols., 2nd edn, London: Saunders and Otley, 1835, vol. 2, pp. 171–9.

128 Hannah Lawrance, 'Modern Painters', *British Quarterly Review* 23 (1856): 442–67. Quoted in Dabby, 'Female Critics', p. 152.

129 Hannah Lawrance, 'The Education and Employment of Women', *British Quarterly Review* 52 (July 1870): 31–57 (47).

130 E. F. Ellet, *Women Artists in All Ages and Countries*. London: Richard Bentley, 1859, p. v.

131 *Athenaeum* (24 December 1859): 849.

132 Ellet, *Women Artists*, pp. 209–10, 210–11.
133 Ellen C. Clayton, *English Female Artists,* 2 vols. London: Tinsley Brothers, 1876, vol. 1, p. 2.
134 Ibid., pp. 5, 8, 21–9. See volume 2 for nineteenth-century female artists.
135 Clayton, *English Female Artists*, vol. 1, p. 4.
136 Ellen C. Clayton, *Female Warriors.* London: Tinsley Brothers, 1879, pp. 2–3.
137 Helen Zimmern, 'The Work of Miss Bessie Potter', *Magazine of Art* (1900): 522–3.
138 See Clarke, *Critical Voices*, pp. 53–8, 60–1.
139 See ibid, pp. 95–6, 94–5.
140 'Wares of Autolycus', *Pall Mall Gazette* (10 August 1893). See also Fenwick Miller's less positive review of the Women's Building, 'Art in the Woman's Section', *Art Journal* (1893): xii–xvi.
141 Waern, 'Some Notes on French Impressionism', p. 540.
142 N.N., 'The Impressionists in London', *Nation* (9 February 1905). Reprinted in Meyer, ed., *Brushes with History*, pp. 80–5.
143 Elizabeth Robins Pennell, *Chautauquan* 13 (1891): 83.
144 Elizabeth Robins Pennell, 'Art and Women', *Nation* (1 June 1918). Reprinted in Meyer, ed., *Brushes with History*, pp. 120–3.
145 Ibid., p. 123.
146 Virginia Woolf, *Mr Bennett and Mrs Brown.* London: The Hogarth Press, 1924, p. 4.
147 Linda Nochlin, 'Why Have There Been No Great Women Artists?' *ARTnews* (January 1971): 22–39, 67–71.

Conclusion

1 Hannah Lawrance, 'Our Epilogue on Books: Art', *British Quarterly Review* 58 (April 1859): 553–60 (553). Likewise, in her view, women were not best served by separatist histories of female art, such as Elizabeth Ellet's *Women Artists in all Ages and Countries*, published two years later in 1859, but were better judged alongside their male peers, in comparison with whom they would not be found wanting See Dabby, 'Female Critics', pp. 152–3.
2 See Clarke, *Critical Voices*, pp. 56–8.
3 Florence Fenwick Miller, 'Ladies' Page', *Illustrated London News* (26 February 1898): 310. Quoted in Clarke, *Critical Voices*, p. 107. See Clarke's discussion of the controversial issue of separate female exhibitions, pp. 106–13, and 131ff.
4 *Pace* Anna Jameson, who sixty years earlier had argued, just as vigorously, 'I wish to combat in every way that oft-repeated but most false compliment unthinkingly paid to women, that genius is of no sex' (Jameson, *Visits and Sketches*, vol. 2, p. 179).
5 A.U., 'Art and Artists', *Star* (4 June 1895): 1. Quoted in Clarke, *Critical Voices*, p. 131.
6 See Jan Marsh and Pamela Gerrish Nunn, *Pre-Raphaelite Women Artists.* London: Thames & Hudson, 1998.

7 Oscar Wilde, 'The Critic as Artist', in *Complete Works of Oscar Wilde*, introduced by Vyvyan Holland. London: Harper Collins, 1966, pp. 1054–5.
8 Joan Scott, 'Fantasy Echo: History and the Construction of Identity', *Critical Inquiry* 27 (Winter 2001): 284–304 (286–7).
9 Robert Browning, 'Inapprehensiveness', *Robert Browning: The Poems, Volume II*, ed. John Pettigrew, supplemented and completed by Thomas J. Collins. Harmondsworth, Middlesex: Penguin, 1981, pp. 886–7.
10 Crary, *Techniques of the Observer*, p. 7.
11 Vernon Lee, 'A Postscript on Ruskin', *North American Review* (November 1903): 678–90 (678, 681).
12 Ibid., p. 689.
13 Ibid., pp. 689–90.
14 Ibid., pp. 678–9.
15 Ibid., p. 680.
16 Ibid., p. 678.

Bibliography

Ajmar-Wollheim, Marta and Flora Dennis, eds. *At Home in Renaissance Italy*. London, V&A Publications, 2006, p. 219.

Aliquis. 'Art Critics of Today', *Art Journal* (July 1892): 193.

Altick, Richard D. *The Presence of the Present: Topics of the Day in the Victorian Novel*. Columbus: Ohio State University Press, 1991.

'An American Talks about Art', *Magazine of Art* 1 (May 1878): 202–5.

[Anon.] 'E. F. Ellet, *Women Artists in All Ages and Countries*', *Athenaeum* (24 December 1859): 849.

'Ellen C. Clayton, *English Female Artists*', *Art Journal* (1 August 1876): 256.

'Emilia Dilke, *The Renaissance of Art in France*', *Westminster Review* 55 (April 1879): 595–6.

'Handbook to the Public Galleries of Art', *British and Foreign Review* 14 (1843): 55.

'Handbook to the Public Galleries of Art', *Gentleman's Magazine* n.s. 18 (1842): 227.

'The Wares of Autolycus', *Pall Mall Gazette* (May 1893–December 1998).

Armstrong, Isobel. *Victorian Glassworlds: Glass Culture and the Imagination 1830–1880*. Oxford University Press, 2008.

Arnold, Matthew. *The Complete Prose Works of Matthew Arnold*, ed. R. H. Super. Ann Arbor: University of Michigan Press, 1960–70.

Avery-Quash, Susanna and Julie Sheldon. *Art for the Nation: The Eastlakes and the Victorian Art World*. London: The National Gallery Company, 2011.

Badeni, June. *The Slender Tree: A Life of Alice Meynell*. Padstow, Cornwall: Tabb House, 1981.

Barthes, Roland. *Camera Lucida: Reflections of Photography*. trans. Richard Howard. New York: Hill, 1981.

Benjamin, Walter. 'The Task of the Translator', in *Illuminations*, ed. Hannah Arendt, trans. Harry Zohn. London: Pimlico, 1999, pp. 70–82.

Berenson, Bernard. Archive. Villa I Tatti, Florence.

The Florentine Painters of the Renaissance. New York, 1896.

Berenson, Mary. *Mary Berenson: A Self-Portrait from her Letters and Diaries*, ed. Barbara Strachey and Jayne Samuels. London: Victor Gollancz, 1983.

Bhabha, Homi K. *The Location of Culture*. London and New York: Routledge, 1994.

Bohn, Babette. 'The Antique Heroines of Elisabetta Sirani', *Renaissance Studies* 16 (2002): 52–79.
Braddon, Mary Elizabeth. *Lady Audley's Secret*, ed. Jenny Bourne Taylor. London: Penguin, 1998.
Brontë, Anne. *The Tenant of Wildfell Hall*, ed. Stevie Davies. London: Penguin, 1996.
Brontë, Charlotte. *Jane Eyre*, ed. Richard J. Dunn. New York and London: W. W. Norton & Company, 1971.
Villette, ed. Mark Lilly and Tony Tanner. London: Penguin, 1979.
Brown, Alison. 'Vernon Lee and the Renaissance: From Burckhardt to Berenson', in *Victorian and Edwardian Responses to the Italian Renaissance*, ed. John Easton Law and Lene Østermark-Johansen. Aldershot, Hants.: Ashgate, 2005.
Browning, Robert. *The Poems, Volume II*, ed. John Pettigrew, supplemented and completed by Thomas J. Collins. Harmondsworth, Middlesex: Penguin, 1981.
Bryson, Norman. *Vision and Painting: The Logic of the Gaze*. New Haven: Yale University Press, 1983.
Burdett, Carolyn. 'Introduction: Psychology/Aesthetics in the Nineteenth Century', *Psychology/Aesthetics in the Nineteenth Century, 19: Interdisciplinary Studies in the Long Nineteenth Century* 12 (2011) http://19.bbk.ac.uk/index.php/19/issue/view/80.
'"The subjective inside us can turn into the objective outside": Vernon Lee's Psychological Aesthetics', *Psychology/Aesthetics in the Nineteenth Century, 19: Interdisciplinary Studies in the Long Nineteenth Century* 12 (2011) http://19.bbk.ac.uk/index.php/19/issue/view/80.
Caine, Barbara. 'Mothering Feminism/Mothering Feminists: Ray Strachey and *The Cause*', *Women's History Review* 8, 2 (1999): 295–310.
Callcott, Maria. *Essays Towards the History of Painting*. London: Edward Moxon, 1836.
Cartwright, Julia. *Beatrice d'Este, Duchess of Milan 1475–1497: A Study of the Renaissance*. London: J. M. Dent and Sons; New York: E. P. Dutton and Co., 1926.
Christina of Denmark, Duchess of Milan and Lorraine 1522–1590. London: John Murray, 1913.
Isabella d'Este, Marchioness of Mantua 1474–1539: A Study of the Renaissance. 2 vols., London: John Murray, 1903.
Casteras, S. P. '"The Necessity of a Name": Portrayals and Betrayals of Victorian Women Artists', in *Gender and Discourse in Victorian Art and Literature*, ed. A. H. Harrison and B. Taylor. DeKalb: Northern Illinois University Press, 1992, pp. 207–32.
Cherry, Deborah. *Beyond the Frame: Feminism and Visual Culture, Britain 1850–1900*. London and New York: Routledge, 2000.
Painting Women: Victorian Women Artists. London: Routledge, 1993.

Cherry, Deborah, and Griselda Pollock. 'Woman as Sign in Pre-Raphaelite Literature: A Study of the Representation of Elizabeth Siddall', *Art History* 7, 2 (June, 1984): 206–27.

Clarke, Meaghan. *Critical Voices: Women and Art Criticism in Britain 1880–1905*. Aldershot, Hants.: Ashgate, 2005.

'New Woman on Grub Street: Art in the City', in *Gissing and the City: Cultural Crisis and the Making of Books in Late-Victorian England*, ed. John Spiers. Palgrave Macmillan, 2005, pp. 31–40.

'Translating Nudus: Modernity and the British Academy's New Clothes', in *Critical Exchange: Art Criticism of the Eighteenth and Nineteenth Centuries in Russia and Western Europe*, ed. Carol Adlam and Juliet Simpson. Bern: Peter Lang, 2009, pp. 167–89.

Clayton, Ellen C. *English Female Artists*. London: Tinsley Brothers, 1876.

Female Warriors. London: Tinsley Brothers, 1879.

Clifford, Edward. *Broadlands as It Was*. London: privately printed, 1890.

Codell, Julie. 'When Art Historians Use Periodicals: Methodology and Meaning', *Victorian Periodicals Review* 34, 3 (Fall 2001): 284–9.

Colby, Vineta. *Vernon Lee: A Literary Biography*. Charlottesville and London: University of Virginia Press, 2003.

Cooper, Robyn. '"The Crowning Glory of Pisa": Nineteenth-Century Reactions to the Campo Santo', *Italian Studies* 37 (1982): 72–100.

Corbett, Mary Jean. *Representing Femininity: Middle-Class Subjectivity in Victorian and Edwardian Women's Autobiographies*. Oxford University Press, 1992.

Costelloe, Mary Whitall. 'The New and the Old Art Criticism', *Nineteenth Century* (May 1894): 828–37.

Craik, Dinah Mulock. *Olive and The Half-Caste*, ed. Cora Kaplan. Oxford University Press, 1996.

Crary, Jonathan. *Techniques of the Observer: On Vision and Modernity in the Nineteenth Century*. Cambridge, Mass., and London: MIT Press, 1990.

Cruttwell, Maud. *Fire and Frost*. London: John Lane, The Bodley Head, 1913.

A Guide to the Paintings in the Churches and Minor Museums of Florence: A Critical Catalogue with Quotations from Vasari. London: J. M. Dent & Company; New York: E. P. Dutton & Co. 1908.

A Guide to the Paintings in the Florentine Galleries the Uffizi, the Pitti, the Accademia: A Critical Catalogue with Quotations from Vasari. London: J. M. Dent & Company; New York: E. P. Dutton & Co., 1907.

Dabby, Benjamin. 'Female Critics and Public Moralism in Britain from Anna Jameson to Virginia Woolf'. Unpublished PhD thesis, University of Cambridge, 2013.

David, Deirdre. *Intellectual Women and Victorian Patriarchy: Harriet Martineau, Elizabeth Barrett Browning, George Eliot*. London: Macmillan, 1987.

Davis, Natalie Zemon. '"Women's History" in Transition: The European Case', *Feminist Studies* 3, 3/4 (Spring/Summer 1976): 83–103.

de Bolla, Peter. *The Education of the Eye: Painting, Landscape, and Architecture in Eighteenth-Century Britain*. Stanford University Press, 2003.

Dilke, Emilia. *Art in the Modern State*. London: Chapman and Hall, 1888.
'Benefit Societies and Trades Unions for Women', *Fortnightly Review* n.s. 45 (June 1889): 852–6.
The Book of the Spiritual Life, including a Memoir of the author by Sir Charles Dilke. London: John Murray, 1905.
French Architects and Sculptors of the XVIIIth Century. London: George Bell and Sons, 1900.
French Engravers and Draughtsmen of the XVIIIth Century. London: George Bell and Sons, 1902.
French Furniture and Decoration in the XVIIIth Century. London: George Bell and Sons, 1901.
French Painters of the Eighteenth Century. London: George Bell & Sons, 1899.
'Woman Suffrage in England', *North American Review* 164 (February 1897): 151–9.
Dixon, Ella Hepworth. *The Story of a Modern Woman*. London: Methuen, 1894.
Eastlake, Elizabeth. *Five Great Painters*. 2 vols., London: Longmans, Green and Co., 1883.
'Giovanni Morelli: The Patriot and Critic', *Quarterly Review* 173 (July 1891): 235–52.
Journals and Correspondence of Lady Eastlake, ed. Charles Eastlake Smith. 2 vols., London: John Murray, 1895.
'Life and Works of Thorvaldsen', *Edinburgh Review* 142 (July 1875): 1–29.
'Photography', *Quarterly Review* 101 (April 1857): 442–68.
Edson, Mira. 'A Tiffany Lamp', *Keramic Studio* 1 (1899): 226.
Eisler, Colin. 'Lady Dilke (1840–1904): The Six lives of an Art Historian', in *Women as Interpreters of the Visual Arts, 1820–1979*, ed. Claire Richter Sherman and Adele M. Holcomb. Westport, Conn.: Greenwood, 1981, pp. 147–80.
Eliot, George. *Essays of George Eliot*, ed. Thomas Pinney. London: Routledge and Kegan Paul, 1968.
George Eliot: Selected Essays, Poems and Other Writings, ed. A. S. Byatt and Nicholas Warren. London: Penguin, 1990.
The George Eliot Letters, ed. Gordon S. Haight. 9 vols., New Haven: Yale University Press, 1954–78.
The Journals of George Eliot, ed. Margaret Harris and Judith Johnston. Cambridge University Press, 1998.
Middlemarch. Harmondsworth, Middlesex: Penguin, 2012.
Romola, ed. Andrew Brown. Oxford: Clarendon Press, 1993.
Ellet, E. F. *Women Artists in All Ages and Countries*. London: Richard Bentley, 1859.
Elsden, Annamaria Formidella. *Roman Fever: Domesticity and Nationalism in C19th American Women's Writing*. Columbus: Ohio State University Press, 2004.
Emanuel, Angela, ed. *A Bright Remembrance: The Diaries of Julia Cartwright, 1851–1924*. London: Weidenfeld & Nicolson, 1989.
Ernstrom, Adele M. 'Elizabeth Eastlake's *History of Our Lord as exemplified in works of art*: Theology, Art and Aesthetic Reaction', *Art History* 35, 4 (September 2012): 750–77.

Evangelista, Stefano. 'Vernon Lee in the Vatican: The Uneasy Alliance of Aestheticism and Archaeology', *Victorian Studies* 52, 1 (Autumn 2009): 31–41.

Evans, Elizabeth F. '"We Are Photographers, Not Mountebanks!": Spectacle, Commercial Space, and the New Public Woman', in *Amy Levy: Critical Essays,* ed. Naomi Hetherington and Nadia Valman. Athens: Ohio University Press, 2010, pp. 25–46.

Feltes, N. N. *Modes of Production of Victorian Novels.* University of Chicago Press, 1989.

Ferrugia, Gemma. *Woman's Folly*, trans. Helen Zimmern, intro. Edmund Gosse. London: Heinemann, 1895.

Field, Michael. *Sight and Song*. London: Elkin Mathews and John Lane, 1892.

Underneath the Bough: A Book of Verses. London: George Bell & Sons, 1893.

Works and Days, vols. 4 and 5. Ms. British Library, Add. Ms. 46779 (1891); Add. Ms. 46780.

Works and Days: From the Journal of Michael Field, ed. T. and D. C. Sturge Moore. London: John Murray, 1933.

Fleming, George. *Notes by George Fleming on a Collection of Pictures by Professor G. Costa: Exhibited at the Fine Art Society*. London: The Fine Art Society 1882.

Ford, Colin. *Julia Margaret Cameron: A Critical Biography*. J. Paul Getty Trust Publications, 2003.

Foucault, Michel. 'Of Other Spaces', *Diacritics* (Spring 1986): 22–7.

The Order of Things: An Archaeology of the Human Sciences. London: Tavistock Publications, 1970.

Francis, Eliza Warren. 'Editorial', *Ladies' Treasury* 4 (1860).

Fraser, Hilary. 'Women and the Ends of Art History: Vision and Corporeality in Nineteenth-Century Critical Discourse', *Victorian Studies* 42, 1 (Autumn 1998/99): 77–100.

Garrard, Mary D. *Artemisia Gentileschi: The Image of the Female Hero In Italian Baroque Art*. Princeton University Press, 1989.

Artemisia Gentileschi around 1622: The Shaping and Reshaping of an Artistic Identity. Berkeley and London: University of California Press, 2001.

Greer, Germaine. *The Obstacle Race: The Fortunes of Women Painters and their Work*. London: Weidenfeld & Nicolson, 1979.

Grosz, Elizabeth. 'Sexual Difference and the Problem of Essentialism', in *The Essential Difference: Another Look at Essentialism*, ed. Naomi Schor and Elizabeth Weed. Bloomington: Indiana University Press, 1988, pp. 82–97.

Gunn, Peter. *Vernon Lee: Violet Paget, 1856–1935*. London: Oxford University Press, 1964.

Gunning, Tom. 'The Cinema of Attractions: Early Film, its Spectator, and the Avant-Garde', in Thomas Elsaesser, ed., *Early Cinema: Space, Frame, Narrative.* London: BFI, 1990, pp. 56–62.

Hall, Julie E. '"Coming to Europe", Coming to Authorship: Sophia Hawthorne and her Notes in England and Italy', *Legacy: A Journal of American Women Writers* 19, 2 (June 2002): 137–51.

Hawthorne, Nathaniel. *The Marble Faun*, ed. Susan Manning. Oxford University Press, 2002.

Our Old Home, and English Notebooks, 2 vols., 4th edn. Boston: Houghton Mifflin Company, 1912.

Heffernan, James A. W. *Museum of Words: The Poetics of Ekphrasis from Homer to Ashbery*. University of Chicago Press, 1993.

'Speaking for Pictures', *Word and Image* 15, 1 (January–March 1999): 19–34.

Heron, Liz, and Val Williams. *Illuminations: Women Writing on Photography from the 1850s to the Present*. Durham, N.C.: Duke University Press, 1996.

Holcomb, A. M. 'Anna Jameson: The First Professional English Art Historian', *Art History* 6 (1983): 171–87.

'Anna Jameson (1794–1860): Sacred Art and Social Vision', in *Women as Interpreters of the Visual Arts, 1820–1979*, ed. Claire Richter Sherman with Adele M. Holcomb. Westport, Conn., and London: Greenwood Press, 1981.

Howitt, Anna Mary. 'The Sisters in Art', *The Illustrated Exhibitor and Magazine of Art* 2 (1852): 214–16, 238–40, 262–3, 286–8, 317–19, 334–6, 347–8, 362–4.

Israel, Kali. *Names and Stories: Emilia Dilke and Victorian Culture*. New York and Oxford: Oxford University Press, 1999.

'The Resources of Style: Francis Pattison in Oxford', *Radical History Review* 72 (1998): 122–62.

'Style, Strategy, and Self-Creation in the Life of Emilia Dilke', in *Constructions of the Self*, ed. George Levine. New Brunswick: Rutgers University Press, 1992: 213–45.

Jacobs, Fredrika. *Defining the Renaissance Virtuosa: Woman Artists and the Language of Art History and Criticism*. Cambridge University Press, 1997.

Jameson, Anna. 'Andrea Mantegna', *Penny Magazine* 12 (1843): 436. Reprinted in *Memoirs of Early Italian Painters and of the Progress of Painting in Italy*. 2nd edn, London: John Murray, 1868, 108–27.

Letters of Anna Jameson to Ottilie von Goethe, ed. G. H. Needler. London, New York, Toronto: Oxford University Press, 1939.

Memoirs of Early Italian Painters and of the Progress of Painting in Italy. 2nd edn, London: John Murray, 1868.

Visits and Sketches at Home and Abroad. 2 vols., 2nd edn, London: Saunders and Otley, 1835.

Jay, Martin. *Force Fields: Between Intellectual History and Cultural Critique*. New York: Routledge, 1993.

'Scopic Regimes of Modernity', in *Vision and Visuality*, ed. Hal Foster. Seattle: Bay Press/Dia Art Foundation, 1988, pp. 3–23.

Johnston, Judith. *Anna Jameson: Victorian, Feminist, Woman of Letters*. Aldershot, Hants.: Scolar, 1997.

Victorian Women and the Economies of Travel, Translation and Culture, 1830–1870. Aldershot, Hants.: Ashgate, 2012.

Johnston, Judith and Hilary Fraser. 'The Professionalization of Women's Writing: Extending the Canon', in *Women and Literature in Britain 1800–1900*, ed. Joanne Shattock. Cambridge University Press, 2001, pp. 231–50.

Kanwit, John Paul M. *Victorian Art Criticism and the Woman Writer*. Columbus: Ohio State University Press, 2013.
Kelly, Joan. *Women, History and Theory: The Essays of Joan Kelly*. Chicago and London: University of Chicago Press, 1984.
Landon, Letitia Elizabeth (L.E.L.). *The Poetical Works of Letitia Elizabeth Landon (L.E.L.)*, ed. William B. Scott. London: George Routledge & Sons, nd.
Lawrance, Hannah. 'The Education and Employment of Women', *British Quarterly Review* 52 (July 1870): 31–57.
'Legends of the monastic orders', *British Quarterly Review* 12 (1850): 477–500.
'The Manchester Exhibition', *British Quarterly Review* 24 (1856): 462–92.
'Modern Painters', *British Quarterly Review* 23 (1856): 442–67.
'Our Epilogue on Books: Art', *British Quarterly Review* 58 (April 1859): 553–60.
Lee, Vernon. *Althea: A Second Book of Dialogues on Aspirations and Duties*. London: Osgood, McIlvaine & Co., 1894.
Belcaro: Being Essays on Sundry Aesthetical Questions. London: T. Fisher Unwin, 1887.
Euphorion: Being Studies of the Antique and the Mediaeval in the Renaissance. 2 vols., London: T. Fisher Unwin, 1884.
Juvenilia: Being a Second Series of Essays on Sundry Aesthetical Questions. 2 vols., London: T. Fisher Unwin, 1887.
Laurus Nobilis: Chapters on Art and Life. London: John Jane, The Bodley Head, 1909.
Limbo, and Other Essays. London: Grant Richards, 1897.
Miss Brown. 3 vols., Edinburgh: William Blackwood and Sons, 1884.
'A Postscript on Ruskin', *North American Review* (November, 1903): 678–90.
The Sentimental Traveller: Notes on Places. London: John Lane, The Bodley Head, 1908.
The Spirit of Rome: Leaves from a Diary. London: John Lane, The Bodley Head, 1906.
Studies of the Eighteenth Century in Italy. London: W. Satchell and Co., 1880.
Lee, Vernon, and Clementina Anstruther-Thomson. *Beauty and Ugliness and Other Studies in Psychological Aesthetics*. London: John Lane, The Bodley Head, 1912.
Lefevere, André. 'Translation: Its Genealogy in the West', in *Translation, History and Culture*, ed. Susan Bassnett and André Lefevere. London: Pinter, 1990.
Leighton, Angela. *Victorian Women Poets: Writing Against the Heart*. Brighton: Harvester, 1992.
Leonard, Anna B. 'Exhibition of French Pottery at the Tiffany Studios', *Keramic Studio* 1 (1899): 82–3.
'Pottery and Porcelain at the Paris Exposition', *Keramic Studio* 2 (1900): 73–5.
Levy, Amy. *The Romance of a Shop*. Cambridge: Black Apollo Press, 2012.
Lew, Laurie Kane. 'Cultural Anxiety in Anna Jameson's Art Criticism', *Studies in English Literature* 36 (1996): 829–56.
Losano, Antonia. *The Woman Painter in Victorian Literature*. Columbus: Ohio State University Press, 2008.

Ludley, David A. 'Anna Jameson and D. G. Rossetti. His Use of Her Histories', *Woman's Art Journal* 12 (1992): 29–33.

Maharaj, Sarat. 'Perfidious Fidelity: The Untranslatability of the Other', in *Global Visions: Towards a New Internationalism in the Visual Arts*, ed. Jean Fisher. London: Kala Press in association with the Institute of International Visual Arts, 1994, pp. 28–35.

Maltz, Diana. 'Engaging "Delicate Brains": From Working-Class Enculturation to Upper-Class Lesbian Liberation in Vernon Lee and Kit Anstruther-Thomson's Psychological Aesthetics', in *Women and British Aestheticism*, ed. Talia Schaffer and Kathy Alexis Psomiades. Charlottesville: University Press of Virginia, 1999, pp. 211–29.

Mansfield, Elizabeth. 'Victorian Identity and the Historical Imaginary: Emilia Dilke's *The Renaissance of Art in France*', *Clio: A Journal of Literature, History and the Philosophy of History* 26, 2 (Winter 1997): 167–88.

Marsh, Jan. '"The Old Tuscan Rapture": the Response to Italy and its Art in the Work of Marie Spartali Stillman', in Alison Chapman and Jane Stabler, eds., *Unfolding the South: Nineteenth-Century British Women Writers and Artists in Italy*. Manchester University Press, 2003, pp. 159–82.

Marsh, Jan, and Pamela Gerrish Nunn. *Pre-Raphaelite Women Artists*. London: Thames & Hudson, 1998.

Mermin, Dorothy. *Godiva's Ride: Women of Letters in England, 1830–1880*. Bloomington: Indiana University Press, 1993.

Merrifield, [Mary]. *The Art of Fresco Painting as Practised by the Old Italian and Spanish Masters, with a Preliminary Inquiry Into the Nature of the Colours Used in Fresco Painting*, ed. A. C. Sewter. London: Alec Tiranti, 1952.

Merrifield, Mary. *Dress as a Fine Art*. London: Arthur Hall, Virtue, & Co., 1854.

Medieval and Renaissance Treatises on the Arts of Painting. Mineola, N. Y.: Dover Publications, 1999 (1966).

'The Need of Sanitary Knowledge to Women', *Dublin University Magazine* 76 (September 1870): 843–8.

Practical Directions for Portrait Painting in Water-Colours. London: Winsor and Newton, 1851.

Review of Jameson, *Legends of the Madonna*, *Edinburgh Review* 97 (January 1853): 230–9.

Meskimmon, Marsha. *Women Making Art: History, Subjectivity, Aesthetics*. London and New York: Routledge, 2003.

Meyer, Peter G., ed. *Brushes with History: Writing on Art from* The Nation, *1865–2001*. New York: Thunder's Mouth Press/Nation Books, 2001.

Meynell, Alice. *Essays by Alice Meynell*. London: Burns & Oates, 1914.

'Newlyn', *Art Journal* (1889): 97–102.

'Pictures from the Hill Collection', *Magazine of Art* (1882): 80–8.

Prose and Poetry: Centenary Volume, ed. Frederick Page *et al.*, with a bibliographical and critical introduction by V. Sackville-West. London: Cape, 1947.

'A Question of Propriety', *Tablet* (6 June 1885): 882–3.

The Spirit of Place and Other Essays. London and New York: John Lane, The Bodley Head, 1899.
The Works of John S. Sargent, R.A. With an Introductory Note by Mrs Meynell. London: William Heinemann; New York: Charles Scribner's Sons, 1903.
Meynell, Viola. *Alice Meynell: A Memoir*. London: Jonathan Cape, 1929.
Miller, Florence Fenwick. 'Art in the Woman's Section', *Art Journal* (1893): xii–xvi.
'Ladies' Page', *Illustrated London News* (5 June 1897): 790.
'Ladies' Page', *Illustrated London News* (26 February 1898): 310.
'Ladies' Page', *Illustrated London News* (12 March 1898): 380.
'Ladies' Page', *Illustrated London News* (14 February 1903): 244.
'Ladies' Page', *Illustrated London News* (29 January 1910): 174.
Mills, Sara. *Discourses of Difference*. London: Routledge, 1991.
Mitchell, W. J. T. *Picture Theory: Essays on Verbal and Visual Representation*. Chicago and London: University of Chicago Press, 1995.
Morgan, Thais E., ed. *Victorian Sages and Cultural Discourse: Renegotiating Gender and Power*. New Brunswick: Rutgers University Press, 1990.
Mulvey, Laura. 'Visual Pleasure and Narrative Cinema', *Screen* 16, 3 (Autumn 1975): 6–18.
Murphy, Caroline. 'Lavinia Fontana and le Dame della Città: Understanding Female Artistic Patronage in Late Sixteenth-Century Bologna', *Renaissance Studies* 10 (1996): 190–208.
'Lavinia Fontana and Female Life Cycle Experience in Late Sixteenth-Century Bologna', in Geraldine A. Johnson and Sara F. Matthews Grieco, eds., *Picturing Women In Renaissance and Baroque Italy*. Cambridge University Press, 1997.
Lavinia Fontana: A Painter and her Patrons In Sixteenth-Century Bologna. New Haven and London: Yale University Press, 2003.
Nead, Lynda. *The Haunted Gallery: Painting, Photography, and Film c. 1900*. New Haven, Conn.: Yale University Press, 2007.
Newton, Judith Lowder. 'History as Usual? Feminism and the "New Historicism"', in *The New Historicism*, ed. H. Aram Veeser. New York and London: Routledge, 1989, pp. 152–67.
Nochlin, Linda. 'Why Have There Been No Great Women Artists?' *ARTnews* (January 1971): 22–39, 67–71.
Nunn, Pamela Gerrish. 'Critically Speaking', in *Women in the Victorian Art World*, ed. Clarissa Campbell Orr. Manchester University Press, 1995, pp. 107–24.
Oliphant, Margaret. *The Autobiography of Margaret Oliphant*, ed. Elisabeth Jay. Oxford and New York: Oxford University Press, 1990.
The Three Brothers. New York: D. Appleton and Co., 1870.
Palmer, Caroline. 'Colour, Chemistry and Corsets: Mary Philadelphia Merrifield's *Dress as a Fine Art*', *Costume* 47, 1 (January 2013): 3–27.
Parker, Rozsika and Griselda Pollock. *Old Mistresses: Women, Art and Ideology*. London: Routledge and Kegan Paul, 1981.

Passavant, J. D. *Tour of a German Artist in England with Notices of Private Galleries, and Remarks on the State of Art*, trans. [Elizabeth Rigby]. 2 vols., London: Saunders and Otley, 1836.
Pattison, E. F. S. 'Art and Morality', *Westminster Review* n.s. 35 (January 1869): 148–84.
'Germain Pilon', *Portfolio* 2 (1871): 72–5.
'John Ruskin, *Lectures on Art* and *Catalogue of Examples* (Oxford, 1870)', *Academy* 1 (10 September 1870): 305–6.
The Renaissance of Art in France. 2 vols., London: C. Kegan Paul & Co., 1879.
'The Use of Looking at Pictures', *Westminster Review* n.s. 44 (October., 1873): 415–23.
'Walter Pater, *Studies in the History of the Renaissance* (London, 1873)', *Westminster Review* n.s. 43 (1873): 639–41.
Pennell, Elizabeth Robins. 'A Century of Women's Rights', *Fortnightly Review* 54 (o.s.): 48 (n.s.) (September 1890): 408–17.
'Les Arts de la Femme', *Chautauquan* 16 (1892): 212–14.
Chautauquan 12 (1890): 772.
Chautauquan 13 (1891): 83.
Life of Mary Wollstonecraft. Boston: Roberts Bros, 1884.
Nights: Rome, Venice in the Aesthetic Eighties; London, Paris in the Fighting Nineties. Philadelphia and London: J. B. Lippincott, 1916.
Pennell, Elizabeth Robins (A.U.). 'Art and Artists', *Star* (4 June 1895): 1.
Pennell, Elizabeth Robins (N.N.). 'Millais', *Nation* (27 August 1896): 156–7.
Perkin, H. *The Rise of Professional Society: England since 1880*. London: Routledge, 1990.
Peterson, Linda H. *Becoming a Woman of Letters: Myths of Authorship and Facts of the Victorian Market*. Princeton University Press, 2009.
Pollock, Griselda. *Differencing the Canon: Feminist Desire and the Writing of Art's Histories*. London and New York: Routledge, 1999.
Vision and Difference: Femininity, Feminism and the Histories of Art. Routledge: London and New York, 1988.
Probyn, Elspeth. *Sexing the Self: Gendered Positions in Cultural Studies*. London: Routledge, 1993.
Psomiades, Kathy Alexis. '"Still Burning from this Strangling Embrace": Vernon Lee on Desire and Aesthetics', in *Victorian Sexual Dissidence*, ed. Richard Dellamora. University of Chicago Press, 1999, pp. 21–41
Rigby, Elizabeth. 'The Art of Dress', *Quarterly Review* 79 (1847): 372–99.
'Lady Travellers', *Quarterly Review* 76 (June 1845): 98–136.
Letters from the Shores of the Baltic. 2nd edn, London: John Murray, 1842, pp. 28–9.
Ritchie, Anne Thackeray. *Miss Angel And Fulham Lawn*. London: Smith, Elder, & Co., 1908.
Ruskin, John. *The Works of John Ruskin*, ed. E. T. Cook and Alexander Wedderburn. 39 vols., London: George Allen, 1903–12.
Samuels, Ernest. *Bernard Berenson: The Making of a Connoisseur*. Cambridge, Mass.: Harvard University Press, 1979.

Sani, Bernardina. *Rosalba Carriera: Catalogue Raisonné*. Venice: Umberto Allemandi & Co., 2007.

Schaffer, Talia. *The Forgotten Female Aesthetes: Literary Culture in Late Victorian England*. Charlottesville and London: University Press of Virginia, 2000.

Novel Craft: Victorian Domestic Handicraft and Nineteenth-Century Fiction. New York: Oxford University Press, 2011.

Scholl, Lesa. *Translation, Authorship and the Victorian Professional Woman: Charlotte Brontë, Harriet Martineau and George Eliot*. Aldershot, Hants.: Ashgate, 2011.

Scott, Joan. 'Fantasy Echo: History and the Construction of Identity', *Critical Inquiry* 27 (Winter 2001): 284–304.

Seymour, Miranda. *Ottoline Morrell: Life on the Grand Scale*. London: Hodder & Stoughton, 1992.

Shapiro, Harold I. *Ruskin in Italy. Letters to his Parents 1845*. Oxford: Clarendon, 1972.

Sherman, Claire Richter with Adele M. Holcomb, eds. *Women as Interpreters of the Visual Arts, 1820–1979*. Westport, Conn., and London: Greenwood, 1981.

Shires, Linda M. *Perspectives: Modes of Viewing and Knowing in Nineteenth-Century England*. Columbus: Ohio State University Press, 2009.

Siegel, Jonah. 'The Material of Form: Vernon Lee at the Vatican and Out of It', *Victorian Studies* 55, 2 (Winter 2013): 189–201.

Simon, Sherry. *Gender in Translation: Cultural Identity and the Politics of Transmission*. London and New York: Routledge, 1996.

Smyth, Dame Ethel. *What Happened Next*. London: Longmans Green, 1940.

Starke, Mariana. *Information and Directions for Travellers on the Continent*. 5th edn, London: John Murray, 1824.

Information and Directions for Travellers on the Continent. 7th edn, London: John Murray, 1829.

Stein, Richard. *The Ritual of Interpretation: The Fine Arts as Literature in Ruskin, Rossetti and Pater*. Cambridge, Mass.: Harvard University Press, 1975.

Swindells, Julia. *Victorian Writing and Working Women: The Other Side of Silence*. Cambridge: Polity, 1985.

Taylor, Una Ashworth. 'Morris and Rossetti', *Edinburgh Review* (April 1900): 356–79.

'Some Prospects of Modern Art', *Edinburgh Review* (July 1899): 48–69.

Tennyson, Alfred. *The Poems of Tennyson*, ed. Christopher Ricks (Longman's Annotated English poets). London: Longmans, Green & Co, 1969; revised edn in 3 vols., 1987.

Teukolsky, Rachel. *The Literate Eye: Victorian Art Writing and Modernist Aesthetics*. Oxford and New York: Oxford University Press, 2009.

Thompson, Kate. *A Handbook to the Public Picture Galleries of Europe*. London: Macmillan,1877.

Tilley, Heather. 'Blindness and Writing, 1800–72'. Unpublished PhD thesis, University of London, 2009.

Trollope, Frances. *Domestic Manners of the Americans*, ed. Donald Smalley. New York, 1949.

Twining, Louisa. *Workhouses and Women's Work*. London: Longman, Brown, Green, Longmans, & Roberts, 1858.

Vadillo, Ana I. Parejo. '*Sight and Song*: Transparent Translations and a Manifesto for the Observer', *Victorian Poetry* 38, 1 (2000): 15–34.

Vicinus, Martha. 'The Adolescent Boy: *Fin-de-Siècle* Femme Fatale?' in *Victorian Sexual Dissidence*, ed. Richard Dellamora. University of Chicago Press, 1999, pp. 83–106.

Vrettos, Athena. '"In the clothes of dead people": Vernon Lee and Ancestral Memory', *Victorian Studies* 55, 2 (Winter 2013): 202–11.

Waagen, G. F. *Peter Paul Rubens, his Life and Genius*, trans. R. R. Noel, ed. Anna Jameson. London, 1840.

Treasures of Art in Great Britain: Being an Account of the Chief Collections of Paintings, Drawings, Sculptures, Illuminated Mss., &c., &c, trans. Elizabeth Rigby Eastlake. 4 vols., London: J. Murray, 1854 and 1857.

Waern, Cecilia. 'Puvis de Chavannes in Boston', *Atlantic Monthly* 79 (February 1897): 251–7.

'Some Notes on the Art of John La Farge', *Atlantic Monthly* 75 (May 1895): 690–3.

'Some Notes on French Impressionism', *Atlantic Monthly* 69 (April 1892): 535–41.

Watson, Rosamund Marriott. *The Art of the House*. London: George Bell and Sons, 1897.

Whewell, William. *The General Bearing of the Great Exhibition on the Progress of Art and Science*, Inaugural Lecture (25 November 1851).

Wilde, Oscar. *Complete Works of Oscar Wilde*, introduced by Vyvyan Holland. London: Harper Collins, 1966.

Woolf, Virginia. *To the Lighthouse*, ed. Stella McNichol and Hermione Lee. London: Penguin, 1992.

Mr Bennett and Mrs Brown. London: The Hogarth Press, 1924.

A Room of One's Own, Three Guineas, ed. Morag Shiach. Oxford University Press, 1992.

Yeats, William Butler. *W. B. Yeats: Uncollected Prose*, ed. John P. Frayne. 2 vols., London: Macmillan, 1970.

Zimmern, Helen. 'The Work of Miss Bessie Potter', *Magazine of Art* (1900): 522–3.

Index

CAMBRIDGE STUDIES IN NINETEENTH-CENTURY LITERATURE AND CULTURE

General editor

Gillian Beer, *University of Cambridge*

Titles published

1. The Sickroom in Victorian Fiction: The Art of Being Ill
Miriam Bailin, *Washington University*

2. Muscular Christianity: Embodying the Victorian Age
edited by Donald E. Hall, *California State University, Northridge*

3. Victorian Masculinities: Manhood and Masculine Poetics in Early Victorian Literature and Art
Herbert Sussman, *Northeastern University, Boston*

4. Byron and the Victorians
Andrew Elfenbein, *University of Minnesota*

5. Literature in the Marketplace: Nineteenth-Century British Publishing and the Circulation of Books
edited by John O. Jordan, *University of California, Santa Cruz* and Robert L. Patten, *Rice University, Houston*

6. Victorian Photography, Painting and Poetry
Lindsay Smith, *University of Sussex*

7. Charlotte Brontë and Victorian Psychology
Sally Shuttleworth, *University of Sheffield*

8. The Gothic Body: Sexuality, Materialism and Degeneration at the *Fin de Siècle*
Kelly Hurley, *University of Colorado at Boulder*

9. Rereading Walter Pater
William F. Shuter, *Eastern Michigan University*

10. Remaking Queen Victoria
edited by Margaret Homans, *Yale University* and Adrienne Munich, *State University of New York, Stony Brook*

11. Disease, Desire, and the Body in Victorian Women's Popular Novels
Pamela K. Gilbert, *University of Florida*

12. Realism, Representation, and the Arts in Nineteenth-Century Literature
Alison Byerly, *Middlebury College, Vermont*

13. Literary Culture and the Pacific
Vanessa Smith, *University of Sydney*

14. Professional Domesticity in the Victorian Novel:
Women, Work and Home
Monica F. Cohen

15. Victorian Renovations of the Novel: Narrative Annexes
and the Boundaries of Representation
Suzanne Keen, *Washington and Lee University, Virginia*

16. Actresses on the Victorian Stage: Feminine Performance
and the Galatea Myth
Gail Marshall, *University of Leeds*

17. Death and the Mother from Dickens to Freud: Victorian Fiction
and the Anxiety of Origin
Carolyn Dever, *Vanderbilt University, Tennessee*

18. Ancestry and Narrative in Nineteenth-Century British Literature:
Blood Relations from Edgeworth to Hardy
Sophie Gilmartin, *Royal Holloway, University of London*

19. Dickens, Novel Reading, and the Victorian Popular Theatre
Deborah Vlock

20. After Dickens: Reading, Adaptation and Performance
John Glavin, *Georgetown University, Washington D C*

21. Victorian Women Writers and the Woman Question
edited by Nicola Diane Thompson, *Kingston University, London*

22. Rhythm and Will in Victorian Poetry
Matthew Campbell, *University of Sheffield*

23. Gender, Race, and the Writing of Empire: Public Discourse
and the Boer War
Paula M. Krebs, *Wheaton College, Massachusetts*

24. Ruskin's God
Michael Wheeler, *University of Southampton*

25. Dickens and the Daughter of the House
Hilary M. Schor, *University of Southern California*

26. Detective Fiction and the Rise of Forensic Science
Ronald R. Thomas, *Trinity College, Hartford, Connecticut*

27. Testimony and Advocacy in Victorian Law, Literature, and Theology
Jan-Melissa Schramm, *Trinity Hall, Cambridge*

28. Victorian Writing about Risk: Imagining a Safe England in a Dangerous World
Elaine Freedgood, *University of Pennsylvania*

29. Physiognomy and the Meaning of Expression in Nineteenth-Century Culture
Lucy Hartley, *University of Southampton*

30. The Victorian Parlour: A Cultural Study
Thad Logan, *Rice University, Houston*

31. Aestheticism and Sexual Parody 1840–1940
Dennis Denisoff, *Ryerson University, Toronto*

32. Literature, Technology and Magical Thinking, 1880–1920
Pamela Thurschwell, *University College London*

33. Fairies in Nineteenth-Century Art and Literature
Nicola Bown, *Birkbeck, University of London*

34. George Eliot and the British Empire
Nancy Henry *The State University of New York, Binghamton*

35. Women's Poetry and Religion in Victorian England: Jewish Identity and Christian Culture
Cynthia Scheinberg, *Mills College, California*

36. Victorian Literature and the Anorexic Body
Anna Krugovoy Silver, *Mercer University, Georgia*

37. Eavesdropping in the Novel from Austen to Proust
Ann Gaylin, *Yale University*

38. Missionary Writing and Empire, 1800–1860
Anna Johnston, *University of Tasmania*

39. London and the Culture of Homosexuality, 1885–1914
Matt Cook, *Keele University*

40. Fiction, Famine, and the Rise of Economics in Victorian Britain and Ireland
Gordon Bigelow, *Rhodes College, Tennessee*

41. Gender and the Victorian Periodical
Hilary Fraser, *Birkbeck, University of London*
Judith Johnston and Stephanie Green, *University of Western Australia*

42. The Victorian Supernatural
edited by Nicola Bown, *Birkbeck College, London*
Carolyn Burdett, *London Metropolitan University*
and Pamela Thurschwell, *University College London*

43. The Indian Mutiny and the British Imagination
Gautam Chakravarty, *University of Delhi*

44. The Revolution in Popular Literature: Print, Politics and the People
Ian Haywood, *Roehampton University of Surrey*

45. Science in the Nineteenth-Century Periodical:
Reading the Magazine of Nature
Geoffrey Cantor, *University of Leeds*
Gowan Dawson, *University of Leicester*
Graeme Gooday, *University of Leeds*
Richard Noakes, *University of Cambridge*
Sally Shuttleworth, *University of Sheffield* and
Jonathan R. Topham, *University of Leeds*

46. Literature and Medicine in Nineteenth-Century Britain
from Mary Shelley to George Eliot
Janis McLarren Caldwell, *Wake Forest University*

47. The Child Writer from Austen to Woolf
edited by Christine Alexander, *University of New South Wales*
and Juliet McMaster, *University of Alberta*

48. From Dickens to Dracula: Gothic, Economics,
and Victorian Fiction
Gail Turley Houston, *University of New Mexico*

49. Voice and the Victorian Storyteller
Ivan Kreilkamp, *University of Indiana*

50. Charles Darwin and Victorian Visual Culture
Jonathan Smith, *University of Michigan-Dearborn*

51. Catholicism, Sexual Deviance, and Victorian Gothic Culture
Patrick R. O'Malley, *Georgetown University*

52. Epic and Empire in Nineteenth-Century Britain
Simon Dentith, *University of Gloucestershire*

53. Victorian Honeymoons: Journeys to the Conjugal
Helena Michie, *Rice University*

54. The Jewess in Nineteenth-Century British Literary Culture
Nadia Valman, *University of Southampton*

55. Ireland, India and Nationalism in Nineteenth-Century Literature
Julia Wright, *Dalhousie University*

56. Dickens and the Popular Radical Imagination
Sally Ledger, *Birkbeck, University of London*

57. Darwin, Literature and Victorian Respectability
Gowan Dawson, *University of Leicester*

58. 'Michael Field': Poetry, Aestheticism and the *Fin de Siècle*
Marion Thain, *University of Birmingham*

59. Colonies, Cults and Evolution: Literature, Science and Culture in Nineteenth-Century Writing
David Amigoni, *Keele University*

60. Realism, Photography and Nineteenth-Century Fiction
Daniel A. Novak, *Lousiana State University*

61. Caribbean Culture and British Fiction in the Atlantic World, 1780–1870
Tim Watson, *University of Miami*

62. The Poetry of Chartism: Aesthetics, Politics, History
Michael Sanders, *University of Manchester*

63. Literature and Dance in Nineteenth-Century Britain: Jane Austen to the New Woman
Cheryl Wilson, *Indiana University*

64. Shakespeare and Victorian Women
Gail Marshall, *Oxford Brookes University*

65. The Tragi-Comedy of Victorian Fatherhood
Valerie Sanders, *University of Hull*

66. Darwin and the Memory of the Human: Evolution, Savages, and South America
Cannon Schmitt, *University of Toronto*

67. From Sketch to Novel: The Development of Victorian Fiction
Amanpal Garcha, *Ohio State University*

68. The Crimean War and the British Imagination
Stefanie Markovits, *Yale University*

69. Shock, Memory and the Unconscious in Victorian Fiction
Jill L. Matus, *University of Toronto*

70. Sensation and Modernity in the 1860s
Nicholas Daly, *University College Dublin*

71. Ghost-Seers, Detectives, and Spiritualists: Theories of Vision in Victorian Literature and Science
Srdjan Smajić, *Furman University*

72. Satire in an Age of Realism
Aaron Matz, *Scripps College, California*

73. Thinking About Other People in Nineteenth-Century British Writing
Adela Pinch, *University of Michigan*

74. Tuberculosis and the Victorian Literary Imagination
Katherine Byrne, *University of Ulster, Coleraine*

75. Urban Realism and the Cosmopolitan Imagination in the Nineteenth Century: Visible City, Invisible World
Tanya Agathocleous, *Hunter College, City University of New York*

76. Women, Literature, and the Domesticated Landscape: England's Disciples of Flora, 1780–1870
Judith W. Page, *University of Florida*
Elise L. Smith, *Millsaps College, Mississippi*

77. Time and the Moment in Victorian Literature and Society
Sue Zemka, *University of Colorado*

78. Popular Fiction and Brain Science in the Late Nineteenth Century
Anne Stiles, *Washington State University*

79. Picturing Reform in Victorian Britain
Janice Carlisle, *Yale University*

80. Atonement and Self-Sacrifice in Nineteenth-Century Narrative
Jan-Melissa Schramm, *University of Cambridge*

81. The Silver Fork Novel: Fashionable Fiction in the Age of Reform
Edward Copeland, *Pomona College, California*

82. Oscar Wilde and Ancient Greece
Iain Ross, *Colchester Royal Grammar School*

83. The Poetry of Victorian Scientists: Style, Science and Nonsense
Daniel Brown, *University of Southampton*

84. Moral Authority, Men of Science, and the Victorian Novel
Anne DeWitt, *Princeton Writing Program*

85. China and the Victorian Imagination: Empires Entwined
Ross G. Forman, *University of Warwick*

86. Dickens's Style
Daniel Tyler, *University of Oxford*

87. The Formation of the Victorian Literary Profession
Richard Salmon, *University of Leeds*

88. Before George Eliot: Marian Evans and the Periodical Press
Fionnuala Dillane, *University College Dublin*

89. The Victorian Novel and the Space of Art: Fictional Form on Display
Dehn Gilmore, *California Institute of Technology*

90. George Eliot and Money: Economics, Ethics and Literature
Dermot Coleman, *Independent Scholar*

91. Masculinity and the New Imperialism:
Rewriting Manhood in British Popular Literature, 1870–1914
Bradley Deane, *University of Minnesota*

92. Evolution and Victorian Culture
edited by Bernard Lightman, *York University, Toronto* and
Bennett Zon, *University of Durham*

93. Victorian Literature, Energy, and the Ecological Imagination
Allen MacDuffie, *University of Texas, Austin*

94. Popular Literature, Authorship and the Occult in Late Victorian Britain
Andrew McCann, *Dartmouth College, New Hampshire*

95. Women Writing Art History in the Nineteenth Century:
Looking Like a Woman
Hilary Fraser, *Birkbeck College, University of London*

Lightning Source UK Ltd.
Milton Keynes UK
UKHW022014081120
373057UK00009B/64

9 781107 428744